EGYPTOMANIA
GOES TO THE MOVIES

Egyptomania Goes to the Movies

From Archaeology to Popular Craze to Hollywood Fantasy

Matthew Coniam

McFarland & Company, Inc., Publishers
Jefferson, North Carolina

ALSO BY MATTHEW CONIAM
AND FROM MCFARLAND

*That's Me, Groucho! The Solo
Career of Groucho Marx* (2016)

*The Annotated Marx Brothers: A Filmgoer's Guide
to In-Jokes, Obscure References and Sly Details* (2015)

Frontispiece: The unbroken seal on Tutankhamen's shrine
(photograph by Harry Burton).

LIBRARY OF CONGRESS CATALOGUING-IN-PUBLICATION DATA

Names: Coniam, Matthew, 1973– author.
Title: Egyptomania goes to the movies : from archaeology to popular
craze to Hollywood fantasy / Matthew Coniam.
Description: Jefferson, N.C. : McFarland & Company, Inc., Publishers, 2017. |
Includes bibliographical references and index.
Identifiers: LCCN 2017024479 | ISBN 9781476668284
(softcover : acid free paper) ∞
Subjects: LCSH: Egypt—In motion pictures. |
Civilization, Ancient, in motion pictures.
Classification: LCC PN1995.9.E32 C57 2017 | DDC 700/.35832—dc23
LC record available at https://lccn.loc.gov/2017024479

BRITISH LIBRARY CATALOGUING DATA ARE AVAILABLE

ISBN (print) 978-1-4766-6828-4
ISBN (ebook) 978-1-4766-2986-5

© 2017 Matthew Coniam. All rights reserved

*No part of this book may be reproduced or transmitted in any form
or by any means, electronic or mechanical, including photocopying
or recording, or by any information storage and retrieval system,
without permission in writing from the publisher.*

Front cover: Theda Bara in the title role of the 1917 film *Cleopatra*;
background designs by J. C. Rosemann (iStock)

Manufactured in the United States of America

*McFarland & Company, Inc., Publishers
Box 611, Jefferson, North Carolina 28640
www.mcfarlandpub.com*

For Angela
(My first book having been dedicated
to our son Edward, it seems only fitting that this one
should be dedicated to his mummy.)

Acknowledgments

Researching this book has for the most part been a happy affair of reacquainting myself with numerous old favorites from my own library and others; together with scores of articles and dozens of documentaries and movies. Many forgotten memories have risen, Kharis-like, from the dust thus disturbed. But I have also made use of some fresher perspectives, and have additionally benefited from the interest, assistance or input of Mykal Banta, the late Robert Birchard, Anthony Blampied, John V. Brennan, Robin Cook, Bob Gassel, David Kernick, Valerie Leon, David McGillivray, David L. Rattigan, Scott Saternye, Fiona Thompson, Rodney Stewart Hillel Tryster, Ed Watz and Derek Welsby (British Museum). Special thanks are due to ace rare film researcher George White.

As ever I thank my family: my wife Angela, my son Edward (that's him as King Tut, above) and my sister Helen. And in particular, after having written two successive books about the Marx Brothers, I would like to record my pleasure at being able finally to thank my mother and father for a lifetime's selfless practical, material and emotional support, with a book they might actually find reasonably interesting.

Table of Contents

Acknowledgments	vi
Cast of Characters	ix
Introduction: The Dream of Egypt	1
1. Death on the Nile	9
2. Of Mania and Maniacs	21
3. It's an Egyptian Year!	37
4. The Face Behind the Mask	55
5. Good Heavens, What a Terrible Curse!	72
6. Losses and Survivals	89
7. From Lot No. 249 to Law No. 215	107
8. In Many Forms, Shall We Return	121
9. An Egyptian Feast	131
10. The Pharaoh's Razor Blade	141
Epilogue: Graves and Dead Men	152
The Mummy List: A Chronological Concordance of Egyptomania at the Movies, 1849–2015	159
Chapter Notes	177
Bibliography	183
Index	185

Cast of Characters

John L. Balderston: Screenwriter, playwright and journalist, who nearly became the curse's silliest victim.

Theda Bara: Silent film star, born Theodosia Goodman, played Cleopatra and may have been a reincarnation.

Antoine Bovis: Father of "Pyramid Power": the first man who dared to wonder what happens when you put a dead fish inside a cardboard model of the Great Pyramid of Giza.

Howard Carter: Egyptologist and discoverer of the tomb of Tutankhamen: disproved the myth of the curse by living long enough to become completely forgotten.

Lon Chaney, Jr.: The true face of Kharis the Mummy: film actor who started out as rugged hero but became typed in horror for reasons of genetics. Allergic to rubber.

Max Cohen: Enterprising independent film producer responsible for the most tantalizingly lost manifestation of Egyptomania cinematica: *The Mystery of Tut-Ankh-Amen's Eighth Wife* (1923). Also the inventor of "midget comedies."

Cecil B. DeMille: Autocratic American film director whose penchant for Jazz Age social drama and historical spectacle coalesced perfectly in the first and greatest version of *The Ten Commandments* (1923).

Waynham Dixon: British engineer who organized the safe passage of the Cleopatra Needle to England after decades of failure and indecision. Also made a major discovery about the Great Pyramid while damaging it with a hammer.

Sir Arthur Conan Doyle: British novelist and creator of Sherlock Holmes, whose three literary contributions to the subject of Egyptian malevolence more or less provide the complete blueprint for its extension into twentieth century cinema. Also a noted spiritualist and crank, who swallowed whole the curse of the Pharaohs.

Karel Drbal: Czechoslovakian visionary, who built upon the researches of Antoine Bovis and kick-started a Californian cult.

EA6704 (a.k.a. "Prem"): The mummy that time forgot, but Hammer Films immortalized.

Dorothy Eady (a.k.a. "Omm Seti"): London-born Egyptologist and self-declared reincarnation of a handmaiden from the court of Seti I (who was, she insisted, a nice man).

William P. S. Earle: Producer and director of *Dancer of the Nile* (1923) the first dramatic film to capitalize on "Tutmania."

George Gliddon: American Egyptological showman, who received a nasty surprise when he unwrapped a mummy in front of Henry Wadsworth Longfellow.

Bertram Grassby: British film actor, and the screen's original Tutankhamen, who lived in a house with a tree growing inside it.

George Herbert, Fifth Earl of Carnarvon: Howard Carter's patron and the man whose obsession with Ancient Egypt led to the greatest archaeological discovery of all time, even as his death led to its greatest and most enduring myth.

Boris Karloff (a.k.a. "Karloff the Uncanny"): British film actor who invented the ambulatory movie mummy as we know it, in thirty seconds of screen time and one close-up.

Valerie Leon: British film actress and probable reincarnation of the Egyptian lioness goddess Pakhet.

Herschell Gordon Lewis: American film director/producer/writer/composer, creator of the infamous *Blood Feast* (1963), and the world's leading authority on the terrifying Egyptian cult of Ishtar. Last known victim of the curse to date.

President Gamal Abdel Nasser: A wily Oriental.

Sir Matthew William Flinders Petrie: English Egyptologist and eccentric, and proof that it is possible to be in two places at once.

Jack Pierce: American movie makeup wizard; turned the living into the dead and the dead into the immortal.

Ernest Shipman (a.k.a. "Ten Percent Ernie"): Canadian film exhibitor and director and the first to secure film rights to the Tutankhamen excavation—or did he?

Bram Stoker: Irish novelist and creator of Dracula. Met a mummy at the home of Oscar Wilde's father and was never the same again.

Tom Terriss: British actor, film director and prospective producer of the unmade *Curse of Tutankhamen* in 1934. He claimed to have been personally invited to the excavation of the tomb in 1922, and never let the truth get in the way of a good story.

Tutankhamen: Boy king of the Eighteenth Dynasty and global celebrity of the twentieth century: the hero of our story.

William John Warner (a.k.a. "Cheiro," a.k.a. Count Louis Harmon, a.k.a. Count Leigh de Hamong): Irish fortune teller and general purpose charlatan who claimed to have warned Carnarvon of his imminent death, got into a pickle trying to burn a mummy's hand, and spent his spare time defrauding society women of their savings.

Arthur Weigall: Egyptologist and one-time Chief Inspector of Antiquities in Upper Egypt, also theatrical set designer, songwriter, novelist and journalist. May have accidentally invented the myth of Tutankhamen's curse, only to have his own death attributed to it.

Herbert Winlock: Curator of Egyptian Art at the Metropolitan Museum of Art in New York who redefined the term "wishful thinking" by calling a press conference in an attempt to convince journalists that the curse of the Pharaohs was a myth.

Introduction:
The Dream of Egypt

Picture this scene, and imagine yourself there…

It's 2012. Intrepid archaeologist Doug Jenzen and his team are digging beneath the smooth desert sand. Progress is slow at first, the sun hot and high. There is always hope—tantalizing hope—but no realistic expectation of anything ahead of them except another hard day's work.

But then, suddenly, the team make contact with something solid, just below the surface. A shout goes out. The team congregates. Nervous glances are exchanged. Could this be the moment?

Carefully, the sand is sifted away and slowly—oh, so slowly—the past begins to give up its secrets.

Just an inch at first, then a little more … then a little more again, as minutes pile on minutes to make hours. First, iconography becomes visible, then contours distinct…. All mouths are dry, all eyes fixed on the emerging wonder.

Finally, at last, it is free!

A fifteen-foot sphinx, one of 21 that originally lined the path to the Pharaoh's palace.

Ah, yes—that's what it's all about. The irresistible suspense and excitement of high stakes archaeology! Is there anything to match it? The guesswork, the toil, the nail-biting tension, then finally—if you're really, really lucky—the *glory*, as the past comes alive again, and looks back at you, right in the eye.

It certainly sends shivers down my spine, and it's a fair bet, if you've bought this book, that it does yours, too.

But there's a couple of things you need to know about this particular excavation that I haven't made entirely clear. First, Jenzen and his team weren't digging in Egypt. Their sphinx was buried beneath the sands of Guadalupe, California. And far from thousands of years old, it had yet to celebrate its first century. Made of plaster, it was part of the enormous sets constructed for Cecil B. DeMille's original version of *The Ten Commandments* in 1923, and abandoned when production was completed.

Just imagine telling Howard Carter that junk left over from one of the Hollywood movies rushed into production to cash in on his real-life discovery of the tomb of Tutankhamen would now itself be deemed worthy of excavation and preservation. That it might be made subject of solemn archaeological pursuit beneath the shifting sands not of prehistory, but of twentieth century mass culture! The trivia of the ancients; the detritus of the gods...

In that delicious irony is located the focus of this book.

This is a book about ephemera that shows no signs yet of being ephemeral, and about the unusual cast of individuals that came together to create it. Above all it is the story of an unlikely love affair: when mass-culture met world history. It was born in that moment when archaeologists realized their specialism was no longer under their own control, that it belonged to the world, and when the world declared itself intent upon sifting it to find the things it liked and returning the rest to the parched desert sands from whence they came. Dates and dynasties and science: all of these things were basically for the birds. But treasure and tombs, mummies, myth and magic ... that was different. Ancient Egypt's absorption into the clothes fashions, interior décor, music and movies of the 1920s and 30s became its very own curse of the pharaohs: one culture's profoundest mysteries condemned to become another's idle distraction.

On the face of it, few ancient peoples might seem less likely to have inspired a latter-day horror mythology than the Egyptians. And in the eyes of many, when we settle down to watch the Three Stooges explore the tomb of King Rootentooten in *We Want Our Mummy*, we ought to be feeling a little guilty about that. After all, most serious studies of the relationship between ancient civilizations and pop culture are accusatory, indicting the latter, in their ignorance and chauvinism, as relics of the same imperialist attitudes that viewed the ancient sites as fair game for acquisition in the first place. ("I want to explain the problem and the irony that practicing one's own culture can entail the distortion, even denigration of others' culture," writes Jasmine Day in *The Mummy's Curse: Mummymania in the English-Speaking World*. "Hopefully, this will help you to avoid making the same mistake.")

But wagging fingers and shrill denunciations of cultural insensitivity bring us no nearer to answering the question that *really* interests me: *why* Egypt? Why Egypt *specifically*? What does Ancient Egypt have to say to us that is so lastingly potent as to have inspired all this stuff in the first place? Clearly, it is not accidental that the Egyptian mummy is an icon of horror cinema while the Aztec mummy is a novelty footnote.

There is no explanation we can come up with for Egypt's unique power and ubiquity that could not apply equally to other cultures. They all offer, to varying degrees, strange beliefs, esoteric doctrines, obscure rituals, grandiose monuments, art and architecture. The Roman Empire gives us that strange tingle of a vast and powerful civilization that has, nonetheless, disappeared. The Ancient Greeks impress us equally with their imagination. All inspire fascination ... but fascination is not mania, and their manifestations in popular culture are nothing like so varied, persistent and self-supporting.

Neither, for that matter, do the civilizations of ancient Rome or Greece support such a large retrospective body of crank literature, claiming their achievements were influenced by the intervention of little green men, or survivors of the lost continent of Atlantis, or that their architecture is really a 3-D map of the heavens. (As late as 2001, a serious house published *The Tutankhamun Deception*, which claims that Howard Carter discovered a papyrus proving that Tutankhamen and Christ were the same person, and that the supposed victims of the curse were in reality murdered to prevent this truth becoming known, the last of them being Sigmund Freud.) Clearly, there must be something *special* about our concept of Egypt that makes it uniquely supportive of so much mad fantasy.

The Ancient Egypt that the twentieth century enshrined AK (Anno Karloff) is the one that archaeologist Howard Carter and his patron Lord Carnarvon revealed to an enraptured world in 1922. This is the world of Tutankhamen's tomb, "King Tut" (as he almost immediately became popularly known) being a relatively unimportant king of the Eighteenth Dynasty, who ruled for nine years and died in his teens. He is associated with no great monuments, and figures in no significant events in Egyptian history. His very tomb, in fact, was—in size and status—a relatively unexceptional one. However, through the accident of its having been preserved near-intact, he was vaulted to unimagined prominence in the pantheon, and a sensation-hungry world, newly-united by revolutionary mass-media, sat up as one and took notice as never before. They called it "Tutmania," and they weren't joking. Some of its manifestations have had real and lasting influence on our cultural history; others seemed foolish even at the time, but few single events in history had so far-reaching and diverse effects in so many seemingly unrelated areas.

"Egyptomania," the magpie fascination with Egyptian imagery in architecture and design, had been a feature of Western aesthetics for ages, but Tutmania was more frenzied; its reach was wider and more eclectic, to say nothing of more superficial and youthful. Those horror movies, instigated in 1932 just as Carter's work on the tomb was finally drawing to a close a full decade after the great discovery, were at once a culmination and a permanent afterlife for this inchoate fascination: a receptacle for every stray aspect of weirdness and eeriness and wild speculation the story engendered in the popular press, comic books, and short story anthologies.

Even as a boy I knew there was something fundamentally incompatible between the seriousness of Egyptology and the frivolity of the mummy movies, and that my devotion to both placed me somewhat uncomfortably in the middle of a tug of war. Howard Carter, I read, was especially acid in his views on the bastardisation of Egyptian myth and iconography in the 1920s—his opinion of the Karloff film is so far as I know unrecorded but was, I'm sure, piquant. And yet, watching and rewatching my silent, Super 8, one-reel condensation of the movie, it was obvious to me that the pleasure it gave me was, in large measure at least, a respectable (and respectful) one: a sense of awe at what Karloff himself calls the "oceans of time" between we and this strange, poetic culture, and the "dreams of death" it seems to summon up from within us. Yes, of course it was melodrama, hokey and in many ways crude, but it had hovering about it exactly that pervasive commodity—wonder—that the whole subject of Egyptology seemed to brew in my adolescent imagination, and must likewise have animated Carter himself.

There are two "dreams of Egypt." For the original discoverers and explorers, the dream was of the Ancient world itself, pristine and uncontaminated by modern triviality, slowly coming to life again as they sifted the sand. For the travellers who followed in their wake on cruises and package tours, fully as strong was the romance of that very *process* of discovery. No matter that they may come no closer than watching it pass by from the comfort of an air-conditioned boat, or viewing it from a hotel window in toxic, gridlocked modern Cairo—they are all entertaining the fantasy of scraping away the sand themselves, making the breach, clambering inside, lighting the candle, hearing their breath stop and their heart beat louder. The explorers who brought Egypt to the West as a side-product of feeding their own fantasies have themselves become the fantasy fodder of the second generation. And that's what the mummy films tap into, however unknowingly, and however superficially: that dream of Egypt.

What I really wanted as a boy was a book which took those movies seriously. Not, obviously, in the sense of giving credence to their notion that the Egyptian dead are liable to get up and throttle archaeologists, but which took them seriously as *objects of study*. And not merely as movies, divorced entirely from their historical and intellectual inspirations, but as *artefacts*. My feeling was that there *was* a continuity that was intellectually valid here, however remote, and that these films were worth considering not just as fun ways to pass a Saturday afternoon but as another manifestation of our culture's fascination with the strange, twilit beauty of Ancient Egyptian civilization, its monuments, its art, and its arcane beliefs and customs. The mummy subgenre of horror cinema and fiction may be the illegitimate—and highly mischievous—offspring of Egyptology, but there is for all that something to be gained in studying the two in tandem, to see where they threaten rapprochement, as well as the more obvious and amusing ways in which they most overtly diverge, and to account for the one in the tributaries of the other.

This book, then, is the one I was looking for all those years ago. It is both a partial and a personal study, with a decidedly eccentric trajectory, and by no means a straightforward history of its subject. It is not so much a single work as a series of linked essays on a single theme. I tend to the discursive over the methodical, and the subjective over the empirical. I side-track myself constantly. I offer little by way of critical opinion and not even the pretence of completeness. (For any value the book may possess in the latter department I thank my friend George White, whose eye-opening and frequently jaw-dropping

Plastic Imhotep toy standing guard over Castle Films' Super 8 condensation of *The Mummy* (1932) (author's collection).

filmography is located at the end of the expedition.) I aspire to authority only in such areas in which I feel myself qualified: on the history of Ancient Egypt itself, I should stress I am without qualification or tenure. So if, for example, I deal with a matter over which there is dispute among Egyptologists (for instance the causes of Hatshepsut's erasure from the official record, and the identification of her mummy), I prefer to present all sides rather than affect the right to pick a side and bat for it. This does not mean that I don't have opinions, perhaps even certainties, only that there are others far better qualified to hold them, and it is not my place to advance any one position to the certain exclusion of others. From time to time I do speculate, however, and it is up to the reader to decide whether I do so persuasively or naïvely. I will accept either conclusion.

A few other notes, before we start. When quoting 1920s and '30s sources, I have tidied up their grammar, spelling and punctuation only if I feared it necessary for their full comprehension. For the most part, I have left them to speak delightfully for themselves. This is especially the case with variant spellings of the names of Ancient Egyptian places and personages. The spelling used reflects the age in which the piece was written, and so I felt it important to honor the original choices; the only concession to uniformity being that I have standardized the "double-hyphenated" spelling of Tutankhamen, generally used in the 1920s and beyond, as "Tut-Ankh-Amen" (the most popular variant), even when it originally appeared as "Tut-ankh-Amen" (Carter's own preference) or "Tut-ankh-amen." For myself, the reason I spell Tutankhamen with an "e" before the final "n," rather than the now more common "u," is because Carter and Weigall both did, and all the books on the subject that I bought as a child did, and that's good enough for me. I also use "Khufu" rather than "Khnum-Khufu" (or Cheops), and spell "Rameses" rather than "Ramesses." The fact that I use the abbreviation "BC" should not be taken to suggest religious conviction, merely the conviction that "BCE" is ludicrous.

While I imagine most readers will come here as established fans of the movies, what follows will neither presume nor demand deep acquaintance with Egyptian history, and all we need before setting off on our expedition is a general sense of the basic chronology. The established convention for parceling the various episodes of Egyptian history is as a series of dynasties, their division and duration established by an Egyptian priest called Manetho around 300 BC. It's to some extent a rough and ready system, and one founded (as is much seemingly abstract knowledge) on a series of questionable or superseded assumptions. Nonetheless, and with the addition of subsidiary classifications derived from subsequent archaeological findings, it remains invaluable.

Predynastic	c. 4500–3100 BC	Predynastic
Dynasties 1–2	c. 3100–2686 BC	Archaic
Dynasties 3–8	c. 2686–2125 BC	Old Kingdom
Dynasties 9–10	c. 2160–2025 BC	First Intermediate Period
Dynasties 11–13	c. 2125–1650 BC	Middle Kingdom
Dynasties 14–17	c. 1750 -1550 BC	Second Intermediate Period
Dynasties 18–20	c. 1550–1069 BC	New Kingdom
Dynasties 21–24	c. 1069–715 BC	Third Intermediate Period
Dynasties 25–30	c. 747–332 BC	Late Period
Macedonian/Ptolemaic	332–30 BC	Greek
Roman	30 BC–642 AD	Roman/Byzantine

The Predynastic period denotes the years when Egypt was not a single state; the dynasties begin (by most accounts, also questioned) with its unification under the governance of King Narmer around 3100 BC. The intermediate periods refer to interludes of dissolution or invasion, where government was weakened and power was again decentralized and splintered. It will be seen that the Egyptian civilization was both resilient and very long-lasting, thus many of the things we think of as characteristic of Ancient Egypt generally are more properly associated with specific periods. (The great age of the pyramids, for example, was in the era of the Old Kingdom; Egypt's reputation as a wealthy military power was earned in the New Kingdom.) The table also gives us a sense of the vast periods of time separating such well-known names as Khufu (Old Kingdom), Tutankhamen (New Kingdom) and Cleopatra (Ptolemaic). Indeed, the interval between the reign of Khufu (commencing c. 2589 BC) and that of Cleopatra (commencing c. 51 BC) is greater than that between Cleopatra and Elizabeth Taylor.

The most misleading thing about this chronology is its seeming implication that the Predynastic period, all one and a half thousand years of it, is of only peripheral relevance. Far from it: clearly King Narmer could not have appeared overnight, crowned and ready, as if by magic. A partial analogy might be with this introduction: the very term "introduction," leading thence to Chapter 1, rather than grand-sounding Chapter 1 leading to Chapter 2, gives it a lesser, subsidiary status. But as well as—I hope—interesting in its own right it is also formative, and much of that which follows might be unclear or even incomprehensible without it. (For the analogy to be perfect, it would also be the equivalent of four chapters in length!)

In that sense, the Predynastic era is *the* vital and defining one, in which the earliest hunter-gatherers abandon their transient existence in favor of the settled life of an agrarian community in symbiosis with the Nile. With settlement comes a sense of self, and thus self-expression; we find evidence in these first settled communities not only of how they went about their working days but also of such tell-tale signs of self-consciousness as decorated objects, body make-up and portraiture. These things seem to announce, albeit in a whisper, the kind of aesthetics we associate with full-blown pharaonic Egypt. They indicate not the beginning of leisure so much as the first signs of a people imbuing their activities with a sense of meaning as well as mere purpose. The sudden concern with the external reflects the deepening and broadening of the internal. An inevitable consequence of a lifestyle regulated by the unchanging rhythm of the river's annual flood, and the patterns of the seasons upon the land, is an awareness of the distinction between the finite and the infinite. The consequent need to incorporate the fact of death, that most brutal proof of the finite, into their sense of the infinite is the wellspring of Egyptian civilization, and our starting point. Egypt did not step fully formed out of a pyramid—it rose, slowly, from the Nile.

I assure you that in our next class we will concern ourselves solely with the history of Egypt and not with the more lurid and non-curricular subject of living mummies.

—Professor Norman (Frank Reicher)
in *The Mummy's Ghost* (1944)

1
Death on the Nile

> "It is very strange," observed Edric, "that in this age of speculation and discovery, nothing certain should be known concerning them."
> "It is," returned the doctor: "but the thick mysterious veil that has rested upon them for so many ages seems not intended to be removed by mortal hands. They remind one of the sublime inscription upon the temple of the goddess, Isis, at Sais: "I am whatever was, whatever is and whatever shall be; but no mortal has, as yet, presumed to raise the veil that covers me.""—Jane C. Loudon, *The Mummy!—A Tale of the Twenty-Second Century* (1827)

Ninety-five percent of Egypt is desert. Hot, featureless, and incapable of sustaining life, it is nonetheless exceptionally good at one thing: it *preserves*.

So it is the desert that gives us our vital—and iconic—evidences of the great civilization (or civilizations) of Ancient Egypt: the tombs and temples, the Pyramids, the Sphinx, the monuments and the mummies. But there would be none of these things, indeed no Egypt at all, were it not for that other five percent: the fragile strip of fertile land surrounding the river Nile, brought magically to life by its annual flood. If the Nile flooded a fraction too little there would be famine; a fraction too much and the crops would be ruined. The people of the Nile, therefore, lived an ostensibly simple and ordered existence, but one entirely and dramatically at the knife-edge mercy of the processes of nature.

This, then, is the essence of their unique cosmic perspective, its emphases and priorities, and the manner in which they viewed themselves as a part of a wider, unified scheme. Their lives were measured in the changing of the seasons, their work was hard, their pleasures simple, and those things that were within their control they mastered with skill and ingenuity. But the presence of the Nile as constant existential backdrop reminded them that, just as their land was ninety-five percent infertile, so too their destiny was ninety-five percent out of their hands. If ever a society needed the reassurance of supernatural regulation, it was theirs.

The story of Ancient Egypt that we take from the mummy films is one of austere authority, savage vengeance (both earthly and supernatural) and dark mysteries imperfectly grasped even by those who wield their power. Above all, it is a world saturated by death and images of death, a culture in perpetual transit, morbidly tailoring its present to the embrace of its end. It is a world in which stultifying order hovers above a deep well of chaos.

The real story of Ancient Egypt is one of challenge and tradition, played out against millennia of gradual change, development and diversification, and of real people, with everyday passions, concerns and imperatives. That we should somehow perceive an inherently sinister element in Egyptian rite and custom is perhaps accidental, and something we should account for before we get on to the important business of watching Lon Chaney, Jr., drag himself about in bandages in a California film studio.

Egyptian mythology, which can seem such a confused polytheistic and anthropomorphic tangle, is often surprising in the ease with which its symbolism can be unlocked. (Consider, for example, the creation myth that describes the earth emerging from a receding ocean at the behest of frog- and snake-headed deities. Then consider the annual flood, and the creatures that are likely to be seen as the waters retreat and the land "appears"....) There is an ingenuousness to Egyptian belief, an innocent certainty that finds expression in their fixation on order and precision. This in turn reflects and is reflected in the extraordinary simplicity and permanence of their everyday lives, and the lack of curiosity that helped their civilization to endure relatively unchanged for so long.

Without the pressing need to confront and tame the fact of death, Egypt would have no funerary art or architecture, no tombs, no pyramids and, of course, no mummies. For the Egyptians, doubtless again as a side-effect of the otherwise extreme orderliness and routine of their existence, death was a subject into which they poured tremendous enterprise and artistry. The capriciousness of death, its randomness and disregard for human design, had to be incorporated within a rational system to give their lives meaning and purpose. The ritualistic attention to detail that is the hallmark of their funerary practices would have seemed to them merely the reinforcing of continuity and of the essential accountability of the cosmic order. In short, what we see as morbid and spooky, they found reassuring.

Of course, every human society is distinguished by the efforts it makes to incorporate this most inconvenient precondition of existence into its moral, cosmological and institutional schema, and we should never forget that it was the desert to which they donated this more timeless sense of themselves, and which the ageless sands retained, while the evidences of their more prosaic concerns were largely lost in the ever-changing mud of the fertile delta. Our sense of them, therefore, is in that respect partial, and prejudiced in its focus. The idea that they were excessively preoccupied with death, worship, the supernatural and the afterlife is in some degree a mere accident of selective preservation. Nonetheless, it is the specific nature of their funerary system that strikes so eerie and melancholy a chord with later sensibilities—not merely their imperatives, but, more specifically, their choices.

In Western burial, the body is essentially disposed of, because it is presumed that it and the spirit of the deceased have parted ways, and the vessel is no longer needed. It is still, of course, respected, since in its appearance it retains so many aspects unique to the deceased. So it is disposed of solemnly, respectfully and with its equivalent share of ritual. Nonetheless, disposal is the intention, on the understanding that the immortal soul no longer has any use for it. For the Egyptians, likewise, the spirit and body have parted company, but their conception of what happened next seems radically odd to any of us brought up in the Western tradition. Despite the fact that they are now on first name terms with Osiris, the obligations of the living towards them go far beyond reverence. They are still deemed to need all manner of earthly things for use in the afterlife, from clothes and furniture to vehicles, food, servants and, crucially, their mortal bodies, which they will need to return to at a future point. Hence the imperative need to preserve the body as accurately as possible; hence mummification; hence the strange and unique sights that greeted the archaeologists when they began excavating the Egyptian tombs; hence the instant and continued fascination in the popular imagination; hence Kharis. However wild and haphazard the variations have become, this is the central feature that they share and that no other movie monster can claim: this odd half world, between the living and the dead, that metaphorical space we have built ourselves for the majority of our enduring monsters. You could sit down and write a horror story about anything "coming to life," and many have: corpses of all distinction and inanimate objects of every conceivable kind. But they rarely "take" because they are rightly perceived as arbitrary: what the mummy movie has, even in its most trivial variety, is this sense of legitimization by precedent.

It is only fitting therefore that the mummy should in itself become the ultimate visual sym-

The quintessential Hollywood mummy: Lon Chaney, Jr., as Kharis in *The Mummy's Tomb* **(1942).**

bol of the ancients' reflection in the pop cultural mirror: nothing more vividly divides the fact from the fantasy than respective attitudes to this strange, essentially tragic artefact. By performing the act of mummification, the Egyptians were preserving something (the body), not creating something (a mummy). The mummy is in that sense much more an Egyptological concept than an Egyptian one, signifying as it does the preserved corpse that is the *actual* consequence of their funerary practices, *not* the intended one.

To the Egyptians, mummification was a stage in a process, a means rather than an end; its purpose is not the preservation of death but the continuance of life. There *is* no "mummy" at the end of this process because a "mummy" is a corpse. The end of mummification is resurrection: restored life, not preserved death. The walking mummy, dead but alive, that is central to our mythos is paradoxical to theirs: the mummy state is ephemeral, not eternal. This is reflected even in the instances within the ancient culture itself of legends in which the living converse with the dead. According to one tale, dating from the third century BC, an Egyptian priest called Khamaus discovered the means to talk to the dead in their tombs. A year before Karloff, the Egyptologist and oddball Sir E. A. Wallis Budge included an account of the story in his *Egyptian Tales and Romances* (1931):

> The story of the quest of Khamaus for a wonderful Book of Magic which was believed to have been composed by Thoth, and his converse with mummies in a tomb, is found written in Demotic upon a papyrus preserved in the Egyptian Museum in Cairo. The papyrus was written in the fifteenth

year of the reign of Ptolemy III Euergetes I, i.e., 233 B Khamaus was a son of Rameses II by his wife Ast-Nefert, and during the greater part of his life he dwelt at Memphis, where he was a SEM, or SETEM priest, and as high-priest of Memphis he held the title of "Great Wielder of the Hammer." He died in the fifty-fifth year of the reign of Rameses II and was buried near the Great Pyramid of Gizah; Maspero found the remains of his tomb at Kaft al-Batran. He was a very learned man and a great magician, and some have thought that he was one of the magicians who performed such marvellous acts before Moses in connection with the snake-rod. Khamaus discovered by some means that the god Thoth had written a book of magic. Now Thoth was regarded as the heart and tongue of Ra, the Sun-god, and it was he who pronounced the magical words which expressed the thoughts and intentions of Ra, and caused creation to come into being. The book of magic written by Thoth was eagerly sought after by the Egyptians in all ages, but what it was like or what it contained were alike unknown. A tradition exists which stated that it had been sought for and found by Prince Nefer-ka-Ptah, the son of Mer-neb-Prah, a King of Egypt, and that it was buried with this Prince in this tomb, at Memphis. Now Khamaus spent a great deal of time in wandering about the cemeteries. And one day he discovered the tomb of Nefer-Ka-Ptah, which he opened and entered. In it he found the spirits of Nefer-Ka-Ptah, and his wife Ahura, and their child. By the side of them lay the famous Book of Magic written by Thoth. When Khamuas stretched out his hand to take possession of the book, Ahura, the wife of Nefer-Ka-Ptah, prevented him from doing so. When he persisted she entreated him to abandon the idea of doing so, and then she described to him how the book came into their hands, and the disasters which had befallen her and her husband and child in connection with the possession thereof.

Here, still in dynastic Egypt itself, much seems in place for the later mummy fiction—even, note, the book (for which read ring, or scroll) of Thoth. (The Egyptians venerated Thoth as the font of all science and master of magic.) The vital difference, however, is in the attitude revealed towards the mummies themselves. For Khamaus they are represented as spirits, transcending the flesh, even while retaining corporeality. But in the horror fiction of the modern era iconic value is based specifically in the wretched physicality of the mummy form rather than its animating spirituality. Usually it is the servant of a human master compelling it to acts of murder, and its intellectual capacities are limited only to sentience; its behavior is entirely mechanistic. And visual emphasis is placed on the fact of decomposition: the brittleness of the limbs, parchment-like desiccation of the flesh and—most centrally—dank, loose, trailing bandages.

The bandaging of the corpse in reality is a purely logistical act—not a symbolic, aesthetic or sacred one. The illustrated anthropoid outer coffins that became standard from the Twelfth Dynasty are the true exo-form of the deceased—and these show the recumbent figures in attitudes of earthly perfection, not bandaged mortification. *The Mummy* (1932) rightly has Boris Karloff shed his bandages as soon as life and capability are restored: the more common image of the mummy stumbling about still wrapped is, or rather should be, a faintly absurd one.

Yet it is, for all that, one which any would-be mummy moviemaker tampers with at their peril. There are doubtless many good reasons why the mummy films produced in the 1990s by director Stephen Sommers have failed to lodge nostalgically in the popular consciousness as earlier cycles have done, but I think the main one is their revisionist presentation of the titular threat. Call a film *The Mummy* and people expect a shuffling, bandaged monster: even the Karloff original often causes confusion to modern viewers. Newer approaches to the idea are often ingenious—the attacks in the likeable *Talos the Mummy* (1998), for instance, are presented as a flurry of bandages which encircles its victims like a tornado—but you still miss that lumbering monster.

As we shall see, the classic image of the screen mummy is in key regards derived from the appearance of preserved mummies in the major museums, which in many cases are presented misleadingly, for instance in the arrangement of the bandaging, and in a partially wrapped and unwrapped form. In the films these elements are frequently carried over and presented as if historically authentic. But the films also reconfigure the historical record for their own convenience, and many staples of the screen mythology of the mummy movies owe their existence not to dramatic choices but practical ones. Tomb architecture is generally adapted to suit the needs of set designers and camera operators. The reality of multiple ante-chambers, narrow passageways and precarious access points through small entrances and holes—though all highly conducive to cinematic suspense and mood—usually give way to a more practical arrangement, where the body of the deceased is deposited in the center of an enormous single chamber, access to which is often afforded not by penetrating a wall but breaking the seal or rope on a pair of enormous doors, which then glide open silently as if on freshly-oiled casters. These tombs, furthermore, are often amusingly well-lit. (The one in Hammer's first mummy film in 1959 not only glows spectrally green but also gives the impression, surely erroneous, of being carpeted.)

And as Jasmine Day notes in *The Mummy's Curse*:

> Im-Ho-Tep's coffin stands upright in the archaeologists' hut, its lid removed. This assists the mummy's ambulation, allowing him to step out. Whether or not this was suggested solely by the upright placement of coffins in museums, it coincides with their orientation, which evokes in the minds of moviegoers to this day the idea of a sleeping mummy ready to awaken.

And then:

> The mummy must be concealed yet able to see, so a compromise is reached between denial and practicality. The bandages dramatically wound over living Im-Ho-Tep's face have inexplicably disappeared from his mummy.... Hammer's Kharis has just a slit for his eyes...

Similarly, the fact that the mummy Kharis has had his tongue removed "is a plot device contrived to excuse a silence initially imposed by actors' costumes, but thereafter by tradition."

A recurring notion in accounts of these films is that the mummy, as a violator of Egyptian religious law, is sentenced to be mummified alive; we are then shown images of Karloff or Tom Tyler or Christopher Lee struggling as burly hands bind them in lengths of cotton wrap. But "mummified alive" is an oxymoron: mummification is a process performed upon a corpse, you can no more mummify a living person than you can murder a dead one. What actually happens to these unfortunates is that they are *bandaged* alive: no other stage of the mummification process is undertaken (which would, in any event, result in instant death). If one were burying a miscreant alive, to wrap them in bandages first would be simultaneously purposeless and vaguely sacrilegious! (Indicative of the confusion are the competing assertions, voiced by the same character in *The Mummy's Hand*, that Kharis has been buried alive and yet is also "the most amazing example of embalming.") The sole purpose of the bandages, in reality, is to assist in the preservation of a dead body, and the body in its bandaged form is meant never to be seen. Yet the image of the bandaged figure becomes a kind of fetish in the mummy movies, as significant as the tomb art and architecture. This is the boggy ground in which the mummy of fiction stakes its own, cultural afterlife.

Most histories suggest that mummification was, at first, accidental. The Predynastic culture, keen not to bury their dead in land that would be waterlogged in the annual Nile floods, opted instead to inter them further from harm, in the desert. Because the hot, dry sand allowed liquids to dissipate downwards and away, the corpse desiccated rather than putrefied. This was then discovered during later dynasties, perhaps by chance as an ancient burial site was cleared for new construction, and the idea of reverse engineering the process was born. As with most great theories, of course, it is only that, and it would certainly be ironic if this best known element of Egyptian custom was the mere imitation of a natural phenomenon. Early Old Kingdom mummies are often partially reconstructed with plaster and paint, beneath which the body rotted as normal, suggesting that if mummification *was* a chance discovery it was an incredibly fortuitous one that satisfied an already exigent need.

There is some evidence that deliberate mummification may also have begun in the Predynastic period. Excavators in 1997 found large numbers of Predynastic graves dating to around 3500 BC containing bodies whose head, arms and hands were wrapped in strips of linen. This suggested ritual: the preservation of the face making the body recognizable to its spirit in the afterlife, while the intact hands would be necessary for it to be fed. Other bodies had bundled cloth secreted internally, as padding; this was also suggestive of cosmetic preservation. The team also detected the presence of preservative resin on the bodies. This could suggest that artificial mummification may well have begun many centuries before traditionally supposed.[1]

What is certain is that techniques in mummification advanced as the practice went along. The earliest efforts consisted chiefly of wrapping the corpse in bandaging, in the hope that it would somehow contain the decomposition and retain the original form. It wasn't until the end of the Third Dynasty that the grim but logical idea to remove the internal organs was hit upon. Resin-soaked bandages were used to maintain the exterior, while the fast-rotting viscera was extracted from within via small incisions. From the Eighteenth Dynasty the practice of removing the brain through the nose began.[2]

There is an irony here. This process must have been so disgusting, so impersonal and clinical, so revealing of the hopeless materiality of the body after death, that it's hard to believe the very enactment of these various processes didn't convince those engaged upon them that their efforts were futile. Could they really have believed—truly believed—that they were preparing the immortal vessel of a timeless soul, rather than just moving lumps of meat about? It's hard to answer that—like the related issue of tomb curses that were completely ignored by robbers, it points to a fundamental ambiguity that no mere archaeological find could ever settle. Nonetheless, this constant striving for advancement of technique in mummification shows that at some high level it *must* have been felt to serve an imperative rather than merely ritualistic purpose.

The typical movie mummy is a powerful killing machine, a guardian of the tomb protecting it from the assaults of modernity, rationalism and Western contamination. As such they are vast, looming figures, barrel-chested like Lon Chaney, Jr., imposingly tall like Christopher Lee, or fresh from the Wild West like Tom Tyler. Yet stare at a real mummy in a museum case and the overriding impression it will give is of fragility, and poignancy. They are sad things, and usually small. (The Egyptians tended to come in between five and five-and-a-half feet.) Divorced from their trappings and surroundings, there is little that is awe-inspiring about them.

Neither did they inspire much awe in the earliest archaeologists, for whom ancient history, before the science of Egyptology prioritized cataloguing and interpretation, was basically a treasure hunt. Tombs were divested of their valuable jewelry and art, and the mummies, though interesting, were considered of no lasting significance. The numbers thus destroyed is beyond calculation: the great tomb raider Giovanni Belzoni speaks casually in his accounts of the piles of mummies, "some standing, some lying and some on their heads," that he encountered as he ventured through the Theban hills. No need, in such circumstances, for consideration, still less piety: "Every step I took," he writes, "I crushed a mummy in some place or another."

Throughout the centuries, countless corpses were ground up to support a lucrative trade in quack medicine, powdered mummy possessing supposedly beneficial properties. The prized substance, originally, appears to have been specifically the pitch-like bitumen found within the bodies, from which the word "mummy" is itself derived (the Arabic word being *mumia*). But as J. R. Harris writes in *The Legacy of Egypt*, this soon evolved into the medicinal use of the entire corpse:

> The historian 'Abd al-Latif in the twelfth century speaks of the matter taken out of the skulls and stomachs of mummies, and Ibn al-Baiṭār, the celebrated thirteenth century physician, also alludes to the *mumia* of the tombs. But already in the eleventh century certain Arab authorities, such as Ibn Ridwān, had begun to ascribe the therapeutic values of *mumia* to the actual flesh of the embalmed, and it was chiefly in this latter sense that "mummy" was to be understood in Europe.
>
> According to a story handed down by Guyon in his *Leçons*, an Alexandrian Jew named "Elmagar" treated Crusaders and their Muslim adversaries with "mummy" and so was responsible for spreading the knowledge of its properties. In fact, the Salerno school of the eleventh century may have played an important part in this, for certainly Constantinus Africanus was familiar with the bituminous *mumia* derived from ancient corpses. The use of the cadaverous flesh itself is cited in a work written in 1363 by Guy de Chavillac, surgeon to Pope Clemens VI—the earliest English reference being in a manuscript of about 1400—and by the beginning of the sixteenth century it was so highly regarded, notably in France, that François I himself was accustomed, says Belon, to carry a little packet containing "mummy" mixed with powdered rhubarb, in case of accident. During the sixteenth and seventeenth centuries, "mummy" was, indeed, one of the drugs included in the ordinary repertoire of European apothecaries, "Mummy is become merchandise, Mizraim cures wounds, and Pharaoh is sold for balsams," wrote Sir Thomas Browne, and allusions to it are frequent in Elizabethan and Jacobean drama.... It was considered most efficacious for bruises and wounds, but was also taken internally in various forms, and different qualities were recognized. The best was generally considered to be that which was hard but easily pulverized, dark brown to black in colour, with a bitter taste and a strong smell...

So in demand was the raw material that it has even been suggested that a lucrative black market in mummies was profitably supplemented with fakes, derived from the bodies of executed criminals and the dead from hospitals, spirited away, stuffed with asphalt and left to desiccate in the Egyptian sun ... these, then, like the authentic versions, were taken both externally and internally!

But this was far from the full extent of their usefulness. During the American Civil War, paper manufacturer Isaac Stanwood imported mummies by the ton, stripping them of their bandages which he then pulped to make brown paper. Shakespeare's Othello describes a handkerchief as "dy'd in mummy," and their use as pigment in the production of bituminous paint apparently continued into the twentieth century. (The story goes that artists Edward Burne-Jones and Lawrence Alma-Tadema, on discovering that their "mummy brown" paint was exactly that, guiltily buried a tube of it in the garden in a makeshift funeral service, attended by several other mourners.) "Mummy" also served, it has been claimed in some contemporary sources, as a condiment in eighteenth century banquets, and in the nineteenth century mummies burned as fuel on steam engines and in factories. Small wonder that they want to rise from the dead and kill us.

The earliest appearances of the mummy in popular culture tend to be more frivolous than the later horror stories, as befits a commodity all too clearly perceived as disposable. Nonetheless, these early tales do articulate, however flippantly, what will become the standard notion of the "classic" mummy story: that of the ancients redressing the balance against those who would disregard their dignity. Théophile Gautier's *The Mummy's Foot*

Egyptian mummy seller, 1875 (photograph by Félix Bonfils).

(1840), for instance, concerns a man who purchases the foot of an Egyptian princess in a curiosity shop for use as a paperweight. (This was a far from unlikely contingency at that time. Famously, a mummified foot had been discovered in the step pyramid of King Djoser, all that remained after generations of plunder.) This one, however, proves to have a life of its own, and is soon leaping over the narrator's desk "like a startled frog," whereupon the spirit of the princess returns to reclaim her lost appendage.

Such disregard for the mortal remains of the ancients was interrogated only by quixotic sensibilities like Gautier's and in works such as these: the unsentimental attitude they lightly chide was unquestioned both without and within the academy. But sometimes the absence of sentimentality could cross the line from pragmatism to myopia. The great Egyptologist William Flinders Petrie recalled his discovery of an arm "in marvellously fine tissue of linen" in the First Dynasty tomb of King Djer. It is generally supposed to have belonged to either the king himself or his wife, and was still wearing four beautiful gold and turquoise bracelets. Beside its value on those grounds, it was also enormously important in that it appeared to have been the result of the then-earliest known attempts at systematic mummification. Petrie had it transported to the Cairo Museum for analysis, where it was handed to the German archaeologist Émile Brugsch. As Petrie recalled: "Brugsch only cared for display; so from one bracelet he cut away the half that was of plaited gold wire, and he also threw away the arm and the linen." It's tempting to posit a sequel to Gautier's tale, "The Mummy's Arm," in which a vengeful Djer comes looking for Émile Brugsch!

Gautier's later *The Romance of the Mummy* (1857) depicts a tomb excavation that seems to somewhat anticipate the Tutankhamen discovery, but a more colorful adventure is to be found in Jane C. Loudon's *The Mummy!* (1827). Its three heroes journey to Egypt in a balloon and use galvanism to revive the mummy of Khuthu, who then promptly steals their balloon and flies to England. In contrast to the cinematic mummy, Khuthu is seen to be lively, articulate and shrewd, and at the end of the novel's three volumes he is happily re-installed in his tomb.

The book, as befits one set three hundred years after it was written, is essentially a work of science fiction, but it uses this element to introduce a lasting theme: that of the supposed need to account for the achievements of the ancient civilization in general, and the Pyramids in particular, in terms other than those of purely human ingenuity and dedication. Thus Dr. Entwerfen, the book's eccentric hero, speaks for another two centuries of wild theorists when he explains to his assistant Edric that only intervention from some other realm can explain them:

> "You are right," said the doctor, "in your observations upon the religion of the ancient Egyptians; but it does not appear to me that the Pyramids were erected by them."
>
> "What! I suppose you draw your conclusions from the want of hieroglyphics in their principal chambers; and, from what Herodotus says of their having been erected by a shepherd, you think they were the work of the Pallic race."
>
> "No; though I allow much may be said in favour of that hypothesis, particularly as Herodotus says the kings under whom they were erected, ordered all the Egyptian temples to be closed, which we know the shepherd or Pallic sovereigns did; but I cannot imagine that an ignorant, Goth-like race of shepherds, men accustomed to live in tents or in the open air, and possessing no talents but for war, were capable of constructing such immense piles. No, no, the Pyramids required gigantic conceptions, highly cultivated minds, and unwearied perseverance; all qualities quite incompatible with a warlike wandering race. I do not think the Palli were capable of imagining such structures, much less of constructing them. I think they were the work of evil spirits."

"Evil spirits!" exclaimed Edric.

"Yes," returned the doctor. "We are told that the evil spirits, after their expulsion from Paradise, were under the command of the Sultan, or Soliman Giam ben Giam, as he is called by Arabic writers, but who is supposed to have been the same as Cheops; and I think that he employed them in this vast work."

For evil spirits read aliens or Atlanteans or whatever you fancy, but that this element should be so promptly present in popular culture is not an accident, neither were later manifestations simply following its lead. (The book made little impact at the time and remains largely unknown.) Much of the "mystery" of ancient Egypt has been fuelled by the presumed unaccountability of its achievements—a myth that dies hard, even today, when so much definitive work has gone into proving it erroneous. It is precisely this perceived gap that an exaggerated emphasis on esoterica has filled. From the first, in other words, Ancient Egypt and the supernatural were linked in the Western imagination more symbiotically than was the case with any other civilization and its mythology.

Loudon's twenty-second century Egypt, by contrast to Khuthu's, owes its majesty purely to human engineering:

> Improvement had turned her gigantic steps towards its once deserted plains; Commerce had waved her magic wand; and towns and cities, manufactories and canals, spread in all directions. No more did the Nile overflow its banks: a thousand channels were cut to receive its waters. No longer did the moving sands of the Desert rise in mighty waves, threatening to overwhelm the wayworn traveller: macadamised turnpike roads supplied their place, over which post-chaises, with anti-attritioned wheels, bowled at the rate of fifteen miles an hour. Steamboats glided down the canals, and furnaces raised their smoky heads amidst groves of palm trees; whilst iron railways intersected orange groves, and plantations of dates and pomegranates might be seen bordering excavations intended for coal pits. Colonies of English and Americans peopled the country, and produced a population that swarmed like bees over the land, and surpassed in numbers even the wondrous throngs of the ancient Mizraim race; whilst industry and science changed desolation into plenty, and had converted barren plains into fertile kingdoms.

Edgar Allan Poe was among the first authors to contemplate letting the ancients speak for themselves.

An interesting riposte to this reductive sizing up the ancients can be found in Edgar Allan Poe's *Some Words with a Mummy* (1845). Not one of the author's famously morbid tales, the piece is among his rarer exercises in obtuse whimsy, lifted from triviality by a marked and thought-provoking strain of satire.[3] The setting is an unwrapping soirée (a fashionable diversion at the time), in which a mummy is revived (again by galvanism) in the drawing room of a group of nineteenth century savants:

> The application of electricity to a Mummy three or four thousand years old at the least, was an idea, if not very sage, still sufficiently original, and we all caught it at once. About one-tenth in earnest and nine-tenths in jest, we arranged a battery in the Doctor's study, and conveyed thither the Egyptian.

Anyone expecting a nightmarish resurrection scene and resultant mayhem is in for a surprise, however:

> Morally and physically—figuratively and literally—was the effect electric. In the first place, the corpse opened its eyes

and winked very rapidly for several minutes, as does Mr. Barnes in the pantomime; in the second place, it sneezed; in the third, it sat upon end; in the fourth, shook its fist in Doctor Ponnonner's face; in the fifth, turning to Messieurs Gliddon and Buckingham, it addressed them, in very capital Egyptian, thus—"I must say, gentlemen, that I am as much surprised as I am mortified, at your behavior. Of Doctor Ponnonner nothing better was to be expected. He is a poor little fat fool who knows no better. I pity and forgive him. But you, Mr. Gliddon—and you, Silk—who have travelled and resided in Egypt until one might imagine you to the manor born—you, I say, who have been so much among us that you speak Egyptian fully as well, I think, as you write your mother tongue—you, whom I have always been led to regard as the firm friend of the mummies—I really did anticipate more gentlemanly conduct from you. What am I to think of your standing quietly by and seeing me thus unhandsomely used? What am I to suppose by your permitting Tom, Dick, and Harry to strip me of my coffins, and my clothes, in this wretchedly cold climate?..."

The discussion between the mummy and the scientists then takes the form of a debate on the relative advantages of the civilizations to which they belong, in which the latter's certainties are soon left decidedly dented:

I here asked the Count what he had to say to our railroads.

"Nothing," he replied, "in particular." They were rather slight, rather ill-conceived, and clumsily put together. They could not be compared, of course, with the vast, level, direct, iron-grooved causeways upon which the Egyptians conveyed entire temples and solid obelisks of a hundred and fifty feet in altitude.

I spoke of our gigantic mechanical forces.

He agreed that we knew something in that way, but inquired how I should have gone to work in getting up the imposts on the lintels of even the little palace at Carnac.

This question I concluded not to hear, and demanded if he had any idea of Artesian wells; but he simply raised his eye-brows; while Mr. Gliddon winked at me very hard and said, in a low tone, that one had been recently discovered by the engineers employed to bore for water in the Great Oasis.

I then mentioned our steel; but the foreigner elevated his nose, and asked me if our steel could have executed the sharp carved work seen on the obelisks, and which was wrought altogether by edge-tools of copper.

This disconcerted us so greatly that we thought it advisable to vary the attack to Metaphysics. We sent for a copy of a book called the *Dial*, and read out of it a chapter or two about something that is not very clear, but which the Bostonians call the Great Movement or progress.

The Count merely said that Great Movements were awfully common things in his day, and as for Progress, it was at one time quite a nuisance, but it never progressed.

We then spoke of the great beauty and importance of democracy, and were at much trouble in impressing the Count with a due sense of the advantages we enjoyed in living where there was suffrage *ad libitum*, and no king.

He listened with marked interest, and in fact seemed not a little amused. When we had done, he said that, a great while ago, there had occurred something of a very similar sort. Thirteen Egyptian provinces determined all at once to be free, and to set a magnificent example to the rest of mankind. They assembled their wise men, and concocted the most ingenious constitution it is possible to conceive. For a while they managed remarkably well; only their habit of bragging was prodigious. The thing ended, however, in the consolidation of the thirteen states, with some fifteen or twenty others, in the most odious and insupportable despotism that was heard of upon the face of the Earth.

I asked what was the name of the usurping tyrant.

As well as the Count could recollect, it was *Mob*.

These, then, are the dominant themes of nineteenth century mummy fiction: the unchanging mummy is used as symbol to reflect upon the course of progress and the march of civilization (either to trumpet or to lightly satirize Western exceptionalism), and archaeological discovery is presented in the context of an adventure story. By the time a frisson of horror was added to the adventure, everything was in place for the mummy to walk again. Théophile Gautier had led us part of the way, in *The Romance of the Mummy* (1857):

> As they pressed forward into the chamber, Lord Evandale had a strange sensation assail him. Modern life and all that it stood for to him seemed to pass away, out of sight and touch, out of thought. He forgot Great Britain, and the great fact that his name was upon the roll of its nobility, that he was one of its "titled and landed" class. Forgot, too, his home in Lincolnshire, his town house in London's West End, his yacht, and all that made or aided his English life. An unseen hand put back the clock of time, had turned again the hour-glass of the ages. Sand by sand the centuries fell silently, sadly, as hours pass in the silence and solitude of the night. History was there, in the past, not here and now, viewed with the eyes of to-day. Moses lived, Pharaoh reigned, and he, Lord Evandale, felt it strange that he was not coiffured and dressed as an Egyptian noble would be when in the presence of the royalty of Egypt. Then, too, a touch of religious horror came to him, for had he not violated this palace of the half-divine, royal dead—defended though it had been with such care against the hand of the profaner?
>
> The attempt, and its success so far, now seemed to him impious and a sacrilege, and he said—
>
> "If there is a Pharaoh here he might rise upon his couch and strike me with his sceptre!"

But the *real* romance, that would fix the mummy in popular culture for all time, was just around the corner, and not in the pages of a novel but waiting patiently in the timeless sands of Egypt herself. To arrive there best prepared, we need to temporarily abandon the fictional representations, and follow the historical trail of Egyptomania itself.

2

Of Mania and Maniacs

> Gilda Gray, star of the Ziegfeld Follies, who acted as one of the judges at the convention of the Hairdressers' Association held recently at the Waldorf Astoria, New York, will be the first member of the theatrical profession to adopt the new "Tut-Ankh-Amen bob."—*Adelaide Chronicle* (August 4, 1923)

Aesthetic movements have always drawn on other periods and other lands—popular culture likewise. In the history of taste we find Greek revivals, Roman revivals, Gothic revivals ... but, note, these are not "manias." A mania is more than an interest, or a movement, or a moment. It carries other connotations: it's unhealthy, excessive, obsessive; it's lawless, and unbounded by intellectual or artistic propriety.

It also suggests a collective flavor to its effects: the kind of obsession that manifests itself in myriad forms but in some manner and to some degree touches just about everyone. And of Egyptomania, all the above is true. Repeatedly throughout history, this strange, ancient world has risen again to claim our souls and our devotion. Like the walking mummies of movies and fiction, Ancient Egypt itself never stays dead for long.

Edgar Allan Poe's *Some Words with a Mummy*, discussed in the previous chapter, is in its essence an early satire of Egyptomania. Most of the characters in the story share their names with real people, and "Gliddon" refers to George Gliddon, the American Egyptologist and showman credited with bringing the hitherto European fashion for unwrapping ceremonies to America. (Readers well-versed in the mummy movies may here want to picture Fred Clark in Hammer's *Curse of the Mummy's Tomb*.)

Had he lived long enough, Poe would have laughed heartily at Gliddon's elaborate attempt in 1850 to stage a public unwrapping in Boston over a period of three days as a kind of cliffhanger serial. He announced grandly that a series of lectures, attended by such luminaries as Henry Wadsworth Longfellow and Louis Aggasi, would culminate in the revealing of "the daughter of a high priest of Thebes who lived more than 3,000 years ago, or about the time of Moses." Great was the anticipation: according to S. J. Wolfe's book *Mummies in Nineteenth Century America: Ancient Egyptians as Artefacts*, an anonymous poet even wrote a lengthy dirge about the tragic heroine about to be exposed; imagining her passing away (of course) in the first flush of youthful beauty, and mourned by her lover, who "weeps upon the broken stem of the lily of the Nile."

The unwrapping began on a Monday, with Gliddon pontificating on the Pyramids and Sphinx while an onstage carpenter wantonly sawed open the painted sarcophagus. The next episode was staged on the Wednesday—the day's gap intended to instill mounting suspense—and saw Gliddon exercising his jaw still further before the unwrapping began. Racking up the nail-biting tension, he halted before the final reveal, which was to be saved for the final show on the Friday. Friday came, and, before the entire awestruck audience, it was seen beyond doubt that this was most decidedly *not* the daughter of a High Priest of Thebes, for the mummy was "exhibiting in its fossil state the erected unequivocal mark of its sex."[1] Gliddon's attempts to excuse his faux pas by attributing it to unclear hieroglyphs, which he blamed on drunken Egyptian coffin-makers, only added to the general hilarity, and the newspapers gleefully reported on the comedy in terms of resounding mockery.

It is perhaps on the basis of episodes such as these that the very term "Egyptomania" became established as the marker of a phenomenon of which intellectual sobriety is not necessarily to be expected, and whose effects can be located on an extremely broad spectrum of aesthetic respectability, from the highest of high art at one extreme, to the antics of Gliddon and his like at the other.

If you keep your eyes open, Egyptomania is all around you. For instance, a few minutes from my door, in Bath's Royal Victoria Park, two splendid stone sphinxes scrutinize each other impassively from the posts of an impressive iron gateway. Frequently through the course of writing this book I've gone to see them in the hope of absorbing some of their eternal wisdom, but they remain inscrutable at all times. I call them "Mr. Reeves" and "I. Williams Esq.," as these are the names that appear prominently beneath them. Closer inspection of the fading stonework, however, reveals that these are the names of the two local philanthropists who donated them to the city, yet in their quaintness and redoubtable air of Englishness, the names seem oddly to suit them. They date from the park's original construction in 1827–30, which makes them contemporary with that most

A nineteenth century English sphinx: Royal Victoria Gardens, Bath (photograph by Angela Coniam).

notable wave of Egyptomania that was a product of the Napoleonic wars, contemporary with the erection of the so-called Cleopatra Needles in London and Paris.[2]

And Egyptomania, perhaps, is more to be savored in these eccentric side-products than in the full force and pomp of its grandest manifestations. Few today who gaze upon London's Cleopatra Needle notice the accompanying benches that line the north side of the Thames embankment, and those who do probably chuckle at the ornate sphinxes and camels that have been recruited as arm-rests. They were designed by George John Vulliamy, the same architect who designed the pedestal supporting the Needle itself, and were intended to complement the obelisk in an entirely sober and worthy fashion. Now, they inevitably suggest pastiche in their naïve, haphazard exoticism. To the student of

The Sphinx benches by Cleopatra's Needle, London.

Egyptomania, however, they may well be considered the main point of interest, with the monument itself coming in second. Or third, even, after such contemporaneous celebrations of the moment as composer Albert Hartmann's *Cleopatra's Needle Waltz* (1877).

This is not to say that the story of the Needle itself is lacking in that flavor of obsessive eccentricity that we Egyptomaniacs so enjoy.³ Having collapsed in the 14th century AD, it was found half-buried in the sand by the Earl of Cavan in his downtime after defeating Napoleon at the Battle of Alexandria in 1801. No doubt in bullish mood, Cavan decided the fallen obelisk was the perfect souvenir with which to celebrate the victory, and successfully petitioned the Turkish authorities to allow it to return with him to England. Unfortunately, the constructions erected to transport the Needle to a ship, via rollers and a specially constructed jetty, proved inadequate: the jetty collapsed and the plans were abandoned.

As the decades wore on no further attempts were made to retrieve it, and a number of efforts by the new Egyptian government to offer it as a gift to Britain free of charge were received with courteous apathy. Plans to include it in Trafalgar Square, or as part of the Crystal Palace Gardens at Sydenham came to naught, as the simple cost of transporting it was deemed prohibitive. "England appears from her apparent bewilderment about the matter," reflected *Fraser's Magazine* in 1846, "to be in the position of the elderly woman who won an elephant in a lottery." Twenty years later, reports confirmed that the obelisk was again entirely submerged in sand and, perilously, was now resting on land that, as the British Consul squeamishly put it, had been "given by the Viceroy to some Greek or Frenchman." Was there no fine upstanding English madman, patriotic and foolhardy enough to drag this ponderous Egyptian elephant to its new home?

Strike up the band, and welcome Waynham Dixon. A young engineer, in Egypt to build bridges over the Nile, Dixon had acquired a passion for the past that would eventually secure him Egyptological immortality as the man who discovered the still-unexplained "air-shafts" in the Great Pyramid. Less celebrated than the discovery itself is his typically insensitive methodology. On a private inspection of the Pyramid's interior he noticed a small crack in the wall of the Queen's Chamber and, without even the pretence of authority, set about walloping it with a sledgehammer.

Clearly, this was the man to bring the Needle back to Britain, and in 1877, he got the job. Bob Brier tells the story in his fascinating history of *Egyptomania*:

> After his brother raised the funds, Dixon designed an iron caisson, very much like a cigar tube, into which the obelisk would be slid, sealed, and then towed to England by steamer. The voyage was dramatic. The ship hit a gale in the Bay of Biscay, six brave seamen lost their lives, and the obelisk was temporarily lost at sea but remained afloat and subsequently was recovered by another ship. The obelisk coming to London was a major Egyptological event. For the first time in more than a century, a monumental Egyptian antiquity left Egyptian soil.

Finally erected on the Thames Embankment in September of 1878, it was honored as a fine symbol of British pomp, the extraordinarily lengthy and eccentric history of its progress seemingly forgotten. Two grand sphinxes were cast in bronze and erected flanking the monument, but looking the wrong way: inward, towards the needle as if intrigued by it, rather than outward, in its defence. Sealed in the pedestal was a time capsule containing an eclectic selection of items representative of Britain in its multifarious glory, including a portrait of Queen Victoria, a Bradshaw's Railway Guide, a box of cigars and 12 photographs of the best-looking women in England.

Think of it all as a journey: from the Needle and its matching benches, to Messrs

Cleopatra's Needle is encased in its cylinder in preparation for its trip to London.

Reeves and Williams (my English sphinxes), to the prurient unwrappings, and on—to the Singer sewing machine, Lon Chaney, Jr., and *Love Brides of the Blood Mummy* (1973). Viewed in sequence, they tell a cumulative story about the degeneration (and reconstruction) that accompanies the appropriation of alien myth and culture in the popular sphere. This is not, however, to say that such attitudes were necessarily at odds with those of the specialists: Egyptomania is not so much an off-shoot of Egyptology as its cradle: the impetus to serious study was a side-effect of the exact same romantic fantasies as fuelled (and fuels) the mania.

Further, as the story of the Cleopatra Needle illustrates, Egyptology was at first purely acquisitive, and essentially nationalistic. The Wedgwood pottery firm produced an Egyptian-style tea set in 1808 designed less in admiration of Egyptian style itself than as a gesture of military superiority over the French, for whom Egyptian aesthetics were a noted obsession. "When an Englishman poured his tea in the morning from an Egyptian-style teapot," notes Brier, "he was saying, 'We beat Bonaparte!'" Indeed, the main reason why the British government finally resolved to claim the Needle for London after decades of indecision was the suspicion that the French still had their eye on it too. This attitude (and basic conception of archaeology) continued certainly as far as the twentieth century, when expeditions competed for digging concessions that, even if privately funded, were nonetheless conducted in the name and interests of their respective governments. Howard Carter's opinion of the French, if requested, was unlikely to have been much different from Cavan's.

In a sense it was Tutmania itself that helped change all that: though skittish and for the most part devoid of any pretence of academic seriousness, it was nonetheless global, youthful and democratic. In its mix and match aesthetics, and its cheerful adoption of Egyptian iconography not merely as demonstrations of power or affluence but as inspiration to fashion, decoration, advertising and pop culture, it proposed and embraced a world without proprietorial privilege. Ancient Egypt was no longer the province of rival governments, stuffy savants, dusty museum cases, or grandiloquent monuments in municipal parks and private estates. It now belonged to everybody—a notion that, however much it may have annoyed the Egyptians, positively enraged Carter and his fellow Western specialists.

But then, Carter had his feet planted in the sacred ground itself, and the world he was revealing through dust and toil had no connection whatever in his mind with posh frocks and foxtrots. It seems an irony somehow typical of its age that a style so symbolic of the youth and freshness of the 1920s, owed its existence to the tomb of a boy, quietly moldering for thousands of years before being dragged into the Egyptian sun and the glare of flashbulbs. The 1920s could hardly have had a more unlikely hero than this small, lonely corpse, yet hero of the age he clearly was. In that sense, then, the story of the Tutankhamen discovery is exactly analogous to the movies in which mummies stalk and kill: both play out a series of confrontations and collisions, between ancient and modern, the frivolous and the somber, the sacred and the secular, knowledge and commerce, wisdom and triviality.

Egyptomania became Tutmania on November 4, 1922. The story of what happened that day, the events leading to it and those that followed, have passed into twentieth century folklore. Carter, under his patron Lord Carnarvon, had been fruitlessly searching the sand since 1917: six seasons of work, with virtually nothing to show for them. Carnarvon was inclined to tighten his belt a little, and had informed Carter that the 1922 season was in all probability the last.

In preparation for a fresh search, Carter's team had removed a number of workmen's huts, probably erected by laborers in the tomb of Rameses VI. Probing what should have been the soft and yielding ground beneath, they instead met with inexplicable resistance. The sand was cleared away, and it became instantly apparent that what had been found was no mere chunk of stone: it was a step. By the following day enough had been cleared away to reveal a descending stairway. By sunset of November 5 the team had dug deep enough to reach a sealed door. Carter and Carnarvon had found the tomb of Tutankhamen and, as in some Hollywood movie, right at the very last minute.

Indeed, so much of the story that followed played out like a Hollywood movie that it is frankly extraordinary that a lavish Hollywood account of the discovery—with Clark Gable as Carter perhaps, and Lewis Stone as Carnarvon—never did materialize. Could anything be more cinematic than Carter's account of the agonizing moment when all the debris was cleared and the team prepared to enter the tomb itself, on November 26, 1922? Carter calls it "the day of days, the most wonderful that I have ever lived through, and certainly one whose like I can never hope to see again." It is as well-known as anything connected with the saga, or indeed with archaeology itself, but I make no apology for sharing it again, for it never fails to make my scalp tingle:

2. Of Mania and Maniacs

Slowly, desperately slowly it seemed to us as we watched, the remains of passage debris that encumbered the lower part of the doorway were removed, until at last we had the whole door clear before us. The decisive moment had arrived. With trembling hands I made a tiny breach in the upper left hand corner. Darkness and blank space, as far as an iron testing-rod could reach, showed that whatever lay beyond was empty, and not filled like the passage we had just cleared. Candle tests were applied as a precaution against possible foul gases and then, widening the hole a little, I inserted the candle and peered in, Lord Carnarvon, Lady Evelyn and Callender standing anxiously beside me to hear the verdict. At first I could see nothing, the hot air escaping from the chamber causing the candle flame to flicker, but presently, as my eyes grew accustomed to the light, details of the room within emerged slowly from the mist, strange animals, statues, and gold—everywhere the glint of gold. For the moment—an eternity it must have seemed to the others standing by—I was struck dumb with amazement, and when Lord Carnarvon, unable to stand the suspense any longer, inquired anxiously, "Can you see anything?" it was all I could do to get out the words, "Yes, wonderful things."

Howard Carter: he gave the world Tutankhamen, and never forgave it for Tutmania.

And wonderful things were just what a world still reeling from the loss and despair of a devastating war had been waiting for. If Carter had deluded himself he was still operating in the subdued and gentlemanly conditions of the Victorian age he soon saw his error when the first reports of his discovery were made and the public response began to show itself. If any one thing justified and symbolized the Jazz Age's surrender to the moment it was the golden horde of Tutankhamen. Here was a treasure beyond imagining, and all in the possession of "lost youth"—a boy king, struck down in his prime, and entirely unable to enjoy it. Live today, tomorrow we die: the metaphor was so overt it felt somehow inevitable. The world wanted Tutankhamen because the world needed Tutankhamen: it was owed to them. And once the party started, it did not stop.

"Archaeology under the limelight is a new rather bewildering experience for most of us," Carter wrote, with uncharacteristic understatement, in his memoirs:

> One must suppose that at the time the general public was in state of profound boredom with news of reparations, conferences and mandates, and craved for some new topic of conversation. The idea of buried treasure, too, is one that appeals to most of us. Whatever the reason, or combination of reasons, it is quite certain that, once the initial *Times* dispatch had been published, no power on earth could shelter us from the light of publicity that beat down upon us. We were helpless, and had to make the best of it.

What he could not have perceived, almost entirely sealed as he was from the drift of Western popular culture, was that ultimately, true though his observations were to a point, this was a phenomenon beyond rational analysis. It was a mass capitulation to a kind of benign psychosis: when he made his hole in the wall, so too was a rupture made in Western high culture. What came bursting through, like the hot air of the sealed tomb, was a long-subdued and liberating insanity, and its message was of fatalistic but sincere joy.

Two elements of Tutmania can be said to have had cultural-historical permanence.

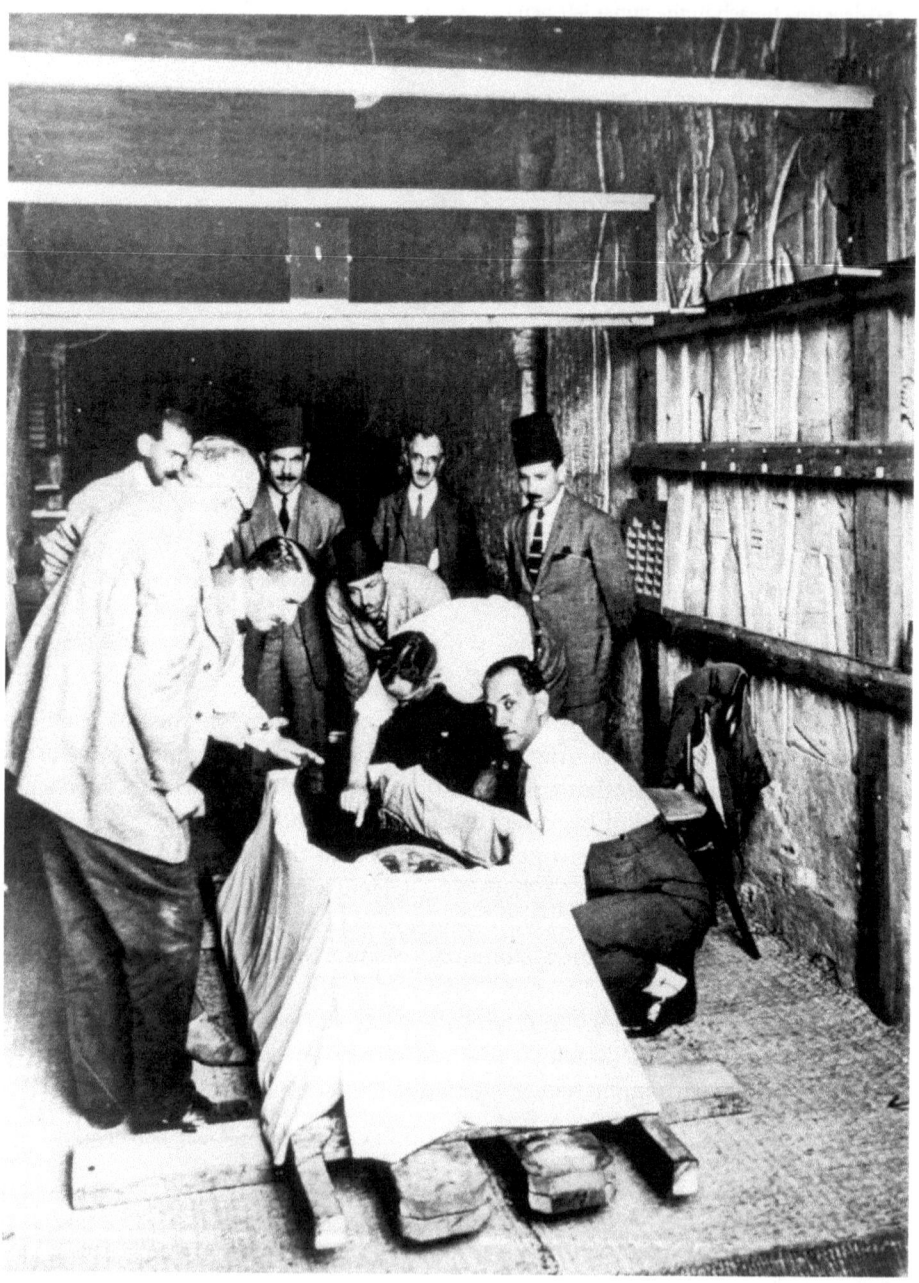

The serious business of exploring the tomb and cataloguing its contents ran in uneasy parallel with the carnival-like reception it was receiving in the outside world—as the team's guarded expressions seem to suggest.

One was the deferred phenomenon of the mummy movie and, in a broader sense, the enshrinement of the Mummy in the pantheon of monsters by which the classical horror genre in all media is defined. The other, quicker to manifest and unique, ultimately, in the respectability it achieved out of context, was Art Deco. Though the term itself only came into common use in the 1960s (derived from the name of the Parisian *Exposition Internationale des Arts Décoratifs et Industriels Modernes* in 1925) the forms we now associate with the movement were instantly recognized, albeit summed-up more trivially as "the Nile Style." While history has sifted the products of Art Deco to construct a canon of great masterpieces in architecture, jewelry and design, at first the magnificent and the mundane jostled against each other in a mad parade that was bewildering, democratic and exhilarating.

Previous eras of Egyptomania inspired their full share of the tacky and trivial, but Tutmania put all that had gone before in the shade. Egypt, pyramids, sphinxes, mummies and camels were everywhere, and "King Tut" was used to sell everything from soap to cigars to pencils to canned foods. Fashionable dances spuriously declared themselves informed by ancient rhythms, furniture and fittings were adorned with sphinxes and crocodiles, and popular songs appeared with titles like "Old King Tut Was a Wise Old Nut." (*He got into his royal bed, three thousand years BC / And left a call for twelve o'clock in nineteen-twenty-three.*) Music hall team Wilson, Keppel and Betty began performing their "Cleopatra's Nightmare" sand dance act in the late 1920s (and didn't stop until the 1960s). Minneapolis-born lightweight boxer Herbert Tuttle fought under the name "King Tut" throughout the second half of the decade. Herbert Hoover named his dog King Tut, while still another dog of that name appeared in movies with Harold Lloyd, Harry Langdon and Clara Bow.

And, of course, the Nile Style conquered the catwalks. As the *Adelaide Chronicle* observed:

> You cannot be in style if you do not wear Tut-Ankh-Amen embroidery, is the latest cry of the Parisian fashion fixers who have induced the Lyons silk mills to turn out millions of yards of special Egyptian designs which would make even Tut-Ankh-Amen's beautiful mother-in-law envious.
>
> Instead of the customary angular designs, this embroidery is so fashioned as to tell whole stories of Egyptian history taken from manuscripts in the Louvre and from carvings found on the ancient temples. One shawl is thus embroidered with several chapters of the Book of the Dead, the characters being faithfully reproduced, while thousands of coats next season are to be lined with embroidery reproducing the frescoes found in the tombs of Tut-Ankh-Amen and other pharaohs.[4]

Through all this, Carter shrugged his shoulders, swore under his breath, and went about his business. But one development in 1924 so incensed him that it compelled him to ill-advised action. As the *Madera Tribune* explained it:

> Untold millions of people have wished that they could see the tomb of Tut-Ankh-Amen in the Valley of the

King Tut, canine star of Hollywood, meets a fan (*Picture Play*, May 1929).

Kings, Egypt, and all the wonderful relics of an early civilization shrouded in the mists of antiquity. Owing to the distance involved and the dispute between the discoverers and the Egyptian government, this is not an easy accomplishment, but the British Empire Exposition which opens in London April 23 and of which the Prince of Wales is president, has built an exact reproduction of the tomb and the various interesting relics found therein. Thousands of dollars worth of gold has been beaten for the gilding of many of these treasures which are about thirty centuries old. The Exposition will remain open until October.[5]

For Carter, this reduction of the find and its wonders to the level of a carnival sideshow was simply intolerable, and he promptly brought legal action against the display's creators, Wembley Amusements, Ltd. Though his motives were essentially proprietorial jealousy and disgust at the commercialization of the discovery, there was also a personal factor. The technical advisor to the exhibition was the popular Egyptological writer, and former Chief Inspector of Antiquities, Arthur Weigall. There was no love lost between the pair, partly because they differed on the subject of how much say in Egyptian excavations the Egyptians themselves should be allowed (Weigall thought Westerners should tread carefully and think themselves lucky; Carter thought the same of the Egyptians.)

But the main issue between them was Weigall's part, while covering the excavation on behalf of the *Daily Mail*, in fomenting a revolution against Lord Carnarvon's attempt to sell exclusive photographic and reporting rights to the London *Times* (of which more later). In this disgusting peepshow, therefore, Carter detected a provocative disregard of copyright, and he duly filed suit, alleging unauthorized reproduction of the artefacts. Unfortunately for him, however, Weigall had anticipated that one, and kept meticulous notes to show how every detail of every model had been obtained from photographs published in other papers showing the objects being transported *out* of the tomb. Anything that appeared only in an official *Times* photograph had been scrupulously avoided. Even errors in his original drawings were deliberately retained in the models if the only accurate version had appeared in a copyrighted image. Carter was left without a leg to stand on and—worse—with copious amounts of egg on his face. The case was dismissed and the public drew the obvious lesson: science, sobriety and the academy had lost, and showmanship, sensation and the new mass-media had won. The exhibition was allowed to continue, and proved a conspicuous success.[6] The party went on.

Of course, the obvious place to capitalize on all this fascination was in the new and ultimate temple of make-believe: the movie theater. In fact the first collision between Egyptomania and the projected image as mass attraction had occurred as far back as 1849, in *Panorama of Ancient Egypt*, exhibited at the Egyptian Hall in Piccadilly (one of the earliest and most impressive buildings in England in the Ancient Egyptian style, sadly demolished in 1905). The prototype of every Egyptian sensation ever to hit a movie house in the decades to follow, the *Panorama* was a huge roll of painted fabric, which was fed past a backlit frame to create the effect of a Nile journey, passing the Pyramids and other landmarks as it went. The result was roughly equivalent to watching a moving image, the proto-cinematic experience completed by a running commentary by artist and Egyptologist Joseph Bonomi. Projected twice daily, it was ballyhooed by a horse-drawn advertising van, which trotted around central London exotically painted with Egyptian scenes exactly analogous to a theater or cinema poster. (It was just one of many panoramas that were bewitching London; *Punch* that year commented upon this epidemic of "Panorama-mania"—there's that suffix again!) After its successful London exhibition it was purchased and toured around America by none other than George Gliddon, as an added

Tutmania hits the American heartland.

attraction to his mummy unwrappings, including the notorious Boston one, previously discussed.

As movies became the dominant form of commercial entertainment in the twentieth century, Nile-style architecture was felt to lend itself especially to the picture palaces that sprouted in profusion to meet the demand for projected entertainment. In the films themselves, however, Egyptian subjects tended to be eccentric affairs, with much of the puckishness of Gautier's literary romances. Such faux-exotic escapism was doubtless felt to be of especial value in 1918 Germany, where Ernst Lubitsch, of all people, contributed a curious chamber piece called *Die Augen der Mumie Ma* (*Eyes of the Mummy*). It begins with a young artist looking for inspiration in Egypt, who encounters a dusky beauty (Pola Negri) among the dunes, who appears to vanish without trace in the open desert. Back at his hotel, he hears talk of a tomb capable of driving to insanity those who stumble upon it. "Would you be so kind as to tell me what happened to you?" he asks one such unfortunate, whose only reply is to rise briefly from his recumbent posture and yell: "The eyes are alive! The eyes are alive!" Sure enough, he visits and finds a coffin whose carved eyes open and meet his own…

It's a wonderfully creepy effect, but the film soon reneges on this promise of a prototype mummy film, devolving instead into romantic melodrama, with echoes of both *Pygmalion* and *Othello*. The eyes belong to none other than the mysterious beauty, concealed behind the eyeholes, and kept prisoner in the tomb by a villainous Arab (played by Emil Jannings, whose bizarre characterization is tipped still further into eccentricity by ebony make-up that covers his face but not his exposed upper-chest and arms). Our hero overcomes him and transports the girl to the modern world, where she becomes a smash hit in the London nightclubs as a sexy oriental dancer. But her fiendish oppressor follows, and the stage is set for the expected tragedy.

Obviously, then, this is not a piece that troubles the historical record too often for factual reassurance (Jannings swears to recapture his unwilling concubine in the name of "Osiris, the high priestess") and the Egyptian elements are deployed solely in the capacity of exotic backdrop. The desert locations (shot in Berlin) are charming, as are the sweetly detailed tomb sets. More importantly, it establishes the idea, central to the Karloff film and recurring often thereafter, of a central female character torn between the ancient and the modern, and east and west, pulled in both directions by the men who want her to be theirs, in one world only.

But for all that it is a small film, clearly meeting a naïve curiosity rather than feeding an obsession. (The film played in America in September of 1922, just two months before the Tutankhamen discovery.) *Cleopatra*, made in Hollywood in 1917 as a vehicle for the pioneer screen vamp Theda Bara, was much more lavish, and pointed the way to the more expected style of Egyptological epic. Hard to judge from the few remaining seconds, but the film was among the most elaborate of its time, with huge battle scenes, massive sets and enough eroticism to compel the Chicago Board of Aldermen to decree that it would "have to be toned down considerably before it may be exhibited"[7] (they needed two viewings to reach this conclusion).

In the *Los Angeles Herald*, the star was recorded on the set explaining: "The moon has a tremendous fascination for me and its cold rays seem to harmonize with my very soul. It seems to look upon this terrestrial globe with a cold unblinking stolidness, mixed with a certain stern cruelty that fits in with my mood while I am portraying the role of Cleopatra."[8]

Despite this, the same paper reported her slight reservations as to the characterization: "When one reflects that Caesar was at the time he is supposed to have been fascinated by Cleopatra a bald-headed man of 54, veteran of many wars and an equal number of amours and orgies, with children of his own older than Cleopatra, and that the young queen was only 20, broke, without a country and in danger of her life, one is moved to wonder did the 'vamping.'"[9]

If that sounds like a more than usual degree of immersion in a role for a star of the time, reflect on this, again from the *Los Angeles Herald*:

> Is Theda Bara the reincarnation of Cleopatra, as well as the first actress to impersonate this famed siren of the Nile on the screen? Her personal press agent declares she is.... Here are the reasons for the P. A.'s claim:
> 1. The character of Theda Bara and the character of Cleopatra are similar in many respects. The great queen was much maligned by contemporary historians because she was believed to be responsible for the downfall of the Roman republic. In the same way the chroniclers of today assign to Miss Bara many of the vampirish vices which she assumes for her screen work.
> 2. In appearance, so far as can be definitely ascertained, Miss Bara and the "Siren of the Nile" were similar. Only one authentic representation of Cleopatra is now extant. This is a bust in the British Museum, and it shows a remarkable likeness to the star of the modern screen.
> 3. Miss Bara's last name is similar to an Egyptian word meaning "Soul of the Sun." One of the titles of Cleopatra and, in fact, all the rulers of Egypt, was "Spirit of the Sun."

"I felt the blood of the Ptolemies coursing through my veins," said Miss Bara, when she had completed the picture. "I know that I actually am a reincarnation of Cleopatra. It is not a mere theory in my mind. I have positive knowledge that such is the case—I live Cleopatra, I breathe Cleopatra—I am Cleopatra!"[10]

The film was lost in the 1930s when the last known negative was apparently destroyed

Theda Bara's version of *Cleopatra* (1917) introduced Egypt as a source of lavish spectacle to the American screen.

in a fire, but the good news is that the following year's great contribution to Cleopatra studies, the hit song "Cleopatra Had a Jazz Band," still survives:

> Cleopatra had a Jazz Band in her castle on the Nile,
> Ev'ry night she gave a jazz dance in her queer Egyptian style.
> She won Mark Anthony with her syncopated harmony,
> And while they played, she swayed—
> She knew she had him all the while
> In the shadow of the Pyramids 'neath the old Egyptian moon,
> A sphinx was looking on and said, "There'll be a wedding soon!"
> But the real historic scandal was Cleo lost her sandal
> As she danced to the strains of the Egyptian Jazz Band tune.

Ultimately, the mantle of Hollywood's Cleopatra would be passed to Claudette Colbert, who in a stunning and thankfully extant 1934 caper drew upon two decades of Egyptian stylization on the American screen to produce a pastiche of exceptional beauty and simultaneous absurdity. Its director, Cecil B. DeMille, was at that time cementing his reputation as the great articulator of modern sensation, after an apprenticeship in sparkling and often supremely witty dissections of modern manners. His shift towards spectacle occurred incrementally and organically, as shown by his immediate response to the Tutankhamen discovery: his first and most interesting version of *The Ten Commandments* (1923).

Unlike the 1956 remake with Charlton Heston, the film is not really an historical spectacle so much as another of his then-trademark commentaries on modern morals, with the Exodus recreation occupying the first half only, whereupon the film shifts to the present day to illustrate what relevance the commandments still hold in the 1920s. This contrasting of ancient and modern was a recurring tic of DeMille's work in its first phase from *The Dream Girl* (1916) onwards, along with the parallel notion that the same old blood beats beneath our sophisticated modern skins, and that all it takes is a freak of circumstance to cause us to revert to prototype. The Babylonian flashback in *Male and Female* (1919) may well have been a specific influence on the deleted sequence in the Karloff *Mummy*, in which we observe the reincarnation of Zita Johann's soul through various historical epochs, including a scene in a lion's den strikingly similar to one with Gloria Swanson in the DeMille film.

In the event, the intention to use the Egyptian section of *Commandments* as merely a kind of *hors d'oeuvres* was entirely undermined by its unprecedented epic splendour: watch the film in a gleaming modern print and it is still easy enough to be caught up in its sweep and grandeur. It will also give the lie to the popular saw that DeMille was an historical comic book artist, cheerfully anachronistic in design, costume and set construction. It is true that he would not allow reality stand between himself and a particular effect or plot device—if the two actually lock antlers then reality must be the loser—but wherever possible (and far more than only when strictly necessary) his attitude to verisimilitude was exacting and painstaking, and invariably rewards the eye with its near-fanatic attention to detail. In pre-production DeMille had instructed his team to obtain and scrutinize the finds that Carter was unearthing simultaneously in Tutankhamen's tomb, much of which made its way intact to the screen. A far cry from Lubitsch's human-scale ancient land, DeMille's Egypt is colossal, a vast canvas in which the human figures are resoundingly dwarfed, exactly mirroring the process by which the ancients had rendered themselves mere footnotes to their own architecture and lore.

The *Healdsburg Tribune* laid out the statistics: "Cecil B. DeMille employed the services of 2500 people and caused to be erected mammoth replicas of several masterpieces of Egyptian architecture. The costuming of these hosts of players; the building of hundreds of chariots; the making of ancient harness and arms, and the construction of devices for such stupendous effects as the parting of the waters of the Red Sea, were the work of many months and supervised by noted archaeologists and Biblical authorities."[11]

Further numbers, courtesy of the *Prahran Telegraph*:

> Statistics reveal that the Egyptian city constructed by Cecil B. DeMille at Guadalupe, Cal. for the Biblical prologue of his new picture, *The Ten Commandments*... was the biggest set ever built in the history of motion pictures. Thirty-three thousand yards of cloth were required for the costumes, which numbered more than 3000; and $18,000 worth of special harness, of ancient design, had to be made. Transportation over the loose sand, where motors and horse wagons were out of the

Enough to make her hop right out of her mummy case: *Cleopatra Had a Jazz Band* (1918).

question, was accomplished by means of 20 big sand sleds. Three fast touring cars provided nightly film service between the camp and Los Angeles. The big set representing the ancient walled city of Rameses was 750 feet wide and 109 feet high. It was the largest ever constructed for a motion picture, and was approached by an avenue of twenty-four sphinxes, each of which weighed nearly four tons. This avenue was designed by and built under the direction of Paul Iribe, Mr. DeMille's art director. It will never be possible to trace the multitude of influences for good that *The Ten Commandments* will spread over the earth. The theme of the picture is contained in the Book of Exodus. It is a story both wonderful and replete with adventure. It will entertain thoroughly, but, while it is doing so, the picture is having a greater effect in moulding the mind towards a cleaner and saner outlook upon life.[12]

Overt though DeMille's homage to Tutmania may now seem, his original plans were for something still less subtle, as *Exhibitors Herald* noted:

LOS ANGELES, Feb. 27.—King Tut-Ankh-Amen of Egypt, who has been making the front pages of newspapers throughout the country recently, is going to appear in motion pictures. All this despite the fact that he has been dead some 3,000 years.

Example of the stunning set design and art direction that distinguished Cecil B. DeMille's 1923 version of *The Ten Commandments*.

> Cecil B. DeMille is going to use him as one of the characters in his Paramount picture *The Ten Commandments*. He has instructed Mrs. Florence Meehan, who has been abroad doing research work for this photoplay for some time, to assemble all possible data for reproduction of his features, figure, raiment and the many relics found in his grave.[13]

Mania, indeed—but it was just the beginning.

3

It's an Egyptian Year!

> About the only thing they didn't find in old Tutankhamen's tomb, who died early in the spring, about 3,000 years ago, was a five-reel super-production. There's a lot of 'em that might have come from King Tut's grave but so far nobody's claimed that distinction. However, it is now up to the press agents to use the publicity Tut's getting, and we'll be looking for a story built around his royal nibs soon. Won't the customers who read the subtitles aloud have a fine time pronouncing "Tutankhamen." Wow.—*Exhibitors Herald*, March 3, 1923

In 1923, in part to quell the rising but not yet—quite—engulfing tide of popular sensationalism, Howard Carter published the first volume of his account of the excavation, *The Discovery of the Tomb of Tutankhamen.* (Subsequent volumes were published in 1927 and 1933.) Rushed to print, and intended to precede a detailed scientific account that he in fact would never get around to writing, it was a masterly account, as fine and stirring as any of the journalism the ill-effects of which it was designed, in part, to counter. Carter's prose is far from dry, and by no means plays down the exciting and thrilling aspects of the tale. But if his defiant emphasis on the value of the discovery to the enlarging of our historical and scientific knowledge was intended to stifle in its cradle the frivolity of Tutmania, it didn't have a chance. The world received it with delight, put it on the shelf next to its King Tut cigar case, and carried on dancing.

Once 1923 was underway, it no longer needed to make sense to make money, and it was everywhere you looked. The popular duo of Gallagher and Shean were featured in a Ziegfeld Follies sketch set in the tomb's interior. Vaudeville double-act Chick Yorke and Rose King took to billing themselves as "the only living relatives of Old King Tut." Jack George was touring *King Tut in Vaudeville*, an "absolutely original" act, with "special scenery." Such was the demand, it seems, that one James Madison, "writer of laughs and thrills for stage and screen," took out an ad in *Variety*[1] offering his "comedy service': guaranteed new and original jokes "including a dialogue about Old King Tut." Strangest of all, perhaps (though it's a fierce fight) is this ad for singer Maureen Englin:

SCIENTIST MAKES DISCOVERY AT TOMB OF KING TUT
Prof. Carter, in charge of research work and excavations at the tomb of King Tut-Ankh-Amen, acquired the services of several eminent archaeologists to decipher some mysterious writing on the stone tablets which were the first to be discovered among the King's favorite treasures by the excavators. After several days of studious application of their knowledge of hieroglyphics and ancient languages, these scientists report the inscription on the tablets are bulletin announcements from

King "Tut" to his subjects that in all his vast kingdom his favorite entertainer was a young lady whose name when translated from the Egyptian to English read MAUREEN ENGLIN.
   Note:—This has nothing to do with my age![2]

As on the stage, so at the movies—1923 was the year that Tutmania's cinematic floodgates broke wide open. "I don't know whether or not anyone has signed up King Tut-Ankh-

A flapper tickling the sphinx with a feather: the perfect image for cinema's collision with Egyptomania in 1923.

Amen for the screen, but he sure would be a big attraction," noted *Exhibitors Herald* on March 3. "And oh, baby, what a press agent that guy has!" *Motion Picture News* on March 17 added: "Already, along Fifth Avenue, the Egyptian note has been struck in gowns, and the screen, always in the lead of fashion, will shortly reflect that tendency. It's an Egyptian year!"

From the first, movie cameras had circled like vultures around the excavation, hoping to get exciting shots for the newsreels. But vastly complicating the issue had been the complicated, unworkable (and possibly unlawful) copyright arrangements Carnarvon had made. Regardless both of the fact that an international news event cannot in itself be copyrighted, and especially of the fact that the tomb belonged to the government of Egypt, Carnarvon independently struck a series of lucrative deals designed to place a blanket around the story, the images, even the basic facts, making them accessible only to the highest bidder. Reporting rights were sold to the London *Times*, along with rights to all still photographs, in exchange for five thousand pounds. Any other newspapers wishing to make use of either would have to separately buy them from the *Times*, and Carnarvon was in for 75 percent of that, too. (The contract demanded that "neither the Earl nor his agents will authorize or permit personal friends, acquaintances or other persons whatsoever to be present at [the excavations] or to inspect any of the results thereof" unless they "first pledge themselves to grant no interviews to and to make no communication and give no information whatsoever as to what such persons shall have seen or heard whether to representatives of the Press in any part of the world or to any persons whatsoever.")

But Carnarvon was far-sighted enough to know that this was the age of the moving picture, and he wrote to Carter on Christmas Eve of 1922 to announce the big plans he was cooking. Among those stepping up for the film rights, he said, were Pathé—we can presume the deal was struck successfully, judging by the contents listings for *Pathé News* in 1923. In January it promised "FIRST AND EXCLUSIVE PICTURES OF THE FAMOUS EGYPTIAN TOMB JUST DISCOVERED." In February it offered "new pictures of tomb, its surroundings and excavators." By way of diversion, March brought a special report on "HOW TUT-ANKH-AMEN IS INFLUENCING STYLES," noting: "The world has gone crazy over the ancient Egyptian king. His dictates are now law in women's styles." But the cameras were back at the tombs later that month—or close enough, at least: "LUXOR, EGYPT—American scientists direct researches within stone's throw of Tut-Ankh-Amen's tomb." (What's a stone's throw between friends?) In June, there was "Transporting Tut-ankhamen treasures down the Nile to Cairo Museum, guarded by soldiers." And even when the boy king wasn't officially reporting for duty, it was hard to get away from the subject entirely. One of the few Tut-free editions that year had journeyed to England to film the winning horse at the Epsom Derby. It was called Papyrus.

Newsreels were all very well, but the world's insatiable demand for images suggested the possibility of more substantial exploitation. In March of 1923 the trades announced that months of negotiation had concluded with the exclusive rights to feature coverage awarded to exhibitor Ernest Shipman. The story feels somewhat fishy: that is to say that the fish Carnarvon had been frying hitherto were of the bigger sort.

Shipman, known affectionately as "Ten Percent Ernie," was a pioneer of Canadian independent cinema, specializing in stories of the great outdoors, which he would film on authentic locations encouraging as many locals as possible to participate. In an age of studio productions, he made waves with his adamant insistence upon the use of real

What Killed Old King Tut?

A LOT of people who didn't know he was sick are just finding out that Old King Tut is dead.

The question naturally arises: *What killed the King?*

During my recent visit to Egypt in the interest of PREFERRED PICTURES, I learned the answer.

Back in those good old days, Tut was King of the Independent Exhibitors. A slick city salesman, driving up on his camel, induced Tut to sign up for his series of 78 Super Specials.

Tut played 77 of the 78 and, as usual, was borrowing on his life insurance to pay his bills.

Along came the 78th picture, which turned out to be good enough for him to make a profit on.

The shock killed him. Poor King Tut! *Requiescat in pace!* Meaning *olav hasholem!*

B. P. SCHULBERG
presents

RICH MEN'S WIVES
SHADOWS
THORNS AND ORANGE BLOSSOMS
THE HERO
POOR MEN'S WIVES
ARE YOU A FAILURE?
(Prints at your exchange now)
DAUGHTERS OF THE RICH
THE GIRL WHO CAME BACK

Coming:— "APPEARANCES"

Produced by
PREFERRED PICTURES, INC.

Distributed by
AL-LICHTMAN CORPORATION

Ernest Shipman, known in the trade as "Ten Percent Ernie."

King Tut was everywhere in 1923, and even films with no actual connection managed to utilize him in their publicity. This lively advertisement appeared in *Motion Picture News* in April.

backgrounds, telling *Exhibitors Herald*: "I have two pet aversions. One is Fifth Avenue traffic when I am in a hurry; the other is picture camouflage." By the latter he meant elaborate and unrealistic studio sets: so unnecessary, he explains, when to the truly adventurous producer the whole world is one big set, waiting to be utilized. His attempts to film the Tutankhamen excavations were an ambitious extension of the same principles and commitments: to authenticity, natural splendor, and local color.

Though it is unclear whether he would have actually been allowed inside the tomb (indeed, it is unclear to what extent any of Shipman's claims are not mere hyperbole), the trades were buzzing with the news that Shipman had secured exclusive rights in the USA and Canada for the pictorial record of the excavation and finds, which *Exhibitors Trade Review* predicted could well be "the 'scoop' of the year":

The negative is now on the high seas, bound for New York, but advance notices from Europe declare the pictures to be remarkable not only for their historical and educational value but for their wealth of beauty and pageantry as well. The principal characters brought to view in the film are Lord Carnarvon, Lady Herbert, the Queen of Belgium and Howard Carter, the latter being the American archaeologist [sic] who is accredited with having carried on the work of exploration when all previous efforts seem to have failed.

Discussing his prize, Mr. Shipman said: "You can add about twenty millions to the normal moving picture patronage, and you will have, I believe, a conservative estimate of the attendance that these pictures will induce. From scientists and students of research to curiosity seekers, all undoubtedly will flock to see this 'picture of the hour.' Anticipating this vast volume of business and to cope with the demand we are prepared to order at once upon the arrival of the negative no less than 300 prints."

Shipman lost no time in taking out double-page ads in the movie trades, offering "The most amazing novelty in the history of motion pictures!" and, as incentive to snap it up quick, quoting a sobering warning from C.W. Barron, owner of the *Wall Street Journal*, advising that "the rising tide of self-determination that is bedevilling the world may cause modern Egypt to deny the right of the archaeologist in his find." Thus, the ad concludes, Shipman's exclusive pictures may prove "the only records of their kind, for posterity." Best of all, the ads proclaimed, "Tut-Ankh-Amen Has Already Received in America $100,000,000 Advertising":

The great Pharaoh lived in an age of wise men! This, too, is an age of wise men! And the wisest of them are the exhibitors who will make capital of the Pharaoh's advertising! But $100,000,000 is not all! The campaign has just commenced! King Tut-Ankh-Amen will grace the front pages of our dailies for months to come!

But Shipman seems oddly to disappear from the story at this point, and his films seem not to have been made. Tempting though it is to concoct conspiracy (or curse) stories, it may be simply that he had too many irons in too many fires, and this one fell through. Consider—in 1923 alone, the trades report him forming the Long Island Film Corp., sponsoring a competition to find (and cast) Long Island's most beautiful blonde and brunette, traveling to Morocco to try to set up a film project there, acquiring exclusive U.S. rights to the film of Shackelton's expedition to the

Ten Percent Ernie stakes his claim to exclusive visual rights to the excavation—what happened next is uncertain.

South Pole, acquiring exclusive Canadian rights to the fights at Yankee Stadium, buying out the Luporini Brothers' interest in the Ultra Company of Rome, settling a lawsuit against Renco Film Co. out of court, announcing thirty other films and making five (including the big hit *The Man from Glengarry*), and, in his spare time, fathering a son. Even so, landing the film rights to the story of the decade would surely have dwarfed all but the latter of these concerns, and one has to wonder if he bolted to the press before all stable doors had been officially opened, or even if he was chancing his luck in an altogether complete and outrageous fashion.

Either way, as Shipman fades from the picture, the more prestigious Fox Film Corporation moves in: *Motion Picture News* announced on March 21 that the company "had just received the first and exclusive moving pictures of the scenes surrounding the excavations of the tomb." This seems much more like the kind of deal Carnarvon would have gone for, though, surprisingly, in the reports Fox's plans seem no less shady than Shipman's. The film was called *Land of Tut-Ankh-Amen*, and while the footage may well have been exclusive, it still doesn't sound strictly authorized:

> The Valley of the Kings, the native helpers clearing away the debris from the entrance to the tomb, princesses of the Court of Egypt entering the tomb under the guidance of Howard Carter who is in charge of the work, the camp of the scientists built near the tomb where the priceless treasures are sheltered and packed for shipment and the actual removal of the first relics from the tomb, are all interestingly set forth in the news pictures.
>
> Lucian Maes, Fox news staff cameraman at the Paris office, arrived early at the scene of the excavations and secured some excellent shots with the aid of a long focus lens. He concealed his camera in a box and ground out complete pictures showing the work going on at the tomb before the guards discovered him.

One wonders if maybe the team struck a deal with Fox for exclusive images after being presented with the fait accompli of their more furtive coverage. Even so, it seems an odd thing for an official outfit to brag of in press coverage. Nonetheless, official endorsement must be presumed, since, unlike Shipman's film, Fox's made it to the screen, and elaborate saturation advertising stood as a measure of their unprecedented expectations for what was, after all, basically just a newsreel. A beautifully designed poster appeared in the trade journals, with the unavoidable sphinxes, pyramids and camels, advising exhibitors of "special advertising material available at every Fox exchange" and proclaiming: "You know what a money-maker it will be for you. Clean up quick—and please your patrons with your enterprise."

It was still doing the rounds on May 19, when *Motion Picture News* reported that to further assist its exhibitors Fox had arranged with Harry Von Tilzer for a special and complete orchestration titled "Old King Tut." Von Tilzer's song of that name became an enduring and much-recorded popular hit:

> His tomb instead of tears, was full of souvenirs,
> He must have travelled greatly in his time—
> The gold and silverware, that they found hidden there,
> Was from hotels of ev'ry land and clime.
> While going thru' his royal robes they found up in his sleeve,
> The first love letter Adam wrote to Eve.

Sheet music showed an image of "Old King Tut" with wrinkles, cigar and a general air of dissipation, leering at a slinky Egyptian handmaiden: a reminder that, while it is instinctive to imagine a dead king as greatly advanced in years, it was not yet generally

As Shipman fades from the scene, Fox move in—and this time successfully.

known that "old King Tut" died in his youth. But what it lacked in veracity the song only gained in appeal: by the end of 1923 pretty much everyone was singing it. Sophie Tucker performed it in *The Pepper Box Revue* and recorded it for Okeh Records, both with sufficient success to prompt her to take out an ad in *Variety* thanking Von Tilzer for "the best novelty comedy song I have had in years."

All this hoopla did its job: *Exhibitors Herald* on May 12 reported "many favorable

Top: Harry Von Tilzer's song *Old King Tut* outlived and overshadowed the project for which it was devised. *Bottom:* Hebrew, Italian, Dutch or Rube—everyone, it seems, was King Tutting.... Harry Von Tilzer plugs his big hit of that Egyptian year, 1923.

reports and hundreds of bookings" for Fox's essentially modest one-reel attraction, but some exhibitors were less convinced. "Don't let them kid you, small town exhibitors," warned Harry Hobolth of the Maxine Theatre, Imlay City, Michigan. "Patrons called it a news reel, and you can buy a news reel for $1.50."

Newsreels were one thing, but clearly this was a subject with dramatic potential. Indeed, the mystery and exoticism of Egypt generally had always had dramatic potential, so it wasn't long before studios were raiding their back catalogues to see if any could be hastily converted to cash-in. Canny exhibitors, too, got wise quickly. *Moving Picture World* tells of how Ernest Shipman's advertisement "about the millions of dollars' worth of publicity Tutankhamen had acquired without cost" had inspired Wilfred Le Doux, manager of the Empress Theater, Omaha, to grab a copy of Lubitsch's 1922 German epic *The Loves of Pharaoh* and give it an instant upgrade: "He didn't wait for the excavation pictures.... It proved what Shipman said, so you can imagine what the authentic pictures are going to do for the box office."[3] According to *Exhibitors Trade Review*: "A big banner in his lobby read: See the Romance of Pharaoh Tut-Ankh-Amen in *The Loves of Pharaoh*, now playing. His newspaper ads and copy also called the Pharaoh in the picture Tut-Ankh-Amen, which he just as much was as wasn't."[4]

The same trick worked with the 1921 melodrama *The Lure of Egypt*, as *Motion Picture World* noted on April 7:

> *The Lure of Egypt*, according to Pathé, has taken on a recent strong spurt of new and re-booking, perhaps as a result of the volume of King Tut publicity.... Its story is based on archaeological explorations on the Nile in the region of Luxor, and the plot centers in trouble with the native chiefs over the actual opening of the tomb and the securing of the treasures buried with the father-in-law of Tut-Ankh-Amen—the young religious innovator King Akhnaton.... At the present stage of the renewed activity of more than twenty Pathé features which have been before the public continuously for upwards of two years, *The Lure of Egypt* is reported to be outstripping them all.

But the rosette for enterprise surely goes to the nameless entrepreneur who took out an ad in *Film Daily* that read:

> **For Sale:**
> King Tut Picture. Have negative of an Italian production with ten to twenty thousand people in cast—a reincarnation story—massive sets; easily adaptable for King Tut story. Picture in present form measures about 5,400 feet and have some cut outs. Will take $6,000 cash for same. Apply Box 5–23[5]

Current production plans, too, were scrutinized for last-minute tie-up potential. So *Exhibitors Trade Review* had this exciting news to tell about Nita Naldi's forthcoming appearance in *Lawful Larceny*:

> She is to be a modern with a pure Egyptian flavor and according to plans will wear gowns that will cause Tut-Ankh-Amen to turn over in his sarcophagus ... "Miss Naldi is Cleopatra reincarnated," declared (director Alan) Dwan. "Many leading artists have said that she is the nearest to the famous Egyptian charmer to be found in America. With her long slender arms and legs, piercing black eyes and raven black hair she will be a wonderful being in Egyptian clothes. Not only will Miss Naldi be clad in Egyptian gowns but she will have a complete Egyptian background for her machinations against men. The art department at the Paramount studio has been busy preparing drawings for the Egyptian scenes. Every photograph of King Tut-Ankh-Amen's tomb printed in this country has been studied for ideas.[6]

Pola Negri's Hollywood debut in *Bella Donna*, with its stylish Egyptian backgrounds, was another obvious candidate. "*Bella Donna* will have scenes laid in the very locale now receiving such wide notice," noted *Motion Picture News*, and made the following recommendations for "exploitation angles": "The Egyptian theme suggests an oriental dance prologue.... The rage of King Tut-Ankh-Amen will help you in your tie-ups with merchants, etc."[7]

Biblical subjects were among the more inevitable to receive this kind of make-over. DeMille eventually decided against giving Tutankhamen a starring role in *The Ten Commandments* but *The Shepherd King*, a rival account of the Exodus from the producer and director of the Theda Bara *Cleopatra*, apparently bested him in the locations department, according to *Motion Picture News*: "It was photographed in Egypt almost in the identical location where the tomb of Tut-Ankh-Amen has been unearthed. The entire company was taken to Egypt by (producer J. Gordon) Edwards where, augmented by a mob of Egyptians, they went to the Pyramids and the Sphinx and thence up the Nile." The production apparently entailed the services of "5,000 Egyptians, 485 camels and nearly as many donkeys."[8]

"It is something more than local color that these graphic Egyptian scenes in *The Shepherd King* will bring to the millions who have read of the excavations now being conducted in the Valley of the Kings," a Fox spokesman told the same journal on July 7. "They are really a page of history, significant, colourful and soul-stirring—scenes that arouse the imagination and thrill the heart as could no romance sprung from the mind of man. The realism of these scenes stamp this production as something unique in pictorial art on the screen."

Alongside all this redressing, the race was on to bring the first original Tutankhamen drama to the screen. First out of the gate was producer W.P.S. Earle, who announced production of a life of Tutankhamen in March, although according to *Picture Play* magazine, planning for the production was already underway before the discovery:

> The story on which it is based was written some months before the actual excavation announced early in the year. However, in this early version, King Tut was only a lesser character. As soon as the news assumed prominence, the producers decided that the worthy Tut didn't have enough to do in their picture. "Tut, Tut!" they said, "we'll have to rewrite this," and as a result, King Tut is to become a very important personage in a tale of the times of the Pharaohs.[9]

But how could a small independent picture match the grandeur of DeMille or *The Shepherd King*? With ingenuity, as *Motion Picture News* explained: "The new process in which artist's drawings are used as backgrounds will be employed, making possible an elaborate production at a reasonable expenditure."[10]

By mid–March Earle had announced he had assembled his production staff, including set designer Paul Dodge, scenic artist Xavier Mochado, technical advisor Captain Dudley S. Corlette and, most importantly, publicity director Tamar Lane.[11] The following month he unveiled his cast list, headed by Bertram Grassby as Tutankhamen.[12]

Grassby was a British actor living in Hollywood in a house with a live sycamore tree growing inside it. The latter according to *Motion Picture Magazine*, which noted as far back as 1921 that he was possessed of "a curious, intangible suggestion of the oriental":

Bertram Grassby—the perhaps unlikely face of Hollywood's first Tutankhamen.

I don't mean Japanese, of course: he makes one want to ask if he has lived in India. He has the leisurely manners that belong to older civilizations.... He is tall—six feet, or possibly a little over, and exceptionally handsome. His hair and eyes are black and his skin swarthy. He is probably intensely emotional; the rare emotional type of Englishman.[13]

Picture Play magazine noted that Carmel Myers had been given "the difficult role of the heroine in this film of old Egypt," and had high hopes for her performance and the film both: "With hands stiffened, face hardened, and a coiffure of sausage-like curls, Carmel is picturesquely engaged in looking like what a mummy was before she was a mummy. The splendour and richness of the vast Egyptian palaces gives an opportunity for many magnificent settings, and this picture will abound in them."[14] Little boxed ads started appearing in the trades in April, announcing simply that "TUT-ANKH-AMEN, A Wm. P. S. Earle Classic" was now "in production." Completion was announced at the end of May.[15]

What happened next is slightly mysterious. On June 12 *Film Daily* reported that Earle was in New York (at the Astor) with a print of the film, "a six-reeler he completed just before leaving for the east," and hoping to snare a distributor. On June 25 the same journal announced that Charles R. Rogers of Resolute Film Sales, Inc. had agreed to take it on.

But then, all is silence for over a month. Finally, on August 4, the silence was broken by a contradictory announcement from *Motion Picture News* that "work is almost completed" on what is plainly the same film that had already been announced completed (and sold) in June, but which is now apparently being produced under the auspices of Film Booking Offices, and called The *Dancer of the Nile*:

> The general idea of the picture is based on the life of King Tut-Ankh-Amen and a romance during his regime of a dancer of the Royal Court. An entire kingdom was erected to get the proper effects and the production as a whole promises to be one of the biggest released in the history of the F.B.O. Thousands of dollars have been spent to date on sets that cover many blocks. City walls wide enough to allow two chariots to pass each other have been erected in addition to a small city which covers about nine city blocks with Egyptian buildings, three, four and five stories tall. An entire valley in the southern end of California was utilized with a telescopic camera to get distances. A telescopic lens was also used on the interior of the "Hall of Kings," a massive roofed set covering 100 by 150 feet and standing four stories tall. The roof is held up by ten foot pillars sixty-five feet tall. In this set over four thousand people were used as guests at King Tut-Ankh-Amen's annual feast. The making of this sequence took ten days during which time the four thousand extras were fed and lodged on location.

If even half-true, this might suggest the delay was caused by a late infusion of big money, after completion of production, enabling Earle to re-shoot and massively improve its settings and backgrounds. Even if there is a healthy chunk of hyperbole in the above report, we've still clearly moved on substantially from having the poor actors perform in front of paintings of sets.

And yet, even with this new and highly commercial addition to the mix, reaction to the film when it finally appeared was disappointing, with critics responding negatively to the plot, the dialogue and the performances. *Motion Picture News* attended the premiere, and reported back with a long face:

> This picture has been inspired by the expeditions of the English Egyptologists to the tomb of Tut-ankhamen and pretends to uncover some vivid chapters in the short but hectic life of the ancient ruler. According to the screen conception King Tut was pretty much a bad actor. And the intelligent

The Dancer of the Nile (1923) marked Tutankhamen's dramatic debut on the American screen.

spectator will probably wonder where the sponsors dug up their information. The civilization of the past has been respected by the English expeditionary forces, but the producers, in an attempt to make capital, have conceived a picture which reveals nothing sacred in the life of the monarch who reigned three thousand years ago.

They have doubtless speculated considerably, for it stands to reason that a reproduction of the imperial glamour of a kingdom so remote in history cannot be accurate. So they have fashioned a weird concoction—which might pass for drama in the reign of any ruler of bygone centuries. Judging it from its historical value it carries no pretensions at all. Judging it as a motion picture we see in it nothing of consequence.[16]

As "production highlights" the journal was only able to single out the "atmospheric settings," the photography, and "the climax when girl is offered as a sacrifice to the crocodiles." "Perhaps Carmel Myers, Bertram Grassby, Malcolm MacGregor and June Elvidge thought they were making a knockout of an historical drama but they were fooled," concluded *Picture Play*. "*The Dancer of the Nile*, inspired by poor old King Tut-Ankh-Amen, is the best comedy since Ben Turpin's *The Shriek of Araby*."[17]

Next up to try his luck was another independent producer, Max Cohen. Cohen was a pioneer and outspoken champion of state rights film distribution, who fought against the encroachment of the majors in the distribution field with a variety of eye-catching and easily exploitable subjects. He produced righteous shockers like *It May Be Your Daughter* (1916, produced in association with the Moral Uplift Society of America), patriotic tracts like *America Is Ready* (1917), and a run of "Midget Comedies" (1917): two reel farces starring "a company of midgets." Ads exclaimed that "Never before has the public witnessed so wonderful a novelty as these MINUTE actors performing before the camera."

Sadly, much of Cohen's life is shrouded in mystery and it is not known even when he died, partly due to confusion with another Max Cohen who designed the titles for Universal's *Dracula*, and who has morphed with our man on the IMDB and elsewhere. But while only fragments of his doubtless fascinating story remain accessible to us, we

Whatever its merits as history or drama, *Dancer of the Nile* (1923) was a lively piece of design that captures the fun and energy of Tutmania at its youthful height.

can be sure that it was this Max Cohen who cooked up a confection enticingly called *The Mystery of King Tut-Ankh-Amen's Eighth Wife*, and announced it to the trades in April: "Cash in BIG on the world's Latest Craze and Sensation!" urged the full page ads, which also offered "a full line of paper, photos and exploitation accessories."[18] And lest we be in any doubt, it is stressed that it is:

> NOT a foreign production!
> NOT a re-issue!
> NOT a conglomeration of scenics!
> BUT a Beautifully Produced Egyptian Mystery Play in Five Parts!

Note that "mystery play" description. From the title it sounds like a comedy, taking humorous aim at *Bluebeard's Eighth Wife*, an adaptation of which Gloria Swanson starred in for Paramount the same year (and which itself includes a King Tut party scene, in which Swanson appeared as a beautiful mummy coming to life). But it would seem the film was played straight, judging by the pre-release description in *Exhibitors Trade Review*:

> Max Cohen of the Longacre Building announces the immediate release to independent exchanges of *The Mystery of Tut-Ankh-Amen's Eighth Wife*. The subject is a drama in five reels, and it is stated that it was made in the east and the west.
>
> The story was written and the picture was produced by Andrew Remo. The scenario was the work of George M. Merrick and Max Cohen. John Bitzer was the photographer.
>
> The locale is Egypt. The theme is of the tragedy that pursues those who violate the tombs of the Pharaohs and their families. The subject, it is stated, was produced prior to the illness and death of Lord Carnarvon.
>
> Mr. Cohen announces that a full line of exploitation accessories has been prepared ... there will be mummy cases, miniature mummies, King Tut dolls and Egyptian drapes for lobby display. Arthur J. Lamb of "Asleep in the Deep" fame, has written a song for which the music has been composed by Frederick B. Bower, the vaudeville producer. The National Drug Stores will carry a window display for many weeks in all of their stores. This tie-up, Mr. Cohen believes, will be of especial advantage, as there are twenty-six of these in New York alone.[19]

The reference to it being "made in the east and the west" is, I suspect, a bit of knowing impudence that refers solely to America, but the suggestion that Arthur J. Lamb was writing a song for the production is especially intriguing, not least because Lamb had previously collaborated with Harry Von Tilzer, composer of the Tut song for the Fox newsreel picture. (They wrote "Bird in a Gilded Cage" together, among others.) Lamb and Bower had also earlier collaborated on at least one occasion, that being the immortal "I'll Do Without Meat, I'll Do Without Wheat, But I Can't Do Without Love" (1918). According to *Exhibitors Herald*: "Max is so pepped up about his picture ... that he is having a song written about it. And if you will indicate that you desire it, Max will call around and sing it for you, which he says is part of the service that goes with his method of state righting the production."[20] Alas, I can find no confirmation that the song was ever written, and the reason for that may just be connected with a curious report in the *New York Clipper*:

> The Tut-Ankh-Amen Products Company, Inc., of No. 347 Fifth Avenue has sent out several warning notices to the effect that it would take action against all music publishers, music dealers, singers and vaudeville artists and theatre proprietors who infringed on its title rights of Tut-Ankh-Amen or variations thereof with the result that the matter has been taken up by E. C. Mills, chairman of the executive board of the Music Publishers Protective Association in order to protect the songs of that type published by members of that organization. Frederick M. Burns, president of the Tut-Ankh-Amen Company claims the title as his exclusive property as registered in Albany, N. Y., and alleges that the only song rightfully entitled to use of the title is the one written by Carlo and

Saunders, and published by Jerome H. Remick & Company. One of the notices sent out by Mr. Burns read in part: "Warning—The use of the title Tut-Ankh-Amen or variations thereof is the property of Martin Burns and all infringers direct or indirect using this title in connection with music or amusement of any nature other than the fox-trot song by Carlo-Sanders, published by Jerome H. Remick & Company and featured by Vincent Lopez and his Orchestra constitutes an infringement and the persons or person recording, singing or publishing any other song or dance music with a similar name to Tut-Ankh-Amen such as Tut, etc., will be prosecuted not only for copyright but for unfair competition as well. This warning is final. The notice is signed by Frederick Martin Burns."

Included in the Tut songs being published by members of the Music Publishers Protective Association is Harry Von Tilzer and William Jerome's *Old King Tut*, which has already gathered considerable headway. Another song being released by Irving Berlin, Inc., entitled *Who Did the Strut for Old King Tut (When He said Tut Tut to the Queen)*, comes under the head of alleged infringement claimed by Burns. Although it is realized that the Tut Company may be making a stab for publicity for their products and song, E. C. Mills, of the M. P. P. A., is prepared to fight for the rights of the publishers and on Monday sent the following letter to the Tut-Ankh-Amen Products Company and Mr. Burns: "We are in receipt of your undated warning relative to the use of the title Tut-Ankh-Amen or variations thereof. I believe this is the second notice along these lines that we have received, the first being a postcard.... Please be advised that m our opinion you are claiming rights which you do not, under the copyright law, possess. Our members are being advised accordingly. Inasmuch as there is now published, and in vogue, a song bearing title which is a variation of that to which you claim such exclusive rights, you are invited to initiate the litigation which you so freely threaten, and assert the rights which you claim to possess under the law, in Court..."[21]

If indeed it was rumblings such as these that put paid to Cohen's song idea, there was certainly no way he was going to pass over the publicity to be made from the production's supposed anticipation of the death of Lord Carnarvon (see chapter four for more on the Earl's fate). Later ads hammered home the supposed coincidence, suggesting that although during production "there was no notion entertained that it would almost be a perfect parallel" with "the death of a splendid man and renowned explorer," the coincidence is such that "it would seem the producer and director and author were all three gifted with clairvoyance and the power of prophets." Never one to undersell a gimmick, Cohen went still further in a later ad:

> It was some months ago—long before anyone even dreamt that Lord Carnarvon's end would be so tragic—long before the public

MAX COHEN

1476 BROADWAY   NEW YORK CITY

PHONE BRYANT 4416

To the State Right Exchanges:—

Your Deluge of Inquiries—<u>WINS</u>!

The Mystery of

KING TUT-ANKH-AMEN'S EIGHTH WIFE

Goes Out Via the Independent Market!

The Picture is Ready for Immediate Delivery!

That the picture is a GOLD-MINE—<u>YOU KNOW</u>!

That the picture is the TIMELIEST CLEAN-UP ever presented—<u>YOU KNOW</u>!

THAT'S ALL!

Irresistible hard sell for *The Mystery of King Tut-Ankh-Amen's Eighth Wife* **(1923).**

press began to hire learned writers to expound on Egyptian myth and lore, on poisoned tombs, venomous insects planted ages ago in sarcophagi, and deadly fumes from tombs sealed up when Solomon was a live man. And YET, this picture is an absolute parallel with the main and striking incidents, down to the tragedy itself, of Lord Carnarvon's explorations.

Even down to such a detail as the history of his wife—her desire to wed another even before Tut-Ankh-Amen was entombed—even here our picture parallels the history and the legendary lore.

All of which makes The Mystery of King Tut-Ankh-Amen's Eighth Wife the LIVEST and TIMELIEST FEATURE PRODUCTION ever produced!

Cohen was certainly unstinting when it came to ballyhoo:

The whole population of the United States—from New York to California—are waiting NOW to see the story of King Tut-Ankh-Amen on the screen. If you don't believe it, ask the first man, woman or child you meet on the street!

In all the history of motion pictures, THIS is the timeliest production ever made! It is the colossal clean-up of the year—the mightiest money-making mint ever presented to wide-awake film men looking for big, clean, novel, audience-pleasing sensations. This picture will do for the picture theatres what rubber heels do for shoes—annihilate hard going!

One who definitely felt the proposition to be worth a speculation was Dave Mundstuk of the Exclusive Film Company, who secured distribution rights for Michigan, sight unseen. According to *Moving Picture World*:

He has also ordered a King Tut mummy, being an exact reproduction of one of the mummies found in King Tut's yard. Dave has a full line of paper photos and exploitation accessories, and on account of the great interest in King Tut, he believes it ought to be a great cleanup for exhibitors that give it the proper ballyhoo.[22]

Sadly it seems fair to say that the film failed to live up either to expectation or to claim. Despite the sale to Dave in Michigan, I have found no proof of its having been exhibited outside of New York, where it played the Palace in July (billed as "a rare treat to all" and boasting of a "personal appearance of the original descendent of King Tut"), the Manor Theatre (Richmond Hill) in August as the top half of a double-bill with a Buck Jones western, and the Playhouse (Hillcrest) in December with a Tom Mix western (and this time, tellingly, on the lower berth). I have been unable to locate any review of the film, and not one member of the cast is known for certain. Further, according to the website "Classic Film Aficionados," Cohen and his partner George M. Merrick were sued for $2,000 in November by Republic Laboratories for outstanding film processing bills, suggesting a severe disparity between expectation and fulfillment. The film is now considered lost.

Lastly, in May, Sydney Ascher, still another colorful independent, announced "TO NATIONAL DISTRIBUTORS AND STATE RIGHTS BUYERS—THE *REAL* KING TUT PICTURE IS READY!"[23]

This was *The Vengeance of Tut-Ankh-Amen*, described breathlessly as: "An Inspiring Romance That Had Its Incipiency in Ancient Egypt and Its Happy Culmination in Modern America, Told in Seven Reels Just Teeming With Thrills—Action—Suspense—Surprises and Gripping Appeal." Ads boasted the film would be not only "an exquisitely executed Egyptian drama, but the most fascinating story ever unfolded on the screen," and promised an "excellent cast of more than 300 people." And, of course: "Many scenes actually taken in the Valley of the Kings and at King Tut-Ankh-Amen's tomb!"

The first thing you learn with these splashy trade ads is always to take with a pinch of salt their claims that the film is ready: frequently, it would seem, they relied on the money from the ensuing bookings to actually finance the production. Certainly in this case, there seems to be no evidence to suggest that the film was ever made at all. A pity, since the title would appear to suggest that, rather than a historical pageant set in Tutankhamen's court, it may well have been a contemporary thriller based around the excavation itself.

According to the ad, the film would boast a story by Ernest Mixx and titles by Ralph Spence. Spence, declared (at five dollars a word) "the highest-paid title writer in the world" by *Motion Picture World* in 1926,[24] eventually graduated to stage- and screen-writing: his 126 known screen credits include contributions to the scripts of Laurel and Hardy's *The Flying Deuces* (1939) and several Wheeler and Woolsey comedies; he also wrote the much-filmed play *The Gorilla*. But *The Vengeance of Tut-Ankh-Amen* appears nowhere in any currently available résumé of his work. As for Mr. Mixx, he has sadly proved as elusive as the film, the last mention of which I have been able to locate is a report in *Moving Picture World* claiming that Lewis J. Selznick has opened negotiations with Ascher to distribute the picture: "This deal, however, is still pending, for bidding for the picture are several national distributing corporations."[25]

And perhaps they still are, because that's the last we hear of the film.

Taking all these projects together, we can see, sadly, an awful lot of hoopla coming to very little: Earle's film a disappointment at best; Cohen's barely released; both almost instantly forgotten, and now this last contribution seemingly never even finished—or perhaps never even started.

Indeed, of all films made or planned that year that made explicit mention of Tutankhamen, the most successful on their own terms were probably the unpretentious short comedies. The prolific Eddie Lyons stepped into the bandages in *For the Love of Tut*, Norman Taurog directed *The Mummy*, one of Fox's legendary, largely lost "Sunshine Comedies," and Neely Edwards and Bert Roach appeared in *Tut Tut King*. Meanwhile, over in Austria, the French comedian Raymond Dandy served as writer, director and star for the simply-named *Tutankhamen*, a two-reel parody of Lubitsch's *Loves of Pharaoh*.

Despite this flurry of activity all through 1923—the peak year for Tutmania on the screen—

> **TO NATIONAL DISTRIBUTORS AND STATE RIGHTS BUYERS!**
>
> # THE *REAL* KING TUT PICTURE IS READY!
>
> Not only does it present an exquisitely executed Egyptian Drama, but *the most fascinating story ever unfolded on the screen* is masterfully told in
>
> # THE VENGEANCE OF TUT-ANKH-AMEN
>
> **300 PEOPLE** EXCELLENT CAST OF MORE THAN **300 PEOPLE**
>
> STORY BY ERNEST MIXX—TITLES BY RALPH SPENCE
>
> Many scenes actually taken in the "Valley of the Kings" and at
> **TUT-ANKH-AMEN'S TOMB**
>
> An Inspiring Romance That Had Its Incipiency in Ancient Egypt and Its Happy Culmination in Modern America Told in Seven Reels Just Teeming With Thrills Action—Suspense—Surprises and Gripping Appeal
>
> ASCHER FEATURES, INC.
> 117 W. 46th STREET   8960 Bryant   NEW YORK

"The Real King Tut Picture" was a typically audacious claim, but *The Vengeance of Tut-Ankh-Amen* appears not to have made it to the finish line.

the lavish American screen treatment of the subject so often announced, and so eagerly anticipated, never quite happened. The moment passed, and the opportunity was missed. By 1924 Carter himself was in town, touring his lecture show with accompanying slides and cine film from coast to coast and all points between. The performances were massively over-subscribed despite steep ticket prices, and extra shows had to be added to meet the demand. Carter knew his audience and played to them adroitly, likening mummification to how Americans canned their food, and a cane found in the tomb to the one wielded on screen by Charlie Chaplin. Along the way he met President Coolidge, the Rockefellers, Henry Ford, and Douglas Fairbanks.

The biggest surprise for many patrons may have been the revelation that Carter was, after all, English. He had been described as "the American archaeologist" so often and so widely in stateside news reports of the discovery, one has to assume it was as much wishful thinking as sloppy fact-checking. In any event, the New York *Tribune* happily burst the bubble in their review of the event, suggesting that whoever it was who started the rumor of Carter's American origins should be "captured, stuffed and placed in a glass case."

4

The Face Behind the Mask

> King Tut, the 125 year old alligator on exhibition at the Florida show at the World's Fair, has been ill-tempered of late. His keeper discovered that he had a toothache, resulting from a tooth broken in a fight with another 'gator. Yesterday he was dragged from his pool, and while a squad of assistants sat upon him, Dr. Joseph Lippert, loop dentist, pulled the tooth.—*Chicago Tribune*, July 30, 1932

While the world thrilled to the newsreels and tapped its tootsies to *Who Did the Strut for Old King Tut (When He said Tut Tut to the Queen)?*, Carter and his team were getting on with the serious, demanding and seemingly endless job of exploring, excavating and cataloguing the tomb. And as each new treasure was brought into the light, the quicker the visual arts rushed to claim it for modernity. The visual style of Tutankhamen's tomb was therefore timeless, old and new at once, forbiddingly ancient and superficially du jour. Tutmania, and Art Deco, did not merely unearth a dead past, as Carter and Carnarvon were doing, but breathed new life into it.

The mummy was figuratively walking again: now it would do so literally. As the twenties gave way to the thirties, a parallel development, albeit one perhaps peripherally informed by the fashionable morbidity of Tutmania, was getting underway in Hollywood. It would soon acquire a name of its own: the horror movie.

It is often unrecognized that when Universal codified the Gothic horror film, beginning with *Dracula* and *Frankenstein* in 1931, they transplanted it from its historical setting to the present. (It was the later Hammer cycle in Britain that returned its monsters—even, perversely, the mummy himself—to a faux–Victoriana.

The freshly discovered mask of Tutankhamen, photographed by Harry Burton.

Of the original Universal series, only *Murders in the Rue Morgue* [1932] is not set in the era in which it was made.) Here, even before the Mummy joined the studio's pantheon personally, we observe the mindset of Tutmania being applied to the Gothic legends of Europe in the same way as it was making sport with the mythic sensibilities of the Egyptians.

This can be seen in the first few seconds of the cycle's existence, at the very beginning of *Dracula* (1931). In the first shot of that film we are, just, in the realm of literary Gothic.

Dracula (1931) **invented the American horror film, and paved the way for** *The Mummy* **by allying supernatural themes to Art Deco aesthetics.**

Beautiful glass-painted Transylvanian skylines, the small inn, the nervous peasants, the horse-drawn carriage—all seem to have come straight from Bram Stoker's pages. But almost instantly the spell is broken: "Among the rugged peaks that frown down upon the Borgo Pass, are found crumbling castles of a bygone age…"

These lines are the first heard in the film, spoken by a tourist in cloche hat and glasses, reading aloud from a travel guide.[1] Instantly, then, we realize that this is today, that is to say 1931. And Dracula, though clearly a product of this pre-industrial wilderness, has somehow survived (and kept up, more or less, with the fashions) into a time when pre-industrial wildernesses start turning up on the summer travel itineraries of American college girls. There's something delightful about the fact that this place is both a land of wolves, vampires, dark powers and terrified villagers, and an international tourist stop. But this is exactly the world of Universal horror—a no man's land between the present and the past, with the freedom to pick and choose the best of each. That modern sassiness of speech, the idiom of the wisecrack by which thirties sophisticates identified each other, the latest fashions for the ladies … and the chance that our slumbers might be violated by some demonic fantasy of the pre-scientific imagination.

This is what made the mummy—dark and creepy and not fully explained, and at the same time *already* central to Western culture and familiar to the American filmgoer—an obvious and natural choice for Universal horror. Everything the studio had strained to do with Dracula and Frankenstein in terms of dragging worlds together is already right there, waiting in the source material. In that sense, *The Mummy* was the film they had been trying to make all along.

Note that it was called *The Mummy*—not *The Tomb*, nor even *The Curse*. The mummy itself was the payoff, the endpoint, the meaning. The true climax of the Tutankhamen adventure was the revelation of the king's mummy in 1925, just under three years after the discovery of the tomb and seven years before the last of its contents was shipped to the Cairo museum and the excavation officially declared completed.

The mortal remains were in the last of three coffins, contained within each other like Russian dolls, all placed inside a quartzite sarcophagus and surrounded by three outer shrines. With them came the last and most majestic revelation of all: the discovery that the king's head had been adorned with an almost unbelievably beautiful mask, made from two sheets of pure gold inlaid with quartz, lapis lazuli and other semi-precious stones. Serene, haunting, hypnotic, it became as ubiquitous and defining an image of Ancient Egypt as the pyramids and sphinx of Giza. What lay behind it *had* to be an anti-climax, but the revelation was shocking all the same. Here, at the end of the journey, the mysterious, glamorous fantasy of "King Tut" finally yielded to the shriveled, pathetic remains of an eighteen year old boy.[2]

Which was to be the "real" face of Tutankhamen: the golden one or the sad, almost accusingly mortal one? A lot was riding on the question, and the movie mummy, perhaps, was born in that moment that Carter and his team wrenched the mask from the face, ending their would-be eternal embrace, and drawing a final and irrevocable line between glamour and truth. The history books have voted unanimously for the mask: just look at how many cover jackets it adorns. The horror films went with the crumbling flesh. In a sense, they were more honest.

Symbolically, the narrative trajectories of the mummy movies all pivot on this dichotomy: the fantasies of gold and wonder giving way to the horrors of bodily corruption (whereupon the treasure hunters become the hunted, at the mercy of the world they

Howard Carter and an assistant in 1925 stripping away the last layers of mystery before grim reality regains control.

have defiled). The revenger mummy is not a figure encased in reassuring pomp and finery but an essentially naked corpse, rotting even as it triumphs. It personifies that shock of reality, of disenchantment and, possibly, of guilt, when the end of the game is signaled by the sad, lonely, unavoidable fact of death and decay. Except that in the movies, of course, death itself lives on and becomes its own avenging fury: a receptacle for the doubt and unease that, officially, Egyptology was never permitted to articulate.

So, finally, it arrives. 1932, and a film called *The Mummy*. There had been films about Ancient Egypt before, and there had been supernatural fantasy films about Ancient Egypt before. Indeed, there had been at least five films called *The Mummy* before. But cinematically, that was all prehistory. The moment the movies laid claim to Ancient Egypt, as decisive as the moment when Carter made a hole in a wall and archaeology was reinvented in a second, was now. *The Mummy* is a haunting piece of cinema, in its way more potent even than *Dracula* or *Frankenstein*, which—for all their undoubted brilliance—had essentially translated extant literary and theatrical materials. *The Mummy* was purer—a naked assembly of pristine essentials: the American horror film template perfectly applied, with the real world tang of Tutankhamen to root it both to modernity and to eternity.

Boris Karloff, newly rechristened "Karloff the Uncanny" by studio publicists, is "Imhotep," sentenced to be buried alive for stealing the Scroll of Thoth (in which "are set down the magic words by which Isis raised Osiris from the dead") and attempting to restore life to his late love, the Queen Ankhesenamen. Unearthed by twentieth century

The Mummy finally rose in 1932. This classic shot never actually appears in the film itself.

Egyptologists and accidentally restored when one of them reads the Scroll (for some reason buried with him) he leaves the tomb and returns years later as the shriveled but unbandaged "Ardath Bey." Bey is intent on finding his lost love who, we learn, has been repeatedly reincarnated through the ages, and is currently inhabiting the body of Helen Grosvenor, half–English and half–Egyptian, and part of a present-day British field expedition. Once in his clutches, he wastes no time getting her into a snake headdress and jeweled bikini, resembling one of Claudette Colbert's fetishistic outfits from DeMille's *Cleopatra*. ("Ancient Egypt! Nothing modern!" she coos approvingly when she sees his interior décor.) For some reason his scheme necessitates sacrificing her with a jeweled dagger; presumably the ritual will then permit her resurrection in her true ancient form. The orientalists charge in just in time to re-assert their supremacy but—notably—are not actually called upon to do so. Imhotep is in fact destroyed by Isis herself, who animates her own statue so as to supernaturally strike him down and reduce him to stop motion grave-dust, while the Westerners stand by and gawp.[3]

Karloff, of course, is the film's mesmeric focus, but Zita Johann is equally persuasive as Helen. Indeed, Johann's is widely regarded as the most nuanced female performance in the Universal sequence, and certainly few actresses playing a hypnotic trance have proved so hypnotic themselves. Even so, her reputation is smaller than her fascinating, brief filmography and extraordinary looks warrant: she should be an icon alongside Barbara Steele or even Louise Brooks.[4] Watch the sequence where Karloff summons her

"Ancient Egypt! Nothing modern!" Zita Johann in *The Mummy* (1932).

while she is at a dance, and she walks from the dance floor, out of the building and into a taxi. It is beautifully shot, with an especially well photographed reverse tracking shot as Johann separates from her dancing partner and walks directly towards the camera, short-haired, round-faced, massive-eyed. And I'm not sure what she's wearing in that back-of-the-taxi shot, twenty-two minutes in, but what a fantastic composition!

So here it is, at last: the classic cinematic representation of the living Egyptian mummy. And with incredible restraint and subtlety, we get to see it for just a few seconds, in an opening scene that is a masterpiece of suggestion. First, he is in his sarcophagus; original audiences may well have presumed this was a dummy, until we see him come very dimly to life. In a brilliant shot we see his eyes open just enough to show a twinkle, then one arm moves. A moment later, we see his hand, and, later, a single bandage trailing behind him as he leaves.

And that's it! As an aesthetic decision it's perfectly justified: the scene is suggestive and creepy to a degree far greater than anything in the later Kharis movies, one of the few Universal moments that really do rival the subtle effects of Val Lewton at RKO. But how it was smuggled past the value-for-money front office is mysterious indeed. (Compare it to the self-destructive over-use of the titular fiend in *The Wolf Man*.) The scene is one of the high points not only of the mummy sub-genre but of the horror film entire. The pace is so measured, and all unfolds in such glorious *Dracula* silence; every shot counts, every moment is held just long enough ... until the sudden eruption of horrible laughter, when archaeologist Bramwell Fletcher catches sight of him, and is turned mad by the shock. ("He went for a little walk.... You should have seen his face!")

Two people need to take a bow for this iconic achievement. One, obviously, is Karloff himself, the protean character actor beneath all the gauze and clay. The other is makeup designer Jack Pierce, the Dr. Frankenstein of Universal studios, who ran his department as an entirely separate autocracy within the studio hierarchy and achieved creations that have gone on to define their subjects for all time. After all, Frankenstein's creature had existed on page, stage and screen for over a century before Pierce got the commission. But ask anyone to draw a picture of him—even now, nudging a century later—and what will they draw?

The mummy designs for Karloff (there are two: with and without bandages) were instantly recognized as all-time classics, and earned Pierce the *Hollywood Filmograph* 1932 Makeup Trophy (this is of course many decades before makeup became an Oscar category). Karloff personally handed him the award at a gala presentation in the Roosevelt Hotel on Saturday 21st January 1933, announcing: "I want to publicly acknowledge to you, Jack Pierce, the deep debt of gratitude I owe you, for were it not for your wonderful makeups, the success I had in *The Old Dark House, Frankenstein* and *The Mummy* would have been impossible."

According to the paper:

> During the elimination, over one hundred makeups were considered by the committee of judges. Many marvellously effective character studies were submitted but the judges contended that merely elaborate makeups did not necessarily indicate exceeding cleverness. A makeup must primarily express a character as well as enable an actor to maintain his personality in delineating that character. Grotesqueness that held the actor expressionless may have been artistic but not outstanding.
>
> In deciding in favor of Jack Pierce's masterpiece, the problems that confronted him and the manner in which he overcame them won the admiration of the judges. To make a mummy come to life and appear natural was truly a problem. The manner in which Jack Pierce solved it reads like a romance. He first sculptured a statuette of the character in modelling compound, then proceeded to figure out a practical way of reproducing it on a human.... Max Factor Cosmetics played an important part in the makeups, coupled with Eastman Super-Sensitive Panchromatic Negative used by cinematographer Charles Stumar.[5]

In a 1935 interview from the set of *The Black Room* (then titled "The Black Room Mystery') the star recalled the experience:

> My worst makeup was in *The Mummy*. That took nine hours to get on. There were two makeups in that—one the mummy in the tomb, and the second, the mummy come to life. The nine hour makeup was the first one. Clay was applied, allowed to dry, then covered with wrappings. The second mummy makeup took four hours; it was uncomfortable in the extreme as the wrappings were put on wet and as they dried they tightened, and it was very difficult to speak lines with my throat so constricted.
>
> I don't complain. It's all interesting, this working in horror roles. It's certainly different and for the most I enjoy it tremendously. Jack Pierce, the makeup man at Universal, who has been with me on all these horror roles, is skillful and careful. We work out the new makeup together, well in advance of the actual beginning of the shooting schedule. Then if the makeup proves too uncomfortable or in any way unsatisfactory, we still have time to try again and do something better.[6]

As usual, the final designs came at the end of much costly trial and error. *Hollywood Filmograph* reported that camera tests were beginning on a set closed to all except Pierce, Karloff and cameraman Charles Stumar. At this point, it tells us, the make-ups were taking over three hours to apply, "thus topping the time record of almost three hours consumed in applying the various cosmetics and wigs which turned him into Frankenstein."[7] (Ultimately, as we shall see, the approved design took much longer than three hours to complete!) My favorite statistic from the report: "More than 150 yards of bandage will be twisted about his body each day to give him the appearance of just having risen from a casket."

Here's the final process, as described in meticulous if somewhat melodramatic detail by the *New Movie Magazine*:

> Last, but not least, we come to a make-up triumph which may stand as the greatest in Hollywood history—the changing of Boris Karloff, by Jack Pierce, Universal's makeup expert, into a 3700-year-old mummy. Here is the process, step by step.
>
> Mr. Karloff's entire face, even to his eyelids, is covered with layers of paper—thin cotton tissue, which is next painted with collodion to make it shrivel. This is dried with an electric drying machine, to set the wrinkles. The tip of the nose is built up in the same manner to make it look decomposed.

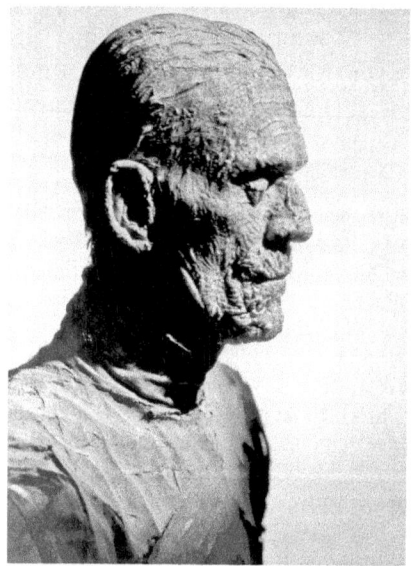 

The two faces of Boris Karloff in *The Mummy* (1932).

His hair is plastered with makeup clay. This is dried, then it is cracked and fluid is poured into the cracks—a clay-solvent to make them look rough, as they naturally would be.

Next, not one but *twenty-two* coloured makeup paints are applied to the base of crinkled cotton and collodion—the colours copied from a coloured photo of the Mummy of the Egyptian Pharaoh Seti II, which is in the Cairo Museum. These paints are dried and set.

Then the arms and hands undergo the same treatments, and, last of all, Karloff is swathed from head to foot in ashen-colored linen bandages, which have been acid rotted and passed through a warm oven. His joints are taped, and he is sprayed with a dusting of Fullers' earth.

Grotesque and inhuman, shrivelled, sunken of cheek and eye, a colorless grayish brown all over, Karloff has to be lifted to his feet. He cannot move a muscle of his face. He cannot talk. For a scene which will last two minutes on the screen he endures *seven hours* of torture, followed by another seven or eight hours of gruelling work on the sound stage. Do you marvel that he twice fainted dead away during the making of the picture?[8]

Of course, it is in the interest of star, studio and designer alike to exaggerate the arduousness of a fantastic make-up, but Pierce's professionalism soon bridled at the excessive melodrama of some of these reports, as *Hollywood Filmograph* reported:

Safety is the primary element considered in concocting the spectacular movie makeup creations which have made Karloff supreme in the field of grotesque characterizations, according to Jack Pierce, chief makeup artist at Universal studios, and responsible in large part for the uncanny forms the actor has assumed on the screen.

Pierce resents sensational reports of extreme pain, discomfort and physical injury endured by Karloff in the weird character creations of *Frankenstein*, *The Old Dark House* and more recently *The Mummy*, in which the actor was made to resemble a 3700-year-old mummy. Reports were largely founded on the fact that Karloff fainted several times on the set of the pictures, and lost weight during their filming.

The makeup artist declares, however, that these evidences of exhaustion while partly due to the ordeal of assuming the makeup, were mainly traceable to the extreme physical effort demanded by the roles Karloff portrayed, and the long hours of work made necessary by the tedious makeup. Nothing ever applied to Karloff in the makeup room was used without a thorough test on himself, Pierce states.

The collodion and spirit gum with which the intricate coating of dampened cotton was applied in preparing for *The Mummy* was carefully kept from injuring the skin of Karloff, and while the completed makeup was uncomfortable, as are all of the spectacular makeups, as a rule, there was never the slightest danger of a skin infection, burns, abrasions or physical injury to any part of the actor's body, Pierce claims.[9]

By the time Lon Chaney, Jr., had taken on the part in the 1940s, however, the cost-conscious Universal slashed the amount of time required in the make-up chair by designing a simple rubber mask for him to wear. This proved no less uncomfortable in the event, however, since Chaney discovered that contact with rubber brought him out in rashes, bumps and welts.[10]

As Jasmine Day notes in *The Mummy's Curse*, the use of real mummies as reference points had some unforeseen legacies:

The unexplained absence of Im-Ho-Tep's outer wrappings obscures the causes of similar conditions of actual mummies (including scientific study and interference by tomb robbers), implying they were interred in this state. Im-Ho-tep's appearance was copied from the mummy of at least one king: Seti I, if not also Rameses III. Both of these mummies were ravaged by tomb robbers and partly unwrapped in the nineteenth century; both retained only their innermost bandages, their arms wrapped separately and their unwrapped and detached heads reattached by ancient priests who restored their burials. A cloth that the priests wound around the neck of Rameses III to disguise the damage reappears on Karloff's outfit.

Day nominates Seti I as Pierce's principal source of reference, though you will note that the contemporary report above opts for Seti II, as does Universal horror expert Gregory William Mank, who states in his book *Bela Lugosi and Boris Karloff* that a photo of Seti II pinned to Pierce's wall provided inspiration as he worked. (And the truth is that there is very little resemblance, except in the broadest sense, between Karloff's make-up and either Seti.) But Day's main point stands, whatever: "These interferences have seldom been mentioned on museum labels," she concludes, "so how were costume designers to know that the bodies they were studying had not originally been interred in their present semi-clad state?"

More ambiguous is the question of the limb-binding displayed in the design. Day again:

> While mummies' separately wrapped limbs were bound to their bodies by outer layers of cloth, Im-Ho-Tep, supposedly discovered intact, has separately bound limbs. This permits his ambulation. His head and hands are uncovered to indicate Ardath Bey's similarity to him.

Ironically, the most authentic of all the screen mummies is probably Prem, designed by George Partleton for Hammer's *The Mummy's Shroud* (1967). I say ironic, because this is also the screen mummy that likely conforms least to our standard concept of what a "real" mummy looks like. It is nonetheless an accurate copy of the unnamed "EA6704," a beautifully preserved specimen in the British Museum collection. The point of confusion lies in the fact that EA6704 is from the Roman period and so has a distinctly exotic look, strikingly different from the "classic" mummies from much earlier periods. His eerie, mournful face painted directly onto the bandaging, individually wrapped fingers and toes, patches of color and decoration, and patterned, geometric bandaging on the arms are all at odds with the unadorned, simply bandaged mummies with which we are more familiar.

It is easy to be too whimsical about such things as this, but let us take a moment, at least, to consider the extraordinary journey that the appearance of Prem concludes.

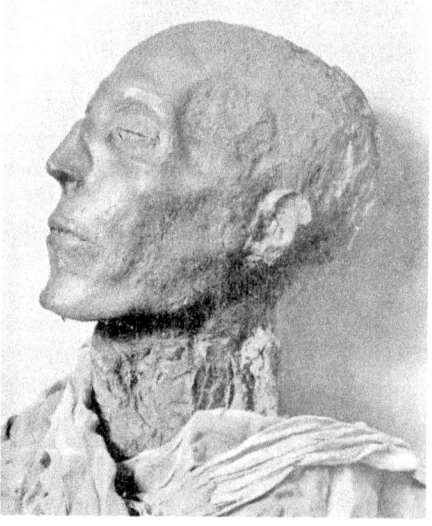 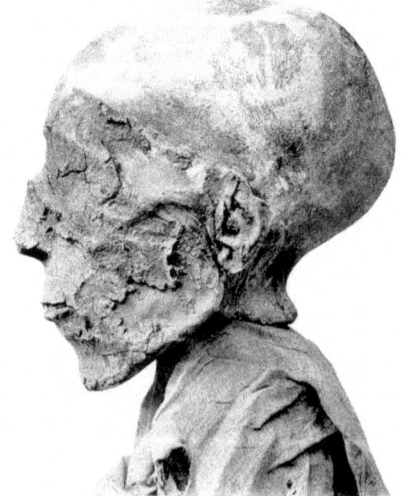

The mummies of Seti I (left) and Seti II (right) have both been suggested as potential models for Jack Pierce's design for *The Mummy* **(1932).**

4. The Face Behind the Mask

Whoever EA6704 was, we do not know him in any regard: not his name, not his physical appearance, not any detail of his life. He had a personality, he had opinions, and his life was shaped by events. The lottery of history has preserved none of them. Then, in death, where the right to individuality more commonly vanishes, he suddenly "wins" a much bigger lottery, of a sort he could have never imagined. Not only is he displayed before millions of enquiring eyes, he becomes a movie star, and a figure of (intrinsic, rather than incidental) fear and menace. It is a trajectory so absurd, it almost seems to rewrite the rules of probability. If that could happen to EA6704, then we must conclude that it could happen to anybody. It could happen to you.

Given the gap between what we presume to be Prem's historical era and that of EA6704, it may be of interest to add that EA6704 was originally in a much earlier New Kingdom coffin (see Chapter 5 for further discussion of coffin reuse) when he was purchased by the museum in 1835. He was bought, under the provocatively Conan Doyle–esque moniker of "Lot Number 580," at Sotheby's auction house, part of a collection amassed by the late Henry Salt, a noted archaeologist and translator of hieroglyphs, and former British consul-general in Cairo. Salt was a voracious collector of antiquities who purchased from Belzoni, and sold on both to major museums and private collectors. (He supplied the British Museum with the head of Rameses II, the Louvre with the sarcophagus of Rameses III, and Sir John Soane with the sarcophagus of Seti I.)

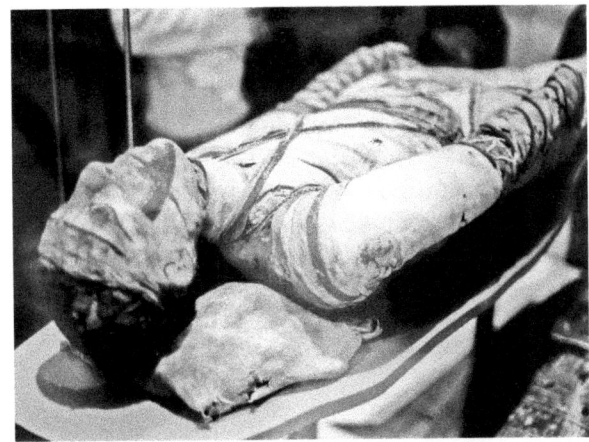

EA6704 in his real form in the British Museum, and a star at last in the form of stuntman Eddie Powell in Hammer's *The Mummy's Shroud* (1967). Maggie Kimberly wishes he was elsewhere.

It was adventurers like Salt who brought Egypt to the West, and helped create the store of essential mental images—in all their partial, often misleading forms—upon which these later cinematic representations draw. As well as the mummy designs of Pierce, Partleton and the rest, this also, of course, applies to the art direction of these films. And equally as fascinating, in *The Mummy*, as Pierce's work on Imhotep himself, are the settings by the Hungarian artist William Pogany, famous for his striking book illustrations of fabulous and mythical subjects, and who had come to movies following a stint at set-designing for the New York stage. (They might have asked Weigall, who had been doing the same in London.) All of the film's settings—ancient, modern and hallucinatory—share the same oneiric quality, making the film more satisfying visually even than *Dracula* or *Frankenstein*. Delightful library shots of 1930s Cairo complete the feast.

The design of *The Mummy* (1932) is for the most part excellent, though perhaps the hieroglyphs could have benefited from a little more attention.

The project travelled a bizarrely convoluted route before landing in correct form and proportions on the studio's shooting slate. It began not as a mummy story at all, but as *Caglisotro*, already with Karloff in the lead, loosely based on some of the wilder accounts of the eighteenth-century Italian adventurer and troublemaker. In Nina Wilcox Putnam's treatment, Karloff's Cagliostro was a three-thousand-year-old alchemist and occultist with an astral projection machine cum death ray; Universal's Carl Laemmle, Jr. (the driving force behind the studio's horror program), declared it too fanciful, too science fiction-styled, and insufficiently spooky. As an obvious means to the desired end he then recruited John L. Balderston to give it more of the intended mood.

Balderston was the obvious choice on two counts: first, because he had written *Dracula* and contributed to *Frankenstein*, but also because, as London correspondent of the *New York World*, he had been sent to Egypt to cover the opening of Tutankhamen's sarcophagus and had actually set foot in the tomb himself. He had even found himself dragged briefly into the limelight in 1924 when editor of the London magazine *Outlook*.

Carter had become embroiled in exactly the antagonism with the Egyptian government that Weigall had warned him of should he continue to view the tomb as his exclusive property, and the feud had concluded with Carter locking the tomb and withholding the keys in response to what he called "impossible restrictions and discourtesies." It was a ridiculous stand-off that left the Egyptians no other option than to force entry and take complete control. In common with many in the West, Balderston had taken Carter's part, referring to the Egyptians as "these hysterical children who are playing at self-government."[11] As a result, an Egyptian lawyer called Shalaby Bey wrote to the magazine with the following proposition:

> To teach you to be polite when dealing with Egyptian affairs, and to wash out with blood your insult against Egypt, I challenge you to meet me in a duel; otherwise, you are a coward.
> If you have any blood in your veins, you won't refuse. You are free to fix the date of the duel, and as regards the place, I suggest the neighbourhood of Paris.

The press were not slow in suggesting that the affair may have been "the most recent outcome of Tutankhamen's malignant influence." Meanwhile Balderston glibly accepted the offer, but selected as his choice of weapon a "submarine equipped with 12-inch guns."[12]

Odd, then, with all this experience to draw upon, that the story Balderston eventually came up with was in so many essentials an only lightly disguised remake of *Dracula*: Edward Van Sloan's Dr. Muller is the Van Helsing of the tombs, subjecting leading lady Zita Johann, under the monster's spell, to leading questions in the drawing room, while David Manners resumes his winning strategy of standing a pace or two behind her looking alternately cross and worried. ("Do you have to open graves to find girls to fall in love with?" Johann mockingly asks him at one point.) Statues of Isis are handed out in place of crucifixes. There is even a civilized dinner party confrontation scene between wise Van Sloan and the monster, with the latter eventually showing his true colors and threateningly acknowledging his opponent's wisdom.

The other key influence, present to a degree that made its absence from the credits quite shameful if not actionable, is Sir Arthur Conan Doyle's superb short story *The Ring of Thoth*. Published in 1890, it is a masterpiece of mood and simplicity: very short, set over one night in one location, with only two characters and told almost entirely in dialogue. And yet in its eerie melancholy it establishes exactly that mood of somber mysticism we associate with the movie.

The central character, Egyptologist John Vansittart Smith, falls asleep during his studies in the Louvre, and awakes in the middle of the night to find that he is not alone: a curious attendant who had caught his attention earlier in the day is busying himself by lamplight near one of the mummy cases. The description of this strange individual reads as a blueprint for Karloff's character:

> Vansittart Smith, fixing his eyes upon the fellow's skin, was conscious of a sudden impression that there was something inhuman and preternatural about its appearance. Over the temple and cheekbone it was as glazed and as shiny as varnished parchment. There was no suggestion of pores. One could not fancy a drop of moisture upon that arid surface. From brow to chin, however, it was cross-hatched by a million delicate wrinkles, which shot and interlaced as though nature in some Maori mood had tried how wild and intricate a pattern she could devise.

The nature of his midnight errand is even more curious:

> He stepped lightly and swiftly across to one of the great cases, and drawing a key from his pocket, he unlocked it. From the upper shelf he pulled down a mummy, which he bore away with him, and laid it with much care and solicitude upon the ground. By it, he placed his lamp, and then squatting down beside it in Eastern fashion he began with long, quivering fingers to undo the cerecloths and bandages which girt it round. As the crackling rolls of linen peeled off one after the other, a strong aromatic odour filled the chamber, and fragments of scented wood and of spices pattered down upon the marble floor.

Vansittart Smith watches in stunned fascination as the mummy is revealed to be a female "of extraordinary loveliness," with "a cascade of long, black, glossy tresses" and "a beautifully curved chin." But the biggest surprise is yet to come:

> Its effect upon the Egyptologist was as nothing, however, compared to that which it produced upon the strange attendant. He threw his hands up into the air, burst into a harsh clatter of words, and then, hurling himself down upon the ground beside the mummy, he threw his arms round her and kissed her repeatedly upon the lips and brow. "Ma petite!" he groaned in French. "Ma pauvre petite!" His voice broke with emotion, and his innumerable wrinkles quivered and writhed...[13]

Sir Arthur Conan Doyle. His influence on Egypt-inspired popular culture was as far-reaching as the tips of his mustache.

Vansittart, exposed, begs the man to tell him more. Thus is revealed a strange saga stretching back to the reign of Tuthmosis, the third king of the 18th Dynasty. The man, named Sosra, was a doctor and savant who had discovered "a substance which, when injected into the blood, would endow the body with strength to resist the effects of time, of violence or of disease." The result is not literal immortality, "but its potency would endure for many thousands of years." In consequence, Sosra has lived through centuries of human history: "I was old when Ilium fell. I was very old when Herodotus came to Memphis. I was bowed down with years when the new gospel came upon earth."

In order to have a companion to share his experiences, he gives some of the substance to "a young priest of Thoth, Parmes by name," and for a while all is well. The situation changes, however, when both men fall in love with Atma, daughter of the governor of Abaris, and turns to tragedy when she dies of plague before taking the serum. His longevity now a curse, he is unable to join her in the afterlife. Worse, Parmes has developed an antidote, and is successfully released from eternal wandering. Sosra discovers from his papers that a quantity of this antidote has been concealed within the Ring of Thoth, but the city is invaded and sacked before he has a chance to locate it. Many centuries later he reads that the tomb of Atma has been discovered, along with the ring. He traces the mummy and its artefacts to the Louvre where, finally, that night, he achieved his goal. The story ends with the discovery of his body next morning, locked in embrace with the mummy.

This, minus the tacit necrophilia, is clearly the start point of the Karloff movie, and specifically inspires one of its most painterly and haunting sequences, in which we observe Karloff loitering in the Cairo museum at night; intoning by candlelight over the mummy of his lost love. It will be seen, however, that in several extremely important respects the two works are opposites of each other. Sosra is not a mummy—he has lived continuously from ancient times to the present, and the Ring of Thoth which he seeks—unlike the film's Scroll—ensures not eternal life but merciful death. There is no notion of reincarnation, which is in any event problematic (see also Chapter 8).

The film's biggest logical problem—that the Egyptians had possessed a scroll, the reading of which restores life to the dead, yet were forbidden to use it, and that Imhotep risks damnation to restore his love's earthly life rather than seeking to join her eternally in the afterlife—is absent entirely; the story is much more logical. Further it is via entirely earthly science that Sosra discovered his eternal life potion. (He stresses: "There was nothing of mystery or magic in the matter. It was simply a chemical discovery, which may well be made again.") He no more violates his sacred religion than he would be willing to. The film's screenplay, then, takes Doyle's story as its central idea, but by tacking on a prologue showing Karloff as a mummy coming to life it forces the whole story to change direction in order to accommodate it. (According to *Variety*, Balderston was summoned to the set by director Karl Freund to assist in daily script revision, possibly to iron out issues such as these.[14])

It should be noted, however, that author Julie M. Schablitsky has suggested some altogether more authentic inspiration in her book *Box Office Archaeology: Refining Hollywood's Portrayal's of the Past*, noting that the early Ptolemaic papyrus *The Story of Setna Khaemwas and the Mummies* in the Cairo Museum "shares a number of plot elements" with Balderston's script and "very likely served as an inspiration" to him:

> In it, Setna tries to steal the cursed book of Thoth from a tomb and is opposed by the mummy of Naneferkaptah and the spirits of his wife and child. Setna fails to heed their tale of the disastrous consequences of their sacrilege in possessing the scroll, which was placed in their tomb to keep it away from mortals. Later, Setna realizes his mistake and returns the scroll, agreeing as a penance to reunite Naneferkaptah's mummy with those of his wife and son, who were buried far away. In an episode strikingly similar to the scene with Karloff's mummy, Naneferkaptah appears as an old man and leads Setna to the tomb of his loved ones.

There's no question that Balderston, long familiar with the subject of Ancient Egypt, has drawn on real aspects of it in the script. Ankhesenamen was a real queen (correctly placed by Balderston in the 18th Dynasty and named as "daughter of Ahmenhotep the Magnificent"). Though never stated in the screenplay, the genuine Ankhesenamen was Tutankhamen's wife, and was indeed a daughter of Akhenaten (a.k.a. Ahmenhotep IV). This is one of two nods to Tutankhamen in the movie, the other being an overt bit of cinematic one-upmanship over Carter and the real-life spectacle from which the film draws its currency, when Karloff, now disguised as Ardath Bey, promises the Egyptologists that he will lead them to "the most sensational find since that of Tutankhamen!"

Bey's real name, Imhotep, is a more audacious bit of plundering. The real Imhotep was a Third Dynasty vizier and wise man, widely credited as the architect responsible for designing the first pyramid (the step pyramid of Djoser). According to Manetho he was "the inventor of the art of building with hewn stone." (He seems also to have been an instructional writer of the "wisdom" genre, taking the form of a series of maxims and instructional observations, supposedly addressed to a son from a father; though much referred to and likely quoted without attribution by later writers, none of this material is known to have survived in its original form.)

His reputation as a genius grew with the telling, so that within two thousand years of his death he was being worshipped as a god—a rare accolade indeed for a commoner. According to Christine El Mahdy in her book *The Pyramid Builder*, Imhotep deserved all his ancient superlatives and then some: she calls him "one of the greatest thinkers of all time," his work on the pyramid reflective of "daring vision, and such ability to bring a concept to fruition, [as is] beyond the ability of ordinary men." Further, he also enjoyed a reputation as a physician, anatomist and healer, and would ultimately be venerated as a god of medicine and wisdom, linked with the cult of Thoth. Though some modern writers dispute all these assertions of his greatness and achievement, there's no question that they made him the ideal real-life candidate for Doyle's Sosra, and he was incorporated into Balderston's schema almost certainly for that reason, overriding his historical incompatibility with Ankhesenamen.[15] (I also fancy I really do see something of Karloff in both the proportions and crouching posture of the Late Period bronze statuette of Imhotep held by the British Museum!)

Of course, the most important deviation from Doyle lies in the fact that it is a film about resurrection; about the Egyptian dead being revived, and loosed, in our own time. And we sense the desire to establish the concept on as sound a mystical footing as possible, hence the caption with which the film opens:

> This is the Scroll of Thoth.[16] Herein are set down the magic words by which Isis raised Osiris from the dead. Oh! Amon-Ra—Oh! God of Gods—Death is but the doorway to new life—We live today-we shall live again—In many forms shall we return-Oh, mighty one.

The myth of Osiris is the well-spring of Egyptian ideas concerning the afterlife, simultaneously inspiring, justifying and sustaining them, as well as forming the bedrock upon which these various ideas could be extended and developed to form an entire belief system. In itself, however, it is simple and unexceptional, just one more mythical story among many, suggesting a shrewd opportunism subsequently at play, and a semi-accidental relevance to belief already established and searching for an origin myth to call its own.

The film is rather stretching things here: Isis did not raise Osiris from the dead in anything like so prosaic a sense as that which Karloff has in mind for his queen. Murdered by his brother Set, Osiris was dismembered, and the pieces scattered throughout the land. When Isis had retrieved them she used magic to reassemble and temporarily reanimate Osiris so as to unite with him and produce their son Horus. Osiris then immediately returned to the afterlife, to become King of the Dead.... Well, the story varies in its fine print from telling to telling, but that's the basic yarn—and clearly, the reanimation of Osiris, such as it is, is of an abstract, spiritual order; he is, after all, a god. It's something of a stretch to use this as a basis for the film's central mythology: the existence of a scroll that is a kind of do-it-yourself manual for bringing any dead mortal back to health and vitality.

'The Scroll of Thoth" (if not taken directly from the manuscript cited by Julie M. Schablitsky) is an attempt by Balderston to integrate Doyle's *Ring of Thoth* with the established Egyptian custom of equipping mummies with sacred scrolls to facilitate their passage into the underworld. These contain the texts known as the Egyptian Books of the Dead, rather than curses, or occult spells. This store-house of myth and incantation can also be found painted on the inside of coffins and gouged into sarcophagi, a practice that persisted unchanged until the very end of Ancient Egypt itself, in the Roman era.

Schablitsky again finds an exception worth noting, however:

> In *The Mummy*, Imhotep uses magic to attack, paralyze, and bend people to his will. These actions and Imhotep's fate share some similarities with real events in New Kingdom Egypt. Administrative documents discovered at Thebes relate how conspirators were caught and convicted of stealing a sacred book of spells and using them for similar purposes in the plot to assassinate New Kingdom Pharaoh Ramses III (ca. 1151 BCE [*sic*]). The papyrus trial transcripts reveal both the offense and "great punishments of death" proscribed for the criminals by the gods. At least one of the conspirators, probably Ramses III's son Pentawere, may have been buried alive in an unmarked coffin found in the Deirel Bahri royal cache of thirty-seven mummies. Bound and tightly wrapped, "Unknown Man E" suffered the further indignity of being sewn up in a ritually unclean sheepskin. This archaeological discovery clearly influenced Balderston's screenplay and had a major impact on the mummy genre.[17]

The Mummy represents the perfection of that formula Universal was tinkering with in the early thirties, yet the film did not prove quite the popular sensation that its two predecessors had been. Perhaps the whole idea of the horror film was now settled, and this was taken as merely the next in a clearly ongoing catalogue, and so less of an individual event.[18] Or, perhaps, it indicated a tailing-off in the public fascination with the tombs after a decade of Tutmania, and with its dazzling excess no longer so intoxicating, as the Depression took hold. It would not be until 1940 that the mummy walked again, and when it did, it was in a very different style, in a very different world.

5

Good Heavens, What a Terrible Curse!

> The sentiment of the Egyptologist, however, is not one of fear but of respect and awe. It is entirely opposed to the foolish superstitions which are far too prevalent among emotional people in search of "psychic" excitement.... Similar tales have been a common feature of fiction for many years, they are mostly variants of the ordinary ghost story, and may be accepted as a legitimate form of literary amusement.—Howard Carter, unpublished essay (quoted in T. G. H. James: *Howard Carter: The Path to Tutankhamun*)

Carter and Carnarvon had electrified the world with a unique mixture of detective story, adventure yarn and fabulous fable, all of it glinting with gold. But even this may not have been quite enough to make of the discovery the worldwide obsession it became, without the final and definitive ingredient: the pharaoh's curse.

Carter's 1923 account of the tomb's discovery sold well, of course, but in tailoring his account to a popular readership he seemed to be writing through gritted teeth, resentful of the massive audience that was, he knew, so unconcerned with the finer points of the subject. The book was a kind of riposte to the very fascination that accounted for the greater part of its sales.

For the popular audience of the time, a far more enjoyable volume—and a far more useful one for the modern student of Tutmania itself—was Arthur Weigall's contribution, *Tutankhamen and Other Essays*, published in 1924. Written in a gentler and more conciliatory tone than Carter's volume, though not without its own axes to grind, it was a series of disconnected chapters that took care to mix the scholarly with the more romantic kind of fare for which the public clamored. A dense chapter on Egyptian chronology (in which he states: "I must warn the reader that the subject is extremely complicated and he will require to give his full attention to it if he would understand it") rubs shoulders with *Boys' Own*-style accounts of his expeditions into the desert that dwell on the sights and sounds and sensations of the land and the tombs. These latter are essentially travel literature, aiming to create the sensation of a journey to Egypt for the frustrated Tutmaniac in Boisie, Idaho, or the London suburbs.

Unlike Carter, Weigall had few quarrels with Tutmania, either in theory or in fact. For one thing he couldn't afford to: as a freelancer, a worldwide Egyptian cult meant guaranteed work for specialists like himself. Accordingly, he threw himself into all areas of the Egyptian revival, from scholarly and popular writing, journalism and novel-writing, to designing theatrical sets and even writing song lyrics. He also contributed, albeit remotely, to the cinema, when his novel *The Dweller in the Desert* was adapted into the 1922 film *Burning Sands*. The money was useful, though he later declared the film "the worst picture I ever saw."

But the biggest difference between Weigall and Carter is that the former was happy to give the public what it *really* wanted: an ambivalent take on the curse. A chapter in his book entitled "The Ancient Egyptian Spirits" begins with one of the most quoted elements of the Tutankhamen curse myth—the story that during the excavations, Carter's caged canary was killed by a cobra, embodiment, perhaps, of the Pharaoh's vengeful spirit. From here, he discusses tomb curses in general, for the most part with clear detachment and skepticism, but nonetheless with a willingness to meet halfway the prurient concerns of the mass audience that, to Carter, would constitute an unconscionable capitulation to the lowest common denominator. He tells of an inexplicable experience of his own, in which he seemed to have been attacked by a mummified cat, among other tall tales vividly related, and finally keeps all options open by concluding:

> I have heard the most absurd nonsense talked in Egypt by those who believe in the malevolence of the ancient dead; but at the same time, I try to keep an open mind on the subject.

It had long been a tradition within Western culture that the Egyptians possessed not just a unique mythology but also commanded mastery of a profound and potent magic. That this is divorced, essentially, from their theology, explains why it was commonplace for it to continue to be treated with credulity within the more esoteric corners of Judeo-Christian society, and generally tolerated by it with bemused resignation. Such

Jacqueline Logan in mortal peril in *Burning Sands* (1922), the worst picture Arthur Weigall ever saw.

accounts of it as were generally available should be expected to be both intrinsically absurd and—more importantly—often invented from whole cloth.

In 1822, contemporary with the Napoleonic Egyptomania boom, one John McGowan of London published a book snappily entitled *The Book of Fate, formerly in the possession of Napoleon, later Emperor of France, and now first rendered into English, from a German Translation, of an Ancient Egyptian Manuscript, found in the year 1801, by M. Sonnini, in one of the Royal Tombs, near Mount Libycus, in Upper Egypt. By H. Kirchenhoffer, Fellow of the University of Pavia; Knight Grand Cross of the Annunciade of Sardinia; and Chevalier of the Legion of Honor.* In the space remaining once all of that had been established, the book was essentially a handbook of astrological fortune-telling, with no verifiable basis in Egyptian mythology at all. It derives, the author claims, from secret incantations discovered on a roll of papyrus secreted about the person of a mummy discovered during Napoleon's campaign. The volume went through over twenty reprints in the next dozen years, repeated this success in translation in France and Spain, and was still being published in popular editions in England as late as 1925.

Foolish as this may be, the important point is that this tradition lays the groundwork for a phenomenon that, to many of us, seems utterly inexplicable and in need of careful explanation: the fact that millions of people in the twentieth century, actively encouraged by the media, came truly to believe, without any real justification (let alone empirical evidence!) that the spirits of Egypt could truly perform acts of vengeance through the centuries.

Even today, the notion persists that *something* strange happened in Tutankhamen's tomb, that *some* series of inexplicable events occurred to strike down the principle figures associated with the discovery. Not an actual curse, perhaps—we don't believe in curses, not *really*—but for all that a set of mysteries that, taken together, surely *test* the limit of rational explanation, if not necessarily find it wanting.

But the sober truth is not that reason is more than up to the task of accounting for the mystery, it is that there really is no mystery to account for in the first place. The whole thing was a journalistic invention with no foothold in reality to any degree. And however many peripheral names are added to the supposed roll call of victims, the stubborn fact remains that Carter himself somehow escaped it with ease, dying of natural causes, many years later, in England.

The idea that the ancients really could rustle up mysterious occult powers to give eternal protection to their sacred tombs would have come as good news to them. The notion is so silly only a sophisticated modern intelligence could ever really give it credence. The Egyptians surely did not: Carter's greatest fear on discovering the tomb, after all, was not that it would kill him but that it had already been robbed in antiquity. This was more than likely, so commonplace was the practice. No robber would have dared enter on so blasphemous an errand if they

NATIVES SAY GODS WATCH TOMB OF TUT

Natives Claim Gods to Blame For Death of Lord Carnarvon

EXAMPLES ARE BEING CITED

Death Curse Because Tomb of Pharaoh Disturbed

The *Madera Tribune* (April 5, 1923) picks up the story.

truly believed that to do so was to risk some eternal supernatural punishment. (The actual, physical punishments meted out were risk enough: according to the written results of a Twentieth Dynasty investigation into an epidemic of tomb robbery, apprehended miscreants were tortured into confession, and subject to death by impalement.) Neither did the intruders display even a token reverence for the physical remains. Mummies were smashed up and ripped apart in the search for the jewels with which they had been buried, and there is evidence at some sites of corpses, including those of children, being burned to provide illumination for the job.

Now, clearly, if the ancients thought curses would work, they wouldn't have bothered strengthening the tombs' defenses with so many elaborate physical mechanisms to deter robbers. The complexity of the tombs' design, the sloping corridors and vertical entranceways, re-filled on exit, the elaborate stone seals, the false doors—all were put in place on the understanding that robbery would inevitably be attempted. Some tomb chapels contain notices advising that anyone "who shall make a disturbance in this tomb, who shall damage its inscriptions or who shall do damage to its statue, they will fall under the anger of Thoth," but surely this is more wishful thinking than warning. Religion, then as now, was a means of stabilizing and accounting for the cosmic order: anyone who actually believes they can rely on it to provide invincibility is soon disabused. Thus if robbers were ever afraid of damnation they would have soon learned not to be, and such curses as exist, especially in Old and Middle Kingdom and Late Period tombs, would have assumed a tone as purely ceremonial as everything else.

This brings us back to the question of just how absolute, and central, religion actually was to the Ancient Egyptians. All surviving data would suggest they were scrupulously diligent in their religious observances. But how then do we reconcile this with the fact of tomb robbing? In *Ancient Lives*, his wonderfully evocative study of the Theban tomb builders in the village of Deir el Medina, John Romer writes both that "the security of the [Valley of the Kings] and its rich graves ultimately depended more upon the reverence in which the kings' tombs were held by their subjects than on cunning architectural subterfuge or an army of perpetual guards," and that "by the end of the first decade of King Rameses IX, the proceeds of tomb-robbery seem to have become an important part of the Theban economy." So why did they not at least fear some form of supernatural comeback for their outrages?

Weigall notes the paradox, in a chapter delightfully called "The Ancient Ghouls of Thebes" in his *Tutankhamen and Other Essays*:

> These ghouls must have been men of very strong nerves thus to penetrate into the subterranean halls and passages where the spirits of the dead monarchs were thought to roam at large. It is not as though they could climb in, snatch up some article of value, and scramble back to safety: they had to penetrate more than 500 feet into the hillside and descend nearly 150 feet. In the tomb of Sety I … the walls were covered with sculpture and paintings representing the gods and demons of the Underworld; and the figure of the king they were outraging was to be seen on all sides in communion with the deities whose wrath they were incurring. Sometimes when I have been sitting alone at the bottom of this great tomb, I have been oppressed by the silence and the mystery of the place; and if, after this lapse of three thousand years, one is still conscious of the awful sanctity of these dark halls cut into the heart of the hills, one wonders what must have been the sensations of the ancient thieves who penetrated by the light of a flickering oil lamp into the very presence of the dead.

This leads us to a radical suggestion indeed: did the practice of tomb robbery itself play a vital role in the reformation and evolution of Egyptian religious beliefs? Imagine yourself a tomb robber, entering a sacred tomb for the first time. Even if they had been or had known tomb builders, the actual funeral ceremony and the processes of embalming and internment would be things of which they could only imagine, the reality known only to a very select few. Their religious instruction would have told them that it was a divine transformation, the preparation for the reunification of the king's spirit and body in the afterlife. (Perhaps they justified their grim errand by convincing themselves that anything remaining at the end of this magnificent event was essentially obsolete, the generous left-overs of an beneficent deity, and no longer "owned" in any specific moral sense.) But then, suddenly, they find themselves in the holy inner chamber and come face to face with the truth in all its shocking banality. Here is their king, their god: a moldering sack, a grotesque parody of the sacred idealized imagery that would have hitherto been their only reference point, and which even now impotently adorned the walls and funerary items. In this light, their ruthless appropriation of the mortal remains as illumination might be read not as blasphemous disregard so much as a gesture of nihilistic anger, a symbolic revenge by the duped against an ultimate authority cruelly revealed as fallacious.

To the truly religious mind, of course, no amount of partial disproof is sufficient to extinguish the fundamental flame of possibility. We might perhaps imagine the ancient sensibilities splintering at this point into two variant perspectives: the thoroughly disillusioned pragmatism of the tomb robber, and a defiantly revisionist optimism among those whose position and purpose depended upon the old certainties being inviolate? (Was the ruthlessness with which tomb robbers were punished as much a matter of protecting the faith as guarding their property?) To those with a spiritual or pragmatic investment in religious observance, the stark fact of the decomposing mummies may have suggested not the obsolescence of the informing faith as much as evidence of purely human fallibility. If it hadn't worked then, that doesn't mean it would not work on other occasions, or in theory: the fault was to be found at the human level. Perhaps the rituals were incorrectly rendered, or even—heaven forbid—the subject unworthy…

Let us now take this speculation just one degree further and propose that this more prosaic attitude to the ancient mysteries helped facilitate a further trend in the re-use of funerary items and materials in later burials. It is tempting to dismiss this as anomalous, but Kara Cooney, in some fascinating recent work, has shown that it was, in fact, commonplace in the Twentieth and Twenty-first Dynasties:

> I am currently working my way through many of the 800 or so 21st Dynasty coffins spread about the globe, and thus far, I have been startled to find that over 50% of 21st Dynasty coffins examined show evidence of reuse. The reuse of funerary arts represented a spectrum of possible appropriative actions. Some coffin reusers inscribed a new name. Others put in a new name and redecorated parts of the coffin lid. Others went further and redecorated all surfaces, over the old plaster and paint. Some went the extra step to scrub away old plaster and paint before starting new decoration, but they retained the old modelling in the wood. Some, I suspect, scrubbed the coffin down, dismantled it, and started a new coffin from scratch, using only the wood and thus giving away no trace of an older coffin visible except by means of further scientific examination.[1]

Inevitably, then, one wonders if a more realistic attitude, the slow transmogrification of ritual from solemn enactment to symbolic gesture, was enabling this increasingly pragmatic code of practice, and further, if a more cynical concept of their mortal remains was to some degree an engine of that progression. The motivation for coffin re-use, according to Cooney, could not have been more rational: "Economic and political circumstances disintegrated after the reign of Ramses III, pushing many Thebans to reuse what they had formerly imported or built from scratch." But its implications to the faith were profound:

> Some Egyptologists may consider coffin reuse to be an immoral crime that happened rarely, but the ancient Egyptians may have considered the non-performance of ritual transformation for those who had just died to be an egregious cultural and social failure. Coffin reuse was a creative negotiation of this economic-social-religious crisis. In other words, it was not the reuse of a coffin that was aberrant; if anything was aberrant, it would have been refusing to provide the recently deceased with transformative ritual activity by means of funerary materiality, just because there was no access to wood that had not been previously used.

All of this, however far one chooses to travel with it, adds further weight to the proposal that curses could never have played a realistic role in tomb protection, nor could they have been perceived so to do. We belittle the ancients when we conceive of them as superstitious pedants, obsessed with obscure ritual. Despite all that, an integral component of the Tutankhamen curse narrative is that Carter discovered a clay tablet above the entrance to the tomb, which warned that "Death shall come on swift wings to whoever toucheth the tomb of Pharaoh."

By some accounts it fell and smashed, ominously, even as they ignored it and proceeded to make their entrance; other versions have Carter contemptuously plucking it from the wall and crushing it beneath his shoes. Still another has Carter carefully documenting and cataloguing it, like the fine unsuperstitious chap he was, but then burying it in the sand, lest the natives catch sight of it and down tools. Feel free to add your own version, by all means: the stubborn truth is that none of those things occurred, and the tablet never existed. As Carter states in his published account of the discovery, "all sane people should dismiss such inventions with contempt."

It is also reasonable to note that of any disparate assortment of middle-aged men, a goodly number are statistically likely to pass away within ten years, even without the common denominator of the grueling, insanitary and congestive working conditions associated with the excavation of an Egyptian tomb. Even then the Pharaoh's death bag makes for a pretty meager haul, and much of it executed, with disappointingly uncinematic imagination, not upon those one might have supposed to be the priority cases, but merely on friends, relatives, acquaintances, attendants at the British Museum, and lecturers in archaeology from Leeds. Indeed, it is unlikely that the whole idea, diverting as it understandably was, would have outlasted the silly season, were it not for the spectacular fate of Lord Carnarvon.

Here, at last, was a victim worthy of the curse, and a demise that seemed tailor made. In early March 1923, Carnarvon was bitten on the cheek by a mosquito, and later nicked the head from the pimple while shaving. The wound became septic, and within a month he was dead. All manner of supplementary details were added to give it the full effect. There was the claim, reliably testified for, that at the exact moment of death his faithful dog, back in England, howled and dropped dead, and the entire electricity supply of Cairo blacked out. (It is apparently the case that this did indeed happen, but still a stretch to presume relevance. It remains obscure why a vengeful Pharaoh should *want* to underline his revenge upon one man by having the entire population of Cairo bump into each other in the dark, looking for candles.)

Better yet—had Weigall predicted it all? He had certainly helped spread the curse stories. As we have seen, he was a key player in the concerted efforts of the world's news media to break the stranglehold placed upon their coverage by Carnarvon's outrageous granting of sole reporting rights to the London *Times*. Sitting about in Luxor, waiting for stray crumbs of news to feed a ravenous public interest, the assembled journalists found their imaginations starting to wander, as much from desperation as mischief. But it was a chance remark from Weigall that may have put the seal on the matter once and for all. Because of his principled objection to Carnarvon's riding roughshod over the rights of the Egyptians and of the press, his pieces for the *Daily Mail* were often critical of the team's arrogant attitude towards the find. To the public at large this smacked not merely of crassness but of irreverence in the face of profound mysteries. The story goes that Weigall, in the company of his fellow journalists, observed Carnarvon behaving frivolously at the entrance of the tomb and commented, "If he goes down in that spirit I give him six weeks to live." Later, trying and failing to make the coincidence seem less spooky, he called it "one of those prophetic utterances which seem to issue, without definite intention, from the sub-conscious brain."[2] In the circumstances, it's easy to imagine anybody annoyed by the man's peacock antics saying it flippantly, but reason be damned—in Carnarvon, the curse had found its superstar.

Best of all was the punchline: when the mummy of Tutankhamen was finally unwrapped, it was supposedly found to have had a blemish on the cheek in the exact same location as Carnarvon's bite! For anyone who expects the story to play out in a manner more akin to the deaths in the *Omen* or *Final Destination* films—rather than, as it mainly does, as a sorry list of vaguely linked second-rankers dying of peritonitis—this is *much* more like it. "An evil elemental may have caused Lord Carnarvon's fatal illness," opined Sir Arthur Conan Doyle, who had long been squandering his reputation for rationalism, earned by proxy from his Sherlock Holmes stories, through his association with the kooks and crooks of the spiritualist movement. "The Egyptians," he noted sagely, "knew a great deal more about this than we do."

It is surprising, on reflection, that no subsequent mummy movie ever attempted to publicize itself by claiming that its production had likewise been cursed: it seems such an obvious device to utilize. Actually, there is one partial exception. Though Hammer's last film in their series, *Blood from the Mummy's Tomb* (1972), was not promoted as a "cursed film," there nonetheless are many who will tell you that cursed is exactly what it was. These include its star, Valerie Leon: "The film was jinxed. Firstly, I started filming with Peter Cushing playing my father. But then his wife got terribly ill, and he left after a day's filming. Tragically, she passed away, and Andrew Keir took over his role. Then a young man from the arts department was killed on his motor bike, just like my fiancé in the film. And finally director Seth Holt died after having hiccups for a week. He had a heart attack."[3]

The centrality of the curse motif to the later mummy movies is shown in the often uncomfortable ways in which it is worked into their narratives. Few strictly speaking concern curses in the Tutankhamen sense of supernatural retribution striking down the protagonists. The unleashed, stalking mummy is a more direct and tangible threat, however esoterically revived. Yet the curse as a component immediately became part of the checklist of required ingredients. Consider *The Mummy* (1932). The Scroll of Thoth is encased in a box which promises death to whoever opens it ("Good heavens, what a terrible curse!") but no such curse actually manifests itself in the movie, and none die by its influence. The character who does open it goes mad, but not as a consequence of doing so. (That Karloff's mummy happens to be in the room with him as he reads its incantations

Valerie Leon in *Blood from the Mummy's Tomb* (1972), often recalled as a cursed film.

aloud would have been a coincidence entirely unforeseen by the ancients, whose curse is of course intended to compel him *not* to read it.)

We see the same opportunism in the margins of the later Hammer versions. No actual curse comes into play in *Curse of the Mummy's Tomb*, valuable though the concept was for the title. Similarly, though there were no curses at work in the 1959 version of *The Mummy*, much sport was made of them in the advertising. One British ad set the film poster in the middle of a mosaic of Tut curse newspaper cuttings. "Believe it or not, these headlines are TRUE!" yells the headline. Underneath, we are asked: "Do You Believe in the Grave Robbers' Curse?"

Even more overt is a poster from France, where the film was in fact re-titled *La Malediction des Pharaons*. No mummies appear anywhere on the design; instead there is only a faint, red-tinted image of Christopher Lee in unbandaged flashback form, entirely covered in text (attributed to *Parisian Libre* journalist Jean Jouquet), all of it entirely unrelated to the film being promoted:

How do you know a mummy can't come to life? Poster for *The Mummy* (1959) linking Hammer's film spuriously to Tutankhamen's curse.

> Is there such a thing as the curse of the pharaohs? In 1923, nineteen people were present at the opening of Tutankhamun's tomb; only one died of natural causes, seventeen others have disappeared under mysterious circumstances and only one German archaeologist is still alive. Will he be the last victim of this curse which has lasted for 33 centuries and which could have wiped out seventeen of his companions?
>
> Many answers have been proposed for this enigma, but what is the real explanation?
>
> The terrifying enigma will be revealed to you in the film *The Curse of the Pharaohs*.

The American oddity *Pharaoh's Curse* (1957) is as anomalous in this regard as it is in several others. Set most unconvincingly in 1902, alternating between Californian desert locations and a studio tomb boasting sliding panels and secret doors operated by wall-mounted Tut masks, and *very* sparsely decorated with comically inauthentic hieroglyphs, the film is nonetheless unusual, perhaps unique, in its plotting. Here we really do have a tomb curse, albeit a most bizarre one, deciphered by one of the team: "It's a precaution against grave robbers. When the king dies, the high priest is to take his own life and then be laid to rest where his soul can guard the king: "And thy soul shall enter into the mortal body, and possess its spirit to do thy bidding. Ye shall still the fires that seek to destroy, and gain thy strength from the blood of the living, until the last intruder shall be no more." As consequence, rather than unleashing the expected mummy from the tomb, the film's luckless expedition frees the high priest's malign spirit by the act of cutting away his bandages. It then lodges in the body of their Egyptian servant, who turns into a decrepit, fanged and corpse-like monster, stalking the rest of the party and draining them of their blood.

But no film used the Tutankhamen curse itself as a plot until the TV movie *The Curse of King Tut's Tomb* in 1980. There was one tempting might-have-been, however, that survives only as an advert that appeared in the trades in July of 1934: "TOM TERRISS announces the production of an original and psychic drama entitled THE CURSE OF TUTANKHAMEN." *Film Daily* had high hopes for the project, largely, it would seem, on the somewhat bizarre grounds of its wholesomeness and family appeal:

> In preparation by Tom Terriss is a timely script, *The Curse of King Tut*, an authentic account of the sensational discovery of King Tutankhamen's tomb and the mysterious deaths of many of the participants that have followed. This is the type of material the screen needs right now to bridge over the period of agitation for clean films. The dramatization of this tale that was front page news for weeks carries all the elements of pop appeal, yet avoids any sexy angles that could possibly arouse opposition.[4]

If you could see what she could see, you'd be scared too. Diane Brewster in *Pharaoh's Curse* (1957).

Terriss, the advertising stated, was "one of the few remaining survivors of those who were present at the opening of the famous tomb." Needless to say, there were of course many healthy happy survivors at this point, but who was Terriss?

Simply put, he was an English actor and film director, but he was also a man who loved to tell a good story, so here's the account of himself he gave to the *Brooklyn Daily Eagle* in 1932:

> The son of an old English theatrical family, Terriss was educated at Oxford, went to Australia as a sheep-farmer, left there on a windjammer, tried silver mining in Colorado. In the Rocky Mountains one day he was caught in a blizzard, suffered snow-blindness and walked off a cliff. His smashed body was found many hours later by prospectors. Eventually he recovered in a Denver hospital but his eyesight was impaired and he has worn glasses ever since. Against the wishes of his actor-parents, Tom decided next to enter the theater. Many mishaps marred his early attempts but success crowned his labors after William Morris cast him in the role of "Scrooge" and other Dickens characters. Among those who played with him was a fellow named Charlie Chaplin. Back and forth across the Atlantic Terriss sailed, playing in England and America before being attracted to the silver screen. He gave up acting for directing and established many records with the megaphone and camp stool before that memorable vacation.[5]

Like Ernest Shipman, Terriss had a fetish for using real locations (in his case, one suspects, not so much an aesthetic imperative as a good excuse to go globe-trotting), and the "memorable vacation" mentioned above was his decision to shoot a movie in Egypt in 1923.

This brings Arthur Conan Doyle into our story again. In 1898 he had written a novel entitled *The Tragedy of the Korosko*, in which a party of tourists on a Nile cruise are taken prisoner by murderous dervishes. Like his Sherlock Holmes stories, it was serialized in the *Strand Magazine*, with illustrations by Sidney Paget:

> It is a singular country, this Nubia. Varying in breadth from a few miles to as many yards (for the name is only applied to the narrow portion which is capable of cultivation), it extends in a thin, green, palm-fringed strip upon either side of the broad coffee-coloured river. Beyond it there stretches on the Libyan bank a savage and illimitable desert, extending to the whole breadth of Africa. On the other side an equally desolate wilderness is bounded only by the distant Red Sea. Between these two huge and barren expanses Nubia writhes like a green sandworm along the course of the river. Here and there it disappears altogether, and the Nile runs between black and sun-cracked hills, with the orange drift-sand lying like glaciers in their valleys. Everywhere one sees traces of vanished races and submerged civilizations. Grotesque graves dot the hills or stand up against the sky-line: pyramidal graves, tumulus graves, rock graves—everywhere, graves. And, occasionally, as the boat rounds a rocky point, one sees a deserted city up above—houses, walls, battlements, with the sun shining through the empty window squares. Sometimes you learn that it has been Roman, sometimes Egyptian, sometimes all record of its name or origin has been absolutely lost. You ask yourself in amazement why any race should build in so uncouth a solitude, and you find it difficult to accept the theory that this has only been of value as a guard-house to the richer country down below, and that these frequent cities have been so many fortresses to hold off the wild and predatory men of the south. But whatever be their explanation, be it a fierce neighbour, or be it a climatic change, there they stand, these grim and silent cities, and up on the hills you can see the graves of their people, like the port-holes of a man-of-war. It is through this weird, dead country that the tourists smoke and gossip and flirt as they pass up to the Egyptian frontier.

In 1909 Doyle adapted the story for the stage, re-titling it *Fires of Fate*, and it was this that Terriss decided to shoot as a film on authentic locations in 1923. As *Motion Picture News* announced, he "will film scenes, no doubt, around the now famous tomb."[6] And that he did—if the likes of *Exhibitors Herald* are to be believed:

Now that they are going to unwrap a few miles of bandages from the mummy of King Tutankhamen and see how the old gentleman looks after being laid on the shelf for 3,000 years, few men in the film business are taking more interest in the peeping than Pedro de Cordoba, popular actor of screen and stage. The reason for this interest is that Mr. de Cordoba, as Prince Ibrahim, visited the tomb of the old time ruler and was accorded all the courtesies that could be showered on a real son of Egyptian royalty.

This happened when director Tom Terriss was filming *Fires of Fate*, many of the scenes of which are laid in and about Luxor, where the tomb is located and in which Mr. de Cordoba had the lead.

"One night some English friends joined us and we determined to see the tomb and the pyramids by moonlight," said Mr. de Cordoba in relating his experience. "There was little time to lose so I joined the party regardless of being attired as Prince Ibrahim, which later proved most fortunate. A bomb throwing episode that day caused our being held up by the Egyptian police when within a short distance of our destination. Just as we were resigning ourselves to being delayed for several days an official espied me in my princely regalia, and taking me for a scion of the Egyptian royalty, we were permitted to continue our trip without further delay."[7]

In an interview with Louella Parsons, Terriss added his own tall tale:

When Tom Terriss first went to the land of the Pharaohs he did not know that he was to become a member of the late Lord Carnarvon's party, but being an Englishman he was received into the bosom of the family and was entertained at the Moslem House, built by Lord Carnarvon's partner Harry [sic] Carter, almost as soon as he reached Egypt.

After Mr. Terriss related his plans for filming *Fires of Fate*, the story by Sir Conan Doyle, Mr Carter invited him to be one of the twenty-four who were present at the opening of King Tutankhamen's tomb. The Queen of Belgium was also in this exclusive party which will go down in history as having been the first expedition of this kind ever planned. The death of Lord Carnarvon, said by the superstitious to be caused by his interference with the last sleep of King Tutankhamen, may prevent other excursions, although Mr. Terriss was loud in his assertion that Lord Carnarvon's death could not have been caused by anything but natural causes.

"Tell me something of your sensation when the tomb was opened," I asked Mr Terriss.

"The actual sarcophagus containing the body was never really opened," he said. "But I will say the excavation of the tomb was the most thrilling experience I have ever had. The tapping of the hammers on the walls was like some unearthly noise, it rang out so loudly in that quiet room where not a word was spoken. We stood in a huge room which led up to the actual burial place of King Tutankhamen. We had expected to find another huge room. Instead of that the sarcophagus was right up against the wall. A cold blast of air that followed the caving in of the wall was the weirdest sensation I have ever experienced. It was exactly as if someone had turned on a faucet of ice cold water down our backbones. The sarcophagus," went on Mr. Terriss, "was never opened because Lord Carnarvon took sick and died."

"Weren't you superstitious?" I asked him. "And weren't you afraid that you would get sick?"

"Well, I have been sick," said Mr. Terriss. "I have had malaria or some darn thing ever since I came home, but I am not in the least superstitious."[8]

With its claim that the opening of the sarcophagus was halted only by the incapacitation leading to death of Carnarvon, this account is plenty eccentric enough even if Terriss does dismiss the curse. But in 1930, *The Freeman's Journal* listed him among the minor casualties in a spurious curse piece, while also making a

The mischievous Mr. Tom Terriss.

new claim as to his involvement: "Tom Terriss, a New York motion picture director, who had accompanied the expedition as official photographer, fell seriously ill."⁹

I'm afraid we must learn to exercise much caution with regards to the claims of Mr. Terriss. The fact that he seems to be mentioned by no other member of the team as present at this historic occasion is suggestive enough, and indeed we will shortly find Terriss attempting to account for that specific anomaly, as if somewhere along the line his bluff had been called. But more importantly, under the suffocating exclusivity terms that Carnarvon had arranged with the London *Times*, it was simply not possible to invite random Englishmen to the opening ceremony, still less to make him official photographer. Terriss does appear to have been in Egypt shooting his movie at the time the tomb was being excavated, but I have found no evidence to suggest he had so much as a peep at its interior, let alone enjoyed privileged access. Unsurprisingly, his stories grew in the telling, and by 1934, when he was attempting to produce his movie, he had abandoned his earlier skepticism with regards the curse.

The direct inspiration for the production seems to have been a series of bizarre one-reel travelogues he directed and appeared in in the early 1930s. For some time, Terriss (no longer finding employment in features, it would seem) had been shooting travelogues all over the world, in which he billed himself as "the Vagabond Adventurer." (These included *The Glacier's Secret* in 1930, in which he seemingly restaged his apparent Rocky Mountains misfortune, and *The Song of the Voodoo* in 1931, which beat to the screen by a year the subject's supposed movie debut in the Halperin Brothers' *White Zombie*.) Beginning in 1933, the Vagabond Adventurer, (with his friend "Jimmy"), embarked on a series of short adventures in which he searched various exotic locales to find the world's most beautiful female, collectively titled *The Quest of the Perfect Woman*. The resulting films are truly weird, filled with staged shots and inserts, ridiculously fictionalized situations (with actors) mixing with reportage, and even some brief nudity. (Because of the two British stars, the *Perfect Woman* films are often mistakenly thought to be British: only adding to the confusion, therefore, is the fact that they were made for "Hammer Film Productions, Inc." But this is not to be confused with the famous British company later to add its own contributions to the mummy movie: this was an American outfit, owned by producer Arthur Hammer.)

Next to nothing is known about the greater number of them, though at least two are still obtainable today: it is not even certain if the projected run of 13 (or 18, depending on source) separate titles was completed. (The Vagabond Adventurer certainly reappeared, however: *Film Daily* confirms the screening of at least one other collaboration between Terriss and Hammer, *North of Sahara*, "a timely short in view of the Ethiopian situation," on October 14, 1935. Weirder still, "Tom Terriss, the Vagabond Adventurer" appears as a comic strip character in *Famous Funnies*—in the 1950s! One wonders if these were reprints of some much older series of strips; one issue from 1953 advertises on its cover: "UNBELIEVABLE BUT TRUE: MR TOM TERRISS, THE VAGABOND ADVENTURER, AND THE CURSE OF KING TUT.")

Hammer and Terriss set sail from New York to begin work on the *Perfect Woman* series on January 28, 1933, initially to Paris, and thence to points many and exotic.¹⁰ The first two films had been shot by the start of 1934, whereupon the pair returned to America to secure distribution before proceeding to shoot further episodes. (DuWorld acquired world rights for them in June of 1934.) But the interesting thing for our purposes is that, according to *Film Daily* on January 9, 1934, this first two (which are the two that can still occasionally be seen today: *The Veiled Dancer of Eloued* and *The Vampire of Marrakesh*), "comprise material gathered in Morocco and Algeria, including the tomb of Tut-Ankh-Amen, which has recently been coming in for new publicity." Now, neither film contains any recognizable shots of the tomb, which in any event was in neither Morocco nor Algeria last time I checked. So it's possible that if any tomb footage was shot, it may have been for a future adventure in the series, or, perhaps, for Terriss's Tutankhamen project. If the latter, it would mean that the project did get as far as turning over, at least.

As to the suggestion that the tomb had "recently been coming in for new publicity," it is true that 1934 did witness a small renaissance of interest in the subject. The initial kick start may have been the publication of the third and final volume of Carter's own account of the discovery in 1933, some six years after the previous installment. And later, in October of 1934, came the exciting news that Carter would be returning to the Valley of the Kings, this time to search for the tomb of Tutankhamen's queen. (These plans sadly came to nothing.) But it was the apparent return of the curse that had really made the newspapers sit up and take renewed interest.

In the first place, Arthur Weigall, the popular historian who may have helped spread the curse story, had died of pneumonia at the age of just 53 at the start of January. Egyptologist E. A. Wallis Budge, just one of many with an axe to grind against him, contributed a scurrilous and outrageously inaccurate summing-up to the *Daily Express*, claiming he had "died in penury in a London hospital as a result of hashish-eating and addiction to other drugs."[11] It was an outrageous libel, untrue in every detail, and Weigall's family immediately filed suit: the *Express* made a substantial out of court settlement and printed a full retraction, but the damage was done, and the curse was back.

Then, at around the same time, Albert Lythgoe, present at the tomb's opening and the former Curator of Egyptian Art at the New York Metropolitan Museum, was admitted to hospital in critical condition, suffering from what the *Hobart Mercury* termed "a baffling malady."[12] In fact, his condition was only baffling because his family were, ironically as it turned out, trying to avoid intrusive publicity about it. There was no real mystery: he was 64 years old and suffering from cerebral arteriosclerosis, the hardening of the arteries around the brain. But sensible explanations came too late, as ever. The papers went through their files to find and rehash the old stories, and the usual motley assortment of opportunists came out of the woodwork to cash in.

One of the most popular of all the curse legends had re-emerged at exactly this moment too, in a book called *Real Life Stories by Cheiro: A Collection of Sensational Personal Experiences*. "Cheiro," real name John Warner, was a palmist and fraudulent stock market advisor, who claimed to be a Count, and who had made headlines in 1909 when various society women in Paris alleged he had embezzled huge sums of money from them; the French police issued a warrant for his arrest and he promptly fled to London.[13] Here he re-established his reputation as clairvoyant and astrologer, despite an admirably robust official attitude towards such practices from which we seem sadly to have retreated a century later.[14]

"Cheiro"'s 1934 collection of *Real Life Stories* included an extraordinary claim regarding the discovery of Tutankhamen's tomb. He writes that on "the night the news was printed in the papers" that "the tomb itself had been found and that Lord Carnarvon who had financed the search was himself going to Egypt for the opening ceremony" he was visited by the spirit of the Princess Makitaten, seventh daughter of the King Atennaten. Materializing in his house in his house before himself and his wife, she took control of his will and compelled him to write a letter of warning to Carnarvon. Cheiro sent the letter to Carnarvon, which "reached him as he was leaving England."

> Lord Carnarvon, as all his friends know, was an extremely strong-headed, obstinate type of an Englishman. Although he admitted to his companion that he was deeply impressed by the warning, he added, "If at this moment of my life all the mummies in Egypt were to warn me I would go on with my project just the same."
> It is common knowledge what happened.

Chilling stuff! And of all the curse stories it has certainly endured and become one of the most popular, still repeated to this day in books on the occult and paranormal phenomena. So can we truly be sure it didn't happen? After all, it's easy to mock. But can we *really* dismiss this strange story, glibly and without the smallest prickle of doubt? Well, given that the first reports of the discovery appeared in the newspapers on November 30, by which time Carnarvon had already been in Egypt for a week: yes, I reckon we can.

But with poor Albert Lythgoe, the curse's latest claim, hovering between life and death, who cared about facts? The current curator of the Metropolitan Museum, Herbert Winlock, became so frustrated by this idiotic new rash of curse stories (allegedly he had found himself repeatedly unable to contact the hospital for an update on Lythgoe's condition because the lines were jammed by time-wasting fantasists) that he called a press conference with the aim of killing the myths once and for all.

Before the assembled journalists he calmly stated the bald facts. Carter, surely number one on the curse's hit list, was alive and well. So, too were over three quarters of those who saw either the inner tomb or the opening of the sarcophagus. Of those who *had* since died, only one was under fifty and none had died of an undiagnosable disease. Scientific tests had proved there were no strange chemicals, bacteria or poisons present in the tomb. Lord Carnarvon had died from a septic insect bite, a far from uncommon health hazard in Egypt. And the claim that there was a written curse found in the tomb was entirely without basis in fact, and had in fact been invented by disgruntled journalists, resentful that exclusive story rights had been given to the London *Times* and therefore in need of a headline-grabbing scoop of their own...

Winlock thanked his audience and left, confident that reason had at last prevailed. Four days after his announcement, Lythgoe died. The headlines were unanimous: Tutankhamen's curse had struck again.

All this would obviously be a factor influencing Terriss's decision to mount his curse movie, possibly expanding his plans considerably for any Egyptian footage he'd already shot, and even, just perhaps, dropping the *Perfect Woman* series in favor of it. Alas, his "original and psychic drama" never saw the light, but even with his film unmade and his claims to authenticity suspect to say the least, Terriss remained a point of contact whenever the subject of the curse was revived.[15]

By 1946, in an article published in the *Milwaukee Sentinel*, his whole account of how he came to be present at the Tutankhamen opening had changed—perhaps because some bright spark of an investigative journalist had noticed that he, in fact, hadn't been present there at all. And he had yet more nonsense to impart on the subject of Carnarvon:

> He has photographs to prove that he attended the opening of the tomb's inner chamber in 1923. The reason his name doesn't appear on the official list, he says, is that he went disguised as a newspaperman. Sceptical of the curse as applied to himself, he has his own theory of what caused Carnarvon's death. The English nobleman, he reports, usually wore gloves, unfastened and turned back at the wrist. Terriss's photographs show him to have been gloveless on Feb. 17, 1923, the day the excavators

broke into the inner chamber. Moreover, in his enthusiasm over the fabulous treasures spread around him, Carnarvon, according to (Terriss), thrust his naked hand into a vase and pricked his finger on a needle-like object. When he died, word got around that he had been poisoned by virulent germs placed in the tomb 3,000 years before to strike down desecrators.[16]

In 1955, aged 73, he claimed that his expertise on the subject had led to his being hired by Warner Brothers as a technical advisor on their 1955 melodrama *Land of the Pharaohs*. Now he was telling the Mansfield, Ohio *News Journal* that he was the only survivor of fifteen men who entered the tomb's inner chamber, and "all fourteen of the others died violent or mysterious deaths." His latest version of the old yarn also ended up in the *Milwaukee Journal*, where he now claimed to have been in Egypt at the time the tomb was discovered (which he unquestionably was not), and personally invited by Carnarvon to photograph its interior. The celebrated curse, he now affirmed, was written on the actual booby-trapped alabaster vase that claimed Carnarvon's life: "Just a few weeks later, Lord Carnarvon died—according to doctors, from a razor-cut on his cheek that had been infected by an insect. Maybe so. But later, the hieroglyphics around the neck of the alabaster vase were deciphered. They read 'Death shall come on swift wings to him who toucheth the tomb of a Pharaoh.'"

Though not a victim of the curse himself, he easily could have been, owing to Carnarvon having personally given him what, depending on when you asked him, was either "a small bust of Tut from the tomb" (Milwaukee, July 21) or "a graphite statuette" (Ohio, July 31). He elaborated in the latter: "There was a time when I returned to this country that my luck went sour, I couldn't sell my movie shorts and I was stricken with a paralysis of the legs. It wasn't until my wife insisted that I get rid of "that horrible little statue" ... that I recovered, my luck turned and the world became bright again." To Milwaukee he added: "I didn't hate anyone badly enough to make him a present of it, so I donated it to the Los Angeles museum. That very same afternoon, I signed a fat movie contract."

This may be the most apposite point to note that I contacted the British Museum's Department of Egyptology to ask if they had any record at all of Mr. Terriss's involvement, however peripheral, in the story of the Tutankhamen excavation. They got back to say that they had never heard of him in any capacity whatsoever, which may be presumed to be the last word on the matter. But before we leave the colorful Mr. Terriss, let us note that he is further linked to the story of the curse in one other peripheral but no less curious way. In 1897, his father, the celebrated matinee idol William Terriss, was stabbed to death at the stage door of the Adelphi Theatre by a jealous and mentally unhinged fellow actor, Richard Prince. (Terriss's ghost is said to haunt both the theater and nearby Covent Garden underground station.) In an interview the following year, Terriss claimed a bizarre happening had occurred at the family home on the night of the murder that involved the family's fox terrier, Davie:

> My brother and I were playing chess ... and the dog was apparently quietly dozing on my mother's lap, and it startled us all considerably as it bounded up and down the room with frantic snaps and rls. My mother was very much alarmed and cried out, "What does he see? What does he see?" convinced that the dog's anger was directed at something unseen by us. My brother and I soothed her as well as we could, though ourselves considerably puzzled at the behaviour of an ordinarily quiet and well-conducted pet. Yes, the incident occurred at the very hour of my poor father's death.[17]

It will be recalled that according to reliable account, at the moment Carnarvon had died and the lights went out all over Cairo, back at the family home of Highclere Castle his own pet dog likewise began to yelp and howl—and dropped dead. But the interesting thing is that this story predates the Carnarvon anecdote, which it would be folly (if tempting) to suggest Terriss had a hand in inventing. So if this *is* an early example of Terriss the fantasist spinning a yarn, and even if that is *all* it is, the coincidence nonetheless remains.

6

Losses and Survivals

> Lon Chaney thinks Universal is kidding. His next is *The Mummy's Curse*. Day before that title was handed down he'd told the studio that his ranch house had burned down and fire had destroyed all the feed for his livestock.—Hedda Hopper—*Chicago Tribune*, July 27, 1944

On the second of March 1939, Howard Carter, the man who made the greatest archaeological discovery of all time, and an individual who changed the course of his century, died in England, alone and largely forgotten. He was sixty-five.

Newspaper accounts strove to remind their readers of the heady days of Tutmania, but the old memories sparked little retrospective enthusiasm for the subject beyond the listless rehashing of the story of the curse, which many tastelessly suggested may have been responsible for the Hodgkin's disease that killed him. Over and over, the old fantasy of the tomb inscription warning that "death will come on swift wings" was repeated as fact in the obituaries, though a few at least had the grace to admit that the wings had not been particularly swift on this occasion.

Courted in his day by kings, presidents, movie stars and the world's media, Carter had spent the greater part of the decade a virtually anonymous presence in his own land, burdened neither by title nor honorary degree. He was buried in Putney Vale Cemetery, the modest stone merely proclaiming him "Howard Carter, Archaeologist and Egyptologist." No mention was made of the discovery of Tutankhamen's tomb. Nine mourners attended the funeral.

As in life, so in the movies: despite Universal's poetic and haunting original it seemed that the subject was now fit mainly for sniggers, and like unsentimental cultural bailiffs, the clowns had moved in and taken possession. There was Harry Gribbon and Shemp Howard in *My Mummy's Arms* for Vitaphone in 1934; Eddie Cantor and some singing mummies in *Kid Millions* the same year; Wheeler and Woolsey in *Mummy's Boys* in 1936[1] and the Three Stooges in *We Want Our Mummy* in 1939. Usually the mummies in these comedies prove to be villains in disguise, as if signaling that the idea of a genuine reanimated mummy was now considered somewhat hokey. (Even so, the specimen in the Stooges' *We Want Our Mummy*, counterfeit or not, is surely one of the scariest on film: his horrid moon face, round bun cheeks and long, sharp talons are genuinely creepy.)

But the most interesting thing about these comedies is that they appear to be spoofing a cinematic formula that, in fact, was still to be established. They in no way evoke *The Mummy* and instead give the impression of riffing on the staple ingredients of the

We Want Our Mummy (1939)—Egyptomania, Three Stooges style.

other four Universal titles—the stalking bandaged mummy, imperiled archaeologists being chased through tombs, and speculation as to avenging curses. But all those sequels were yet to be made: in terms of laying the ground for the quintessential mummy movie the spoofers, somehow, got there first. *The Mummy's Hand* (1940), when it did appear, therefore, was not inventing the mummy film in the form that is most familiar to us today so much as reclaiming it from Saturday matinee farce. (The film—as well as adopting a broadly cartoonish attitude to its thrills throughout—also begins in overtly comedic style, with two unlikely Brooklyn archaeologists wisecracking their way through Egypt in the manner we now associate with Abbott and Costello, or Bing and Bob on the road to Morocco.)

Such light-heartedness was conspicuously absent outside the auditorium, alas. The world that Carter exited barely resembled the one that had greeted his great discovery. Hitler's armies were beginning their conquest of Europe, and on September 3, 1939, British Prime Minister Neville Chamberlain took to the airwaves and solemnly announced that as of that day Britain was at war with Germany. With the neutral world anxiously watching the headlines, *The Mummy's Hand* seemed almost comforting in its old-fashioned *weltanschauungen*. By the time its three sequels came around, America too had joined the conflict.

A world at war has a peculiar relationship with fantasy: one might perhaps expect it to shun it, as a triviality or even as tasteless, a luxury for more pacific times. In fact, the opposite seems to be the case, perhaps, as Leslie Halliwell has noted, because the constant awareness of sudden and tragic loss makes the idea of the supernatural seem attractive. Fantasy could reassure, on one level, and in a more basic sense, could also distract. Paradoxically, then, the horror villains of the Universal pantheon were needed again (and all came dutifully trouping back to the cinematic front lines) but in a lighter, more ironic capacity. The films could no longer take themselves seriously: they have to offer thrills but not to disturb. The graveyard grue that characterized the original *Frankenstein*, and the leering sadism of such as *Murders in the Rue Morgue*, *The Black Cat* and *The Raven* were nowhere evidenced this time around: now the horrors would be almost blessed reliefs from the headlines. *The Mummy* had been imbued with a real whiff of magic, a tingle of the wonder and awe that the Tutankhamen discovery had created in the Western mind and media. *The Mummy's Hand* was made for a new generation inclined to treat its cinematic monsters as old friends, an audience no longer awed by the mysteries of the ancients, merely eager for diversion from headlines fixated upon Europe's despair.[2]

The mummy movies distract from reality in another sense also. When Carter died, the *Sarasota Herald-Tribune's* headline—"KING TUT CURSE CLAIMS ANOTHER VICTIM IN LONDON"—was sadly typical: in the popular imagination, the curse was about all that was left of the story that had once gripped the planet's media. And so the mummy movies of the 1940s do not merely riff on the old stories of Tutankhamen's curse, they act as outlets for our frustration with the truth. They say: this is what a *real* curse looks like! No pussyfooting here; no ambiguity or invitations to skepticism. No subtlety, either: the interlopers are not struck down by some supernaturally-arranged occurrence, they are literally *killed by the past*, by Ancient Egypt itself, in the form of a living mummy.

In reality, as already noted, curses alone were never really expected to deter tomb robbers. But in the mummy movies all that changes. Karloff's Ardath Bey had actually helped the interlopers: he *wanted* Ankhesenamen's tomb to be located and opened. But the guardians of the Temple of Karnak in these later films, played by the likes of George

Zucco and John Carradine (along with later variations such as George Pastell in Hammer's *The Mummy* and Mal Arnold in *Blood Feast*), have a much more fundamentalist take. These twentieth century zealots believe in the old religion with an intensity and certainty that would surely put to shame many of their equivalents in antiquity. After all, they can actually see the ritual and magic work with their own eyes!

In that respect, these films may not be *quite* so absurd as they first appear: the potency of the old myths, it seems, has died a little harder than we might be inclined to believe. Anthony Sattin's fascinating book *The Pharaoh's Shadow: Travels in Ancient and Modern Egypt* reveals a modern Egyptian culture in which a blanket of strict Islamic practice hides a shadowy sub-realm of more ancient observance. The author calls these remnants of the old worship "survivals," a phenomenon he first encountered at the New Kingdom Temple of Pakhet (a.k.a. Speos Artemidos), an underground shrine built by Hatshepsut in the 15th century BC. Here he encountered a woman in one of the shrine's many chambers rocking and intoning, and was told by his guide that she was childless and was praying to Pakhet to become pregnant. "In my country," his guide explained, "it is all the same, all Allah." An Egyptian woman told him that such practices had always been observed, and there had always been only one God, so if it was acceptable then it must still be so now. Satin goes on to record other similar examples, and quotes a 1937 letter from Oxford Professor J. Gwyn Griffiths who noted seeing infertile women raising their dresses and stepping over a prostrate mummy, chanting "May the Lord give me a little boy." Others spent the night inside the Pyramids, or slid down what remained of their limestone casing.

An unrecognized problem for the films, therefore, equivalent to the problem such "survivals" cause for contemporary Islam, is the challenge they represented to Christianity in the Hays Code era. Other supernatural subjects in the Universal films exist within a framework of Christian apologetics. Vampirism is "evil," subdued by Christian iconography and destroyed in act of explicitly Christian ritual. The Frankenstein monster is created through science rather than necromancy, and the studio stressed the story's morality-play value as a warning against the hubris of those who would play God. The Mummy is different: his endurance is ensured as a result of the *validity* of a pre–Christian religion: he is, in that sense, disproof of Christianity's unique claims to revelation. If the Breen Office had been on the ball, or even vaguely inclined to take films like this seriously on a thematic level, that should have caused problems. The Karloff original is even more overt in its complete capitulation to alternative theology: his mummy is not just revived via the old magic but destroyed by it too while the assembled Western heroes watch impotently, their preferred mythology providing neither protection nor solution.

One of the most intriguing things about *The Mummy's Hand* is its title: why *Hand*? No plot significance is attached to either of the mummy's hands as such, so presumably it must refer to the means by which the unbelievers meet their deaths "at the mummy's hand," to the "hand of vengeance" striking them down. Well, yes and no. That is indeed the only means by which the title can be deemed relevant in relation to the film itself, but mummy's hands in general were legion in the body of popular myth and superstition surrounding Egyptian lore, so much of which had been revived and made current in the wake of Tutmania.

Seemingly endowed with talismanic and psychometric properties, they were often kept as curiosities, and the phrase "mummy's hand" would have been as familiar to the film's original viewers as, say, "rabbit's foot" or, indeed, "monkey's paw." (Scanning the

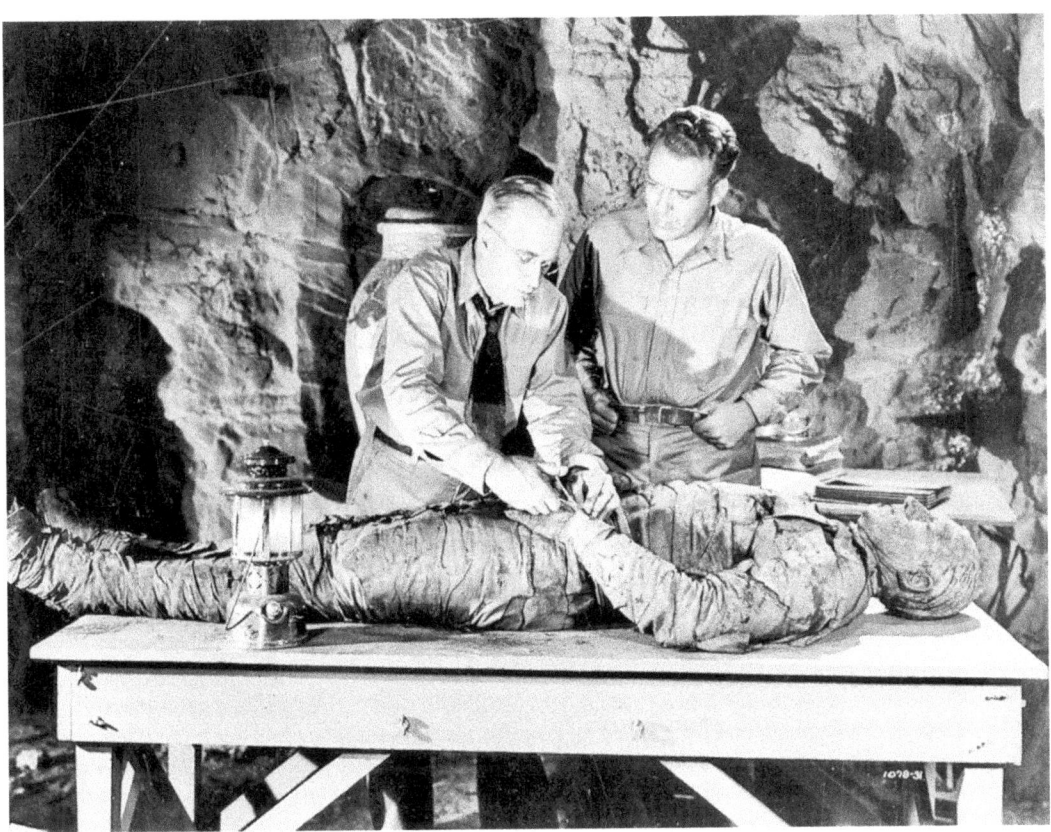

Charles Trowbridge (left) and Dick Foran wonder if it's too early to wake Tom Tyler in *The Mummy's Hand* (1940).

archives, one occasionally encounters the simile "stiff as a mummy's hand" through the thirties, too.) "The hands of colonized subjects—South Asian craftsmen, Egyptian mummies, harem women, and Congolese children—were at the crux of Victorian discussions of the body that tried to come to terms with the limits of racial identification," notes Aviva Briefel in the book *The Racial Hand in the Victorian Imagination*:

> The hands of mummies in particular came to be identified with a resilience that married artistic integrity with gothic horror. Witnesses of mummy unwrappings singled out the hands for their resistance to the ravages of time, a fact that attested to the embalmer's formidable skill....
> Theophile Gautier describes the "gilded nails" of a mummy at the 1957 Paris exhibition as imitating "with sepulchral modesty the gesture of the Venus of Medici." Beauty and permanence were also conveyed through descriptions of mummies' hands grasping still-living plant bulbs or flowers, as in George Wilson's poem *The Sleep of the Hyacinth* (1860). Wilson composed the poem following the exhumation of the mummy of an Egyptian princess clutching a hyacinth bulb, which flowered when it was planted.

There were endless stories equivalent to the latter, in which flora from Egyptian tombs is shown to have timeless powers of rejuvenation. As late as 1939 the papers were telling of one A. A. Aldridge, whose London vegetable garden was sporting a bumper crop of peas that originated from seeds found in Tutankhamen's tomb.[3] Where in the tomb they were found is not specified on this occasion, but in these yarns the record-breaking plant life is usually to be found in the grasp of the mummy's hand, as in the case of a Mr.

White who according to reports in 1892 had produced a crop "of unusual magnitude" after planting "some dried peas taken from the hand of the mummy of an Egyptian princess by an explorer of the ruins of Karnac and supposed to be 8,043 years old."[4] Such stories were so widespread as to warrant parody: Briefel has noted an 1854 *Punch* article which claims that "the original rule of thumb" had recently been discovered clutched in the hand of the "mummy of an Egyptian schoolmaster."

A brief trawl through the newspaper archives yields sundry examples of mummy's hands of all sorts: quaint, menacing and incidental. In 1924, "the right mummy hand of Pharaoh's daughter, who rescued Moses from the waters of the Nile" was left by the late Mrs. Annie E. Petherbridge to the Bradley Polytechnic Institute in Peoria.[5] In the same year, "a human hand found at a cottage at Kurri Kurri recently occupied by a returned soldier ... had been wrenched from a mummy. It was excellently preserved, and the wrist maintained its original life-time flexibility.... His wife took exception to the curio, and threw it under the house 18 months ago."[6] There was the possibility of a supernatural tinge to the tragic death of a young girl in 1930 "in a pond where her father had thrown the hand of an Egyptian mummy."[7] In 1934 we learned of the sudden death of one Jean van der Elst who had been "haunted for three years by a 7,000-year-old beautifully mummified hand of an Egyptian princess...." His "now grief-stricken" wife ("a student of witchcraft") told the press:

> My husband did not want me to keep the hand. It has been a curse ever since we had it. I have been ill and my husband suffered from insomnia. When able to sleep he had fearful dreams that the hand was strangling him. I determined to destroy it, and threw it into a fire. But it was like stone and took three hours to burn. I have been wearing a charm to ward off evil, but when the hand was burned I lost the charm.... I am unable to forget an ancient Egyptian tradition that to enable the dead to be reborn whole, a body must not be dismembered."[8]

In 1937, "the mummified hand of an Egyptian princess, believed to date from 10,000 to 12,000 BC (was) found in the Thames between Wargrave and Henley. A Thames Conservancy waterman saw a glass-topped oak box floating, and when he opened it discovered a hand and an Egyptian scarab."[9]

We could go on virtually forever, but let's round-off with a real creeper from 1937. Headed "Cursed By A Bone From A Mummy's Hand," the report concerns the strange events that befell Edinburgh's Sir Alexander and Lady Seton following a trip to Egypt a year before:

> They visited a tomb that was being opened by excavators. It was the tomb of an Egyptian princess who lived about 3000 years ago. Lady Seton expressed the desire to have a relic of the tomb, and ultimately she brought away one of the bones of the long-dead princess.... It looked innocent enough, harmless enough, as a relic. But since it has been in their possession they have been harassed by a series of incidents that can be explained in only one way—that the spirit of the princess demands the return of her bone to Egypt.
>
> "At first," Sir Alexander told me, "I was sceptical of the stories of a curse following the bone. I couldn't believe that such things happened in this age. But we were told that the bone would be cursed and that it would bring us bad luck. It has lived up to its reputation."
>
> Yet for a time after they returned to Edinburgh, all went on as usual. Then the hoodoo bone struck at its owners. Sir Alexander went down with illness. Lady Seton went down with illness. They recovered, but later became ill again... (Lady Seton) was still ill when a servant came to her and said that she had seen a "hooded figure" in one of the corridors of the house. The girl was afraid of something she could not explain. A friend staying with the Setons came down one morning to breakfast and related that he had had an eerie experience in his bedroom. He had the feeling that "something" or somebody had entered his room. The child of a visitor, a boy entering his

teens, told the same story. He too had seen the "hooded figure" in his room. He was so scared that he had covered his head with the bedclothes and lay shuddering in fear...

Psychic experts were asked to investigate and report their findings. They all agreed that there was an "entity" connected with the bone. One of them had had a communication from the princess. This was to the effect that if the bone was not returned to its original resting-place within two months, blindness would fall on those who kept it...

On April 23 they retired to bed as usual. Early the following morning they were awakened by a loud crash. Sir Alexander rose and made his way to the room where the bone was kept. A strange sight met his eyes. The glass case which had contained the bone lay in fragments on the floor. The bone itself was lying 10 ft away on the carpet. A heavy, valuable vase, which had been placed near the case, was shivered to atoms. The hoodoo bone had struck again. It was impossible for any human being to be responsible for this latest disaster. Not a soul had been near the case or the bone. What had lifted it? How had the wreckage been caused? There was only one explanation. The dead princess was impatient. "I am going back to Egypt with the bone," Lady Seton told me, "as soon as it can be arranged."

That is the story of the strange happenings at Duddingston, the home of the Setons. I have told it without drama or any endeavour to make it theatrical. It is a simple enough story and a terrible one, for there is no saying what next the ghostly princess may do if her orders are not carried out.[10]

We have already noted the colorful Cheiro, who claimed to have warned Lord Carnarvon of his imminent death. What I had neglected to mention earlier was that the conduit by which the dire warning was transmitted was, to quote the title of the piece, *A Mummy's Hand That Came to Life*. It was the right hand of Tutankhamen's sister-in-law, given to him years earlier by a grateful Egyptian he'd cured of malaria.[11] It was, needless to say, "in a magnificent state of preservation" with "even the gold leaf that the ancient Egyptians used instead of the red paint that ladies employ today ... as good as when it had first been put on." Despite being warned that the hand was subject to a curse that had yet to be fulfilled, he brought it back to his English home, where it wasted little time in getting up to mischief. He attempted to burn it, whereupon the spectral vision of the Princess appeared, informing him of Carnarvon's fate. I've no doubt the remarkable Cheiro was more than capable of cooking up all that and much more from his own remarkable imagination, but it's highly likely that these various accounts of malevolent mummy hands helped out, as may have a British movie from 1915, *The Avenging Hand*, in which the ghost of an Egyptian princess persecutes the archaeologist who stole her mummified hand and took it home with him.

In fiction, the locus of the mummy's power was frequently its hands, and severed mummy's hands are legion as conduits for or instigators of curse narratives. One such appears in Bram Stoker's *The Jewel of Seven Stars*, and avenging or jinxing mummy's hands abound in Gothic novels, penny dreadfuls and newspaper serials: *The Beetle* (Richard Marsh, 1897), *The Mummy Hand: A Story of One Christmas Eve (as narrated by Eustace Ormerod)* (Adeline Sergeant, 1901), *The Mysterious Duke* (Anonymous, 1908), and many others. Most important to our line of enquiry, we have H. Carson Marksman's five part serial *The Mummy's Hand* appearing as late as 1938.[12] This is "a strange adventure introducing Dr. Paul Mordred, Psychic Investigator and Criminologist Extraordinary," and I can only urge anyone with a soft spot for pulp fiction to seek out the full adventure. I can give but a taste:

> He brought the box, and lifting the lid disclosed within a large human hand in a mummified condition. It had been severed with skill well above the wrist, and judging by its appearance, was of considerable antiquity. Through some secret process of the embalmers, it had remained perfect in every detail; the skin was of a light brown hue, the true Egyptian colour; the fingers and thumb

were splayed out, with the tips curved over as though the hand, at the moment of severance, had been about to grasp something. The skin of the upper part of the forearm had been left attached to form a flap, which had been folded over the stump of the hand and sewn skilfully into position with some kind of thin sinew. It was a right hand, and on the long middle finger could be seen the indentation of the ring which the Major was now wearing. I saw that he wore the ring In the same position—on the middle finger of the right hand.

Mordred's face was mask-like, betraying no emotion, as he lifted the hand from the box and examined It; but I, who knew him well, could tell from a certain tensity round his eyes that the repulsion, which had swept over him like a wave when first he touched the black ring was strong upon him now. He loathed that hand, and I caught something of his loathing.

"Feel it," he said to me, suddenly.

I touched the hand—and started back in horror. Perfect though it was in form, it had one ghastly characteristic. The skin, still soft and velvety, with a bloom almost like life upon it, dinted at the touch; the flesh within had shrivelled on to the bones, so that the skin slipped round as though the things inside were loose in a bag.

Not long, of course, before the hand's evil influence becomes apparent:

Fear was upon me—fear of that creeping horror coming through the door—fear that clawed at my backbone with icy fingers that gathered inside me like a numbing leaden weight. I would have cried out, but my tongue clove to the roof of my mouth. What was this dreadful thing at which Modred had only dared to hint—this evil presence which I could sense so strongly close at hand? Was that a hand which clawed at the panels? I stood there, staring, staring, taut with trepidation, and the cold sweat from my brow trickled on to my eye-lids. A faint, nauseous stench pervaded the bedroom, a fetid draught as from a sepulchre, and it seemed to come from the table, from the glass box on the table, from the mummy's hand in the glass box on the table by which Paul Modred stood.

Wider, wider, swung the door, the hand reaching from the black gap, poised in exact counterpart of the dead thing on; the table, was plain to see. Something huge bulked in the gloom behind it— Major St. John Courtland. The breath, hard held in my throat, whistled through my teeth. Courtland it was, and yet not Courtland. As he came slowly through the doorway, his hand—on it the blackened ring—upraised, I saw his face, and it was fearfully distorted: his lips, drawn back above the teeth, writhed in a wide, snarling smile that gashed his face like a wound; his brows arched in the strangest fashion over eyes dilated, glittering, devoid of sanity. Nearer and nearer he came, and his left hand rose to join the right, the fingers curving like hooked talons, the tips working slowly in and out as though eager to grasp—and strangle!

So numerous were these stories that one wonders if Gaultier's *Mummy's Foot*, with its outraged appendage hopping like a frog, may have been intended in part as a direct parody of the many malevolent hands of less whimsical accounts. Such is the association that, as if by a kind of generic memory severed hands also feature, in very different contexts each time, in three of Hammer's four mummy films (*Curse of the Mummy's Tomb, The Mummy's Shroud* and *Blood from the Mummy's Tomb*).[13]

This, then, is but a sample of the long, long history by which the phrase "mummy's hand" had entered the lore. It is reasonable to suppose, therefore, that the original audiences for Universal's films would have gone in expecting the action to in some way revolve around a disembodied mummy's hand, so familiar would the object have been to them in both fiction and reportage. But what we actually have is a film about the "long arm" of supernatural revenge, and in that respect it's a witty, clever title; almost postmodern.

Yet again we must here stop to acknowledge Sir Arthur Conan Doyle. Just as *The Ring of Thoth* served as unofficial inspiration for *The Mummy*, so the spirit and structure of its follow-ups (and thus of the mummy film in its most commonly understood formulation) is anticipated by his full-blown shocker *Lot No. 249* (1894). Though only officially filmed once (modernized, as part of the anthology film *Tales from the Darkside:*

The Movie) it finally introduces the idea of a hideous, physically unreformed mummy being sent on a mayhem spree, as an engine of revenge for the mortal who controls it: "a weapon such as no man had ever used in all the grim history of crime." To this it adds the elements of uncommon height and strength ("six feet seven in length, and that would be a giant over there, for they were never a very robust race") and even a possible role played in its resurrection (Doyle's hero remains unsure to the end as to the precise details) by "the dried leaves of some graceful, palm-like plant."

The mummy is described as "a horrid, black, withered thing," and there is an attention to gruesome physical detail that takes it out of the mystic realm of *The Ring of Thoth* and into that of pure horror:

> The features, though horribly discoloured, were perfect, and two little nut-like eyes still lurked in the depths of the black, hollow sockets. The blotched skin was drawn tightly from bone to bone, and a tangled wrap of black, coarse hair fell over the ears. Two thin teeth, like those of a rat, overlay the shrivelled lower lip. In its crouching position, with bent joints and craned head, there was a suggestion of energy about the horrid thing which made Smith's gorge rise. The gaunt ribs, with their parchment-like covering, were exposed, and the sunken, leaden-hued abdomen, with the long slit where the embalmer had left his mark; but the limbs were wrapped round with coarse, yellow bandages.

The most suspenseful passage details the hero's terrified realization that the thing is stalking him down a secluded country lane:

> It was a lonely and little-frequented road which led to his friend's house. Early as it was, Smith did not meet a single soul upon his way. He walked briskly along until he came to the avenue gate which opened into the long gravel drive leading up to Farlingford. In front of him he could see the

Christian Slater is about to come face to face with Lot No. 249 in *Tales from the Darkside: The Movie* (1990).

cosy, red light of the windows glimmering through the foliage. He stood with his hand upon the iron latch of the swinging gate and he glanced back at the road along which he had come. Something was coming swiftly down it. It moved in the shadow of the hedge, silently and furtively, a dark, crouching figure, dimly visible against the black background. Even as he gazed back at it, it had lessened its distance by twenty paces and was fast closing upon him. Out of the darkness he had a glimpse of a scraggy neck and of two eyes that will ever haunt him in his dreams. He turned and with a cry of terror he ran for his life up the avenue. There were the red lights, the signals of safety, almost within a stone's-throw of him. He was a famous runner, but never had he run as he ran that night.

> The heavy gate had swung into place behind him but he heard it dash open again before his pursuer. As he rushed madly and wildly through the night, he could hear a swift, dry patter behind him, and could see, as he threw back a glance, that this horror was bounding like a tiger at his heels, with blazing eyes and one stringy arm out-thrown.

The tale ends with the hero—who survives his ordeal—forcing the villain at gunpoint to dismember and burn the mummy:

> In frantic haste he caught up the knife and hacked at the figure of the mummy, ever glancing round to see the eye and the weapon of his terrible visitor bent upon him. The creature crackled and snapped under every stab of the keen blade. A thick yellow dust rose up from it. Spices and dried essences rained down upon the floor. Suddenly, with a rending crack, its backbone snapped asunder, and it fell, a brown heap of sprawling limbs, upon the floor.
> "Now into the fire!" said Smith.
> The flames leaped and roared as the dried and tinderlike debris was piled upon it. The little room was like the stoke-hole of a steamer and the sweat ran down the faces of the two men; but still the one stooped and worked, while the other sat watching him with a set face. A thick, fat smoke oozed out from the fire, and a heavy smell of burned rosin and singed hair filled the air. In a quarter of an hour a few charred and brittle sticks were all that was left of Lot No. 249.

The Mummy's Hand forsakes Imhotep, the brooding, conspiring mirror of Doyle's Sosra, for an all-new mummy, Kharis. Unlike Imhotep, but like the un-named Lot No. 249, the revived Kharis is a purely physical force, and will sport his bandage wrappings at all times, permanently fixing the classic look of the movie mummy. Kharis reappears in three sequels, a spoof (lightly, perhaps accidentally, disguised as "Klaris") and again in Hammer's ostensible remake of the original *The Mummy*. (It's just possible that his unusual name may have been a cheeky reversal of the middle syllables of Boris Karloff, in the absence of the latter actually making an appearance.)

Whereas Imhotep/Bey was lurking menace and malevolent intelligence both, the Kharis movies split the character in two, providing a guiding villain in the form of some modern devotee of the ancient religious faith (George Zucco, at his pop-eyed best in *The Mummy's Hand*) who controls Kharis and compels him to act: Kharis himself is entirely without autonomy. In *Hand* he is played by cowboy actor Tom Tyler with what looks in stills to be probably the weakest of Jack Pierce's mummy designs: basically a thin and evenly-applied spreading of grey paste over the actor's head, through which his robust twentieth century face, and slicked-back but no less full head of hair, stare plainly. In the film, however, and atmospherically half-lit, it seems much more effective, and agreeably augmented in post-production by the simple expedient of blacking out the eyes frame by frame, giving them the appearance, as Halliwell puts it, of "bottomless pools of quivering black jelly." (The "before and after" effect can be compared in the trailer, which uses undoctored footage.)

Like Imhotep, Kharis wants to restore life to his dead love, but this time it is the Princess Ananka, and he is apprehended stealing not a sacred scroll but the sacred "tana

Tom Tyler as Kharis in *The Mummy's Hand* (1940).

leaves" which can restore the dead when brewed into a liquid. These tana leaves become of much importance in the unfolding Kharis saga—the mummy himself, in the present day, is kept alive through a regular infusion of them, which has to be distilled in complicated variant quantities during the cycle of the full moon. (Three leaves are enough to keep his heart beating, more will make him ambulatory, but nine will turn him into "an uncontrollable monster" with "the desire to kill and kill," giving a whole new meaning to the phrase "it is dangerous to exceed the recommended dose.")

This is also the film that institutes the convention of having the mummy be inordinately slow and lumbering. There seems to be no obvious precedent for it, other than Karloff's brief appearance in the bandages. Here we find Kharis reviving in degrees owing to the quantity of tana fluid he ingests: his first sampling apparently being sufficient only to revive one each of his arms and legs. In the continuing series, however, no matter how much he knocks back, he remains rigid and shuffling. This represents a decisive break with tradition, in that the previous mummies of literature are for the most part rather sprightly fellows—Conan Doyle's Lot No. 249, as we saw, is not averse to running after its victims, or even dropping on them from the branches of a tree. And it inevitably causes problems for the actors portraying the victims, who are obliged to remain motionless, supposedly frozen in terror, but seeming, rather, to have decided that raising their arms and meekly protesting gives them better odds on survival than a brisk walk in the opposite direction. When Hammer abandoned the whole idea in their first mummy film in 1959 (cheekily transferring the limp to Peter Cushing's hero) it pays immediate dividends: a huge part of why its mummy's attacks are so effectively scary is because we are not used to a mummy this agile and resourceful.

It must be left to speculation if these curious tana leaves owe anything to the unspecified dried leaves that figure in *Lot No. 249*. We may also wonder if they take their name from Lake Tana in Ethiopia, source of the Blue Nile. As for the additional complication of the lunar cycles, this might perhaps have been derived from the association of the moon with the god Thoth, who was frequently depicted with a headdress showing a disc and crescent, representing the lunar phases. Further, other images depict him recording the names of the Pharaohs on the leaves on the persea tree. The branches of the persea were often used in funerary bouquets, and the tree features often in Egyptian mythology. At the Temple of Pakhet, aforementioned focus of real-life "survivals," is the inscription: *My divine heart searches for the sake of the future; [my] heart—that which it had not known forever, because of the command which the hidden persea tree, lord of myriads (of years), communicates.* Thus, if we were to propose that the tana leaves might be persea leaves we might, just, contrive a tongue-in-cheek correlation (a difference in interpretation, or even merely translation) between the Scroll of Thoth, familiar from the Imhotep myth, and the sacred leaves of Kharis, source of the "scroll" on which Thoth charts the passing of the years!

The Mummy's Hand was made quickly and without serious intent. The flashbacks from *The Mummy* are re-used to illustrate a different backstory, and the tomb, both interior and exterior, is the Incan jungle temple from *Green Hell*. (It never convinces as Egyptian for a second, despite some token redressing, set into the verdant California hillside with a long flight of steps leading up to it, and decorated with Inca carvings and a stone llama.) Kharis is entombed upright, and when the team remove the decorated outer sarcophagus lid they drop it face down on to the rocky floor and walk on it.

The film also differs starkly from its predecessor in its concept of contemporary Egypt. The Egypt of *The Mummy*, supposedly 1921, is a Western colonial territory, and is quiet and eerie; an ancient land illuminated here and there by the archaeologists' dwellings, a sophisticated nightclub, and the Cairo Museum. The atmosphere is palpable, vividly evoked. The Egypt of this movie, however, is a burlesque: instead of the still and uncanny landscape of the first film we are plunged into a bustling Cairo bazaar, full of camels, veiled temptresses, beggars and souvenir stands. There is nothing atmospheric here: it's noisy and busy, and the American archaeologists bumble through it as huckster tourists, starting brawls in bars and dreaming of Coney Island hot dogs.

And yet, it is a film that seemed to strike many as pretty frightening: *Halliwell's Film Guide*, well into the twenty-first century, still charmingly declared its final third "among the most scary in horror film history." (The author elaborates in *Halliwell's Hundred*, with an amusing story of how he and a number of his young school friends saw it accidentally and emerged terrified, but insists that many others have also since told him they too had been traumatized by it.)

A truly hysterical promotional article that featured in the *Perth Mirror*[14] (and presumably anywhere else willing to run it) substantiates this mood, and hints unfathomably at a real-life inspiration to the movie, under the headline "Frankenstein Was a Sissy Compared to Mummy's Hand":

> Thotmes, Aknaten, Tut-Ankh-Amen; one by one modern scientists have un-earthed the steps leading to their burial places and desecrated the royal grave by carrying the three to 15,000-year-old mummified bodies off to museums. In the Perth museum today are priceless vases and bowls, alabaster and lapis lazuli, dug from the tomb of Tut-Ankh-Amen.
>
> But over those tombs down through the centuries has hung a royal curse. Death to the men who

rob them! Sometimes it has been death in an automobile accident; one archaeologist was impaled on a gold-tipped spear at the entrance to a burial chamber; another scratched his thumb as he lifted a gilded chariot from where it had rested for 10,000 years—and in that scratch was a disease-laden death warrant. Germs from the mummified king killed him with the certainty of those who come under Pharaoh's curse.

It was the late Dr. R. Nicolus who broke the sanctity of an Egyptian tomb and lived to die a natural death. By planning and disguise, learning the number of steps leading down to the ritual chamber, he was able to enter secretly and witness one of the strangest sights ever human eyes have seen.

Guttering gas and candlelight. Hooded Egyptian priests standing around in a semi-circle in the midst of which was something like a tressiled table. And on the table a dead body wrapped in its winding sheet. Like voices from beyond the grave Nicolus heard them chanting unearthly mournful sounds, while one of the priests anointed the dead body with a formulae. Suddenly, to his horror, Nicolus saw the dead man sit up, climb like a sleep walker off the slab, and, eyes fixed and fingers groping, walk unsteadily across the floor of the burial chamber only to collapse in a huddled heap on the other side. He'd seen something beyond the ken of medicine or science. He'd seen a dead man walk!

History; indisputable fact. What a setting for a film photographed in the tombs of Egypt! Hollywood saw the chance, and out of it all came a story that makes Frankenstein read like a prize book given at a Sunday school picnic.... As the camera closes on the Mummy, as he walks towards you, sightless eyes looking, staring at you wherever you sit, you'll long for Frankenstein and think of him as good looking as Robert Taylor. *The Mummy's Hand* is a masterpiece of horror and history, filmed in a desert mountain where, defying the curse of the title, an expeditionary group sets out to discover the tomb.... Groping hands fiddle with the Mummy's winding sheets; dead fingers twitch, dead eyes blink; a 3000-year-dead arm is raised in vengeance...

It's a pity to tell it further. What Howard Carter saw as he walked down those 16 steps leading to Tut-Ankh-Amen's tomb was nothing. In *The Mummy's Hand* is held the greatest mystery-horror Hollywood has given us.

Well, I don't know about that, but if one film deserves the title of "archetypal mummy movie" it is surely *The Mummy's Hand*. (Oh, and as for this extraordinary "Dr. R. Nicolus," the hero of the tale, you'll no doubt be stunned to learn I've found no other trace of his extraordinary experience!) The main change worth noting between *The Mummy's Hand* and *The Mummy's Tomb* (1942) is in Kharis himself. Though briefly glimpsed, even in a restrictive mask that reveals none of his actual facial characteristics, he is now officially played by Lon Chaney, Jr.

Chaney (Universal had dropped the "Jr." by the time he donned the bandages) is one of the most interesting of all Hollywood personalities, long overdue a serious and sympathetic biography. He essayed every major horror role on Universal's books: the Mummy, Frankenstein's Monster, Dracula, and his own creation the Wolf Man, purely and simply because he happened to be the son of Lon Chaney, the versatile creator of macabre and tormented grotesques in the silent era. The son had the surname and no other point of comparison: he was a modern man from head to toe: bulky, urban, and about as ethereal as a Model T Ford. True, there was an almost tormented, intense, Hemingwayesque quality to him, which served him well as the Wolf Man and in his *Inner Sanctum* mysteries, but it's a moot matter how much of that was innate and how much his understandable response to the hand that Hollywood dealt him.

He had begun as Creighton Chaney and set his sights on romantic leads: in his burly handsomeness, before alcohol made him pudgy and vague, he was often compared to Clark Gable. As he himself later said, he had to starve before he would be reduced to making his Faustian pact with Hollywood, taking his father's name, and letting Jack Pierce pile on the greasepaint. But he was not, by any means, a bad actor—though rarely given the chance to play anything other than monsters, thugs and dimwits (or, in later life, ornery sheriffs). He should have been at Warners, in noir and crime films. Recalling his horror roles (from the set of *The Haunted Palace*) in 1963, he was adamant that "the best of the monsters played for sympathy. That goes for my father, Karloff, myself and all the others. They all won the audience's sympathy." (This he contrasted starkly with more recent films that "go after horror for horror's sake. There's no motivation for how the monsters behave. There's too much of that science fiction baloney.")[15]

Whether or not we can call it art, he certainly suffered for it. His allergic reaction to the rubber face mask caused agonizing skin rashes, and the suffocatingly hot body suit resulted in the loss of seventeen pounds during the course of shooting *The Mummy's Curse* (1944).[16] In *The Mummy's Ghost* (1944) he supposedly put his arm through a real glass window when the fake substitute was not ready in time for the shoot, and visibly bleeds from the chin for the rest of the scene.[17] All this for a role that could scarcely be called a role at all, and which he felt to be plainly beneath his dignity.

Chaney's Kharis is limited by being always in the bandages (unlike Karloff or Tyler he features in no Egyptian flashback scenes) and by an unresponsive mask: what acting he is able to do is restricted mainly to one visible eye. Further, as Alan Frank has noted, there is the additional complication of the need to match his scenes with those featuring stuntman Eddie Parker also in the bandages, flashbacks of Tom Tyler as the mummy, and

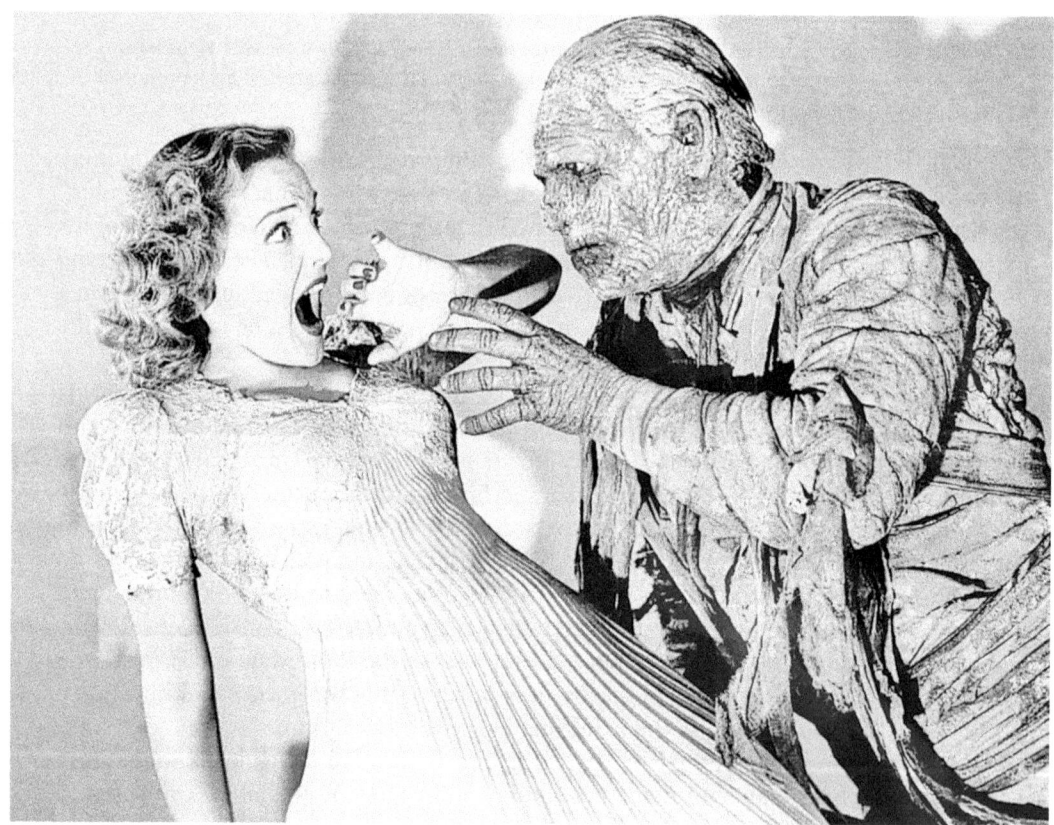

Kharis (Lon Chaney, Jr.) knows how to get a reaction in *The Mummy's Tomb* (1942). Elyse Knox does not disappoint.

unbandaged Egyptian flashbacks of both Tyler *and* Karloff! Easy to see, then, why it was not Chaney's favorite assignment. To reporters on the set of *The Mummy's Curse*, he groused: "I sit up all night learning my dialogue.... My dialogue? What am I talking about? I never say anything. I've no lines, no face. But I have a bet. I've bet that some day one of these pictures will lose money, and then I won't have to do any more. So far, though..."[18]

The decision to retain Kharis as a recurring character has a surprising consequence: only the first of the four films is about the discovery and excavation of a tomb, and the reviving of a mummy. The others begin with Kharis already on the prowl and deal with either his continued vendetta against the previous expedition (in *The Mummy's Tomb*) or his frustrated search for his reincarnated lady love (in *The Mummy's Ghost* and *Curse*). In addition, of course, he is no longer in Egypt: from the second episode onward he enacts his reigns of terror in small American towns. This was a typical move by Universal, both economical and in keeping with the desire to make their monsters more relevant to the home audience. But today, viewers will probably miss the rich Egyptian atmosphere of *The Mummy* and *The Mummy's Hand* in the subsequent variations.

Ten of *The Mummy's Tomb*'s sixty minutes are taken up flashing back to the previous movie, yet when it does bring itself up to date, it pulls a stunt that, though commonplace now, must have seemed shockingly cynical at the time. When we join the new story, we are reintroduced to Dick Foran and Wallace Ford, the two endearing heroes of the previous film whose exploits we have been enjoying in recap, only to then have both of them savagely slaughtered by the revived Kharis. Today we are more used to the survivors of one film getting killed in the sequel; here it must have seemed truly callous.

Even stranger, the film is set thirty years after the events of *The Mummy's Hand*, though no explanation is offered for what Kharis has been doing in the meantime, or why it has taken him so long to get around to completing his campaign of revenge. (George Zucco is back too, now incredibly decrepit, but with hair where he was previously bald and just a stiff arm to show for the multiple bullet wounds that killed him at the end of the last episode.)

Of course, this all means that we are technically in 1970, though there is not the smallest effort to vary the incidental details of a film that couldn't be more forties if it tried, and indeed, at one point a character receives his World War II call-up papers. (Given the multiple absurdities ensuing from the decision to leap three decades—the baby-faced Foran and Ford made up unconvincingly as old men, the inexplicable delay in Kharis's activities, and the World War II–era 1970—it remains mysterious indeed why Universal didn't simply set the film, say, five years later. There is nothing gained, or even made use of, in the absurd time jump.) The idea of Kharis following our heroes back to America, however, gives the film the most overt metaphorical echoes of the Tutankhamen curse, which, the world was told, followed its victims wherever they went, waiting for the right moment to give them their ambiguous deserts.

The Mummy's Ghost brings Zucco back from the dead a third time, completely changes the legend of Kharis and Ananka, and stirs in reincarnation for the first time (heroine Elyse Knox proves to be Ananka in modern form, and in a well-staged and surprising finale joins Kharis in death in an all-engulfing swamp, supernaturally reduced to hideous old age). Like the previous film, all this takes place in New England, but in *The Mummy's Curse*, released the same year, the swamp has inexplicably moved to the Louisiana bayous, and—in a second surprise—the movie opens with a jaunty song number.

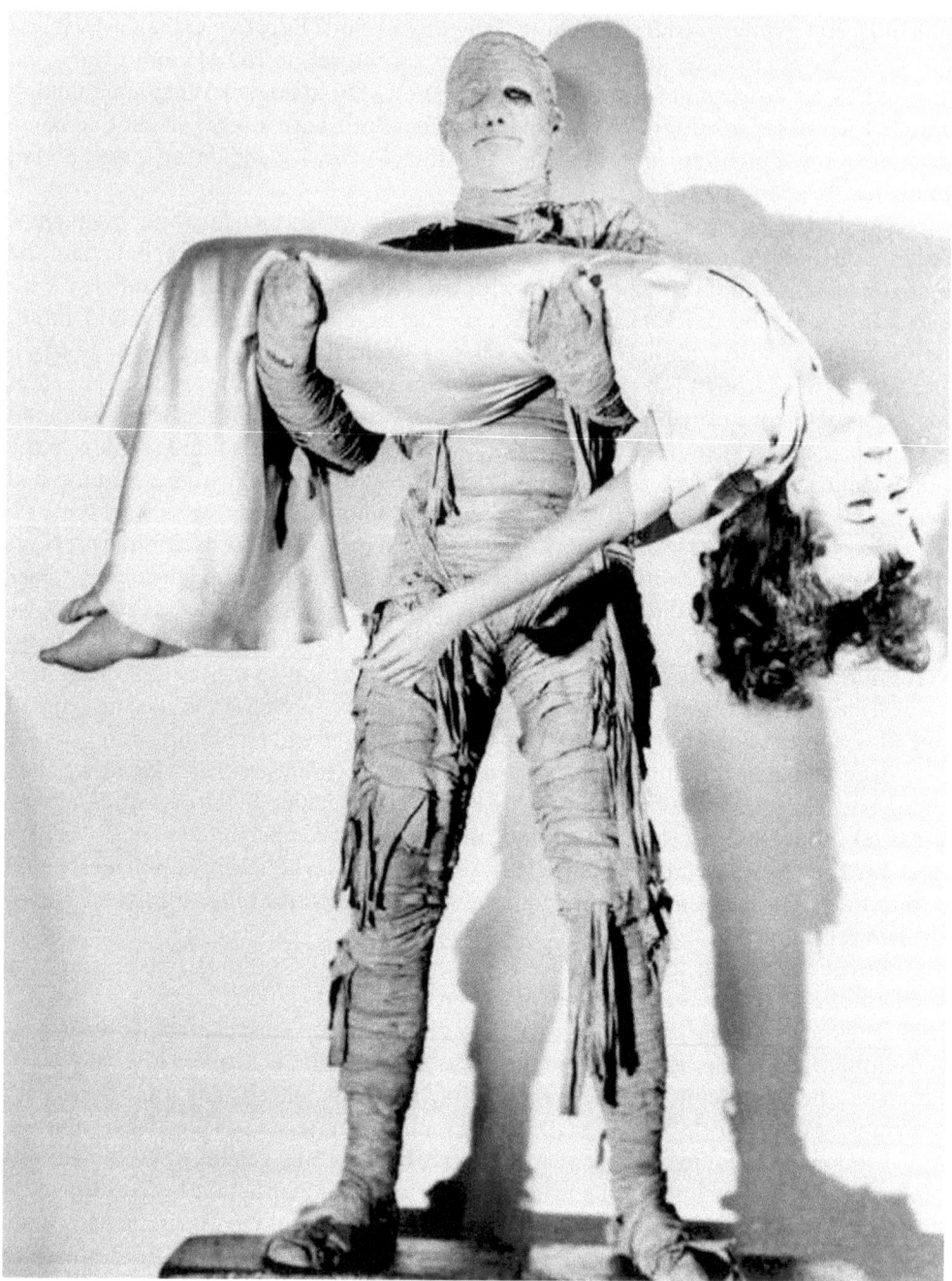

Lon Chaney, Jr., carries off Ramsay Ames in *The Mummy's Ghost* (1944).

The action has moved on another twenty five years, putting us somewhere around the late 1990s.

What all these films deliver, however—in both quantity *and* quality—are what they themselves established as the staple ingredient of the generic mummy movie: great spooky scenes of the mummy stalking, looming, lunging and killing, in country lanes, quiet museums and darkened bedrooms. In this respect, despite the considerable critical ignominy in which they still languish, they still come up fresh as paint—just watch them on a Saturday afternoon with a room full of kids and you'll see for yourself. They are still pacy, and filled with thrills and shudders, if you are willing to meet them on their own terms.

Given their pulp fiction ambiance, the one thing we should not expect of them is the same kind of Egyptological clue-scattering with which John Balderston had streaked *The Mummy*. One impudence worth noting, however, is the decision to name the senior archaeologist in *The Mummy's Hand* "Dr. Petrie." This is unquestionably a reference to William Flinders Petrie, one-time tutor of Howard Carter and, at 87, still very much alive when the film was released. It's fascinating to imagine what he might have made of the film; indeed, one of the best first uses for any functioning time machine would be to gather up my ten favorite Egyptologists and ask them to give a running commentary to a quadruple-bill of Kharis movies. Petrie's would surely have been among the most amusing.

Petrie had made his first visit to Egypt in 1880 and, horrified, would describe it as "a house on fire, so rapid was the destruction." As a result, he dedicated his academic career to two related goals: to replace his predecessors' often flightily imaginative approach to historical analysis with the scientifically quantifiable interpretation of data and, in part as a means to that end, the general redefinition of Egyptology as the pursuit of knowledge rather than treasure. While the whole body of his life and work stands as testament to the latter aim, in the former he is noted especially as the inventor of "sequence dating," a means of breaking the Predynastic era into sub-periods based on observed changes in the design and decoration of the surviving pottery. He perfected this system, still of practical value today, while excavating the massive Predynastic settlement of Nagada in 1895, one of the sites with which his name is most associated. (The others are the Early Dynastic cemeteries of Abydos and the city of el-Amarna, the latter the best-preserved example of a New Kingdom settlement.) Sequence dating has been hailed as a masterpiece of applied mathematics, and Egyptology's only true contribution to empirical statistical analysis.

As well as a brilliant theoretician and an ingenious analyst, Petrie embodies exactly that kind of Englishman that, with thanks to Noel Coward, went out in the noonday sun. According to archaeologist Gabriel Barkai, "he knew the exact distance between his eye and the tip of his finger and therefore could measure distances with great precision. He built a camera out of biscuit tins, and in order to save time, he drew his findings with both hands at the same time, wielding a pencil in each."[19] A more scurrilous recollection was provided by Weigall in a private letter, who described Petrie as a martyr to stomach disorder due to a diet of peas and salad oil, given to anointing himself with green insecticidal powder, and blotting out extraneous noise by putting lumps of plaster of Paris in his ears. The first time he encountered him, he claimed, Petrie tried to avoid the meeting by hiding under a table.[20]

As Petrie himself recalled in his 1932 memoir *Seventy Years in Archaeology*:

> It was often most convenient to strip entirely for work, owing to the heat and absence of any current of air.... For outside work in the hot weather, vest and pants were suitable, and if pink they kept the tourist at bay, as the creature seemed to him too queer for inspection.... The petroleum stove by the door cooked my meals, which I prepared at any time required by the irregular hours of work.

William Flinders Petrie not hiding under a table (Petrie Museum of Egyptian Archaeology).

> When the big theodolite was out, it was needful to finish a stretch of observing within the day, which left only time for a morning and evening feed, and I always reduced the observations every night. On days when work lay inside the pyramid, the morning was spent in writing up observations, and the hours of interior measurement ran from about five till midnight.

As this shows, the real archaeologists simply didn't have the time to be chased about the tombs by mummies. It just wasn't logistically practical. In the movies, however, excavation is insultingly easy! One can almost hear Petrie's tongue clucking at the sight of his cinematic representatives in their immaculate linen suits, as they proceed from finding the tomb at breakfast to exposing the mummy before lunch—a process that in reality would often take arduous weeks or months (or, in the case of Carter and Tutankhamen, years).

Petrie died (sadly long before the age of DVD commentaries) in July of 1942, at the age of 89. On his death it was found that he had donated his head to the London Royal College of Surgeons. Having less use for the ghoulish artefact than he presumably supposed, the college quietly stored it away in their basement where, not long after, the label fell off. As such, it soon became a matter of doubt if it even was Petrie's at all, and positive identification was not established until 1989.

Petrie's body was buried in Jerusalem, but his head remains, to this day, in a jar in London.

7

From Lot No. 249 to Law No. 215

> During the last two or three years a great and astonishing change has taken place in the attitude and bearing of educated Egyptians. In 1882 the nation was bankrupt, and the native government had, by frenzied taxation, reduced the country to such complete chaos, that European intervention was necessary; and this had led to an antiforeign movement which had to be suppressed by force. The British Occupation resulted; and from that time until the outbreak of the great war, Egypt remained under British supervision and guidance, having little more than a nominal control over its own affairs. The British government, however, had always said that this Occupation was only a temporary measure, which would be terminated as soon as the Egyptians showed clear signs of being able to govern themselves; and now the time is fast approaching when we shall honor that promise, and shall leave this interesting people more or less to its own devices.—Arthur Weigall, "The Future of Excavation in Egypt" in *Tutankhamen and Other Essays*, 1924

The Mummy's Curse didn't seem like the last word in the saga, but thus it proved. By the end of 1945, Kharis was finished, World War II was finished, the Universal horror film was finished, and so, it seemed was the Curse of Tutankhamen, according to the *Prescott Evening Courier* on December 11:

> **Last Survivor Dead**
> The last principal survivor of the British archaeological party which opened the fabulous tomb of Tut-Ankh-Amen is dead. He was Alfred Lucas, 79, and it took 23 years for the "curse" of the pharaohs to catch up with him.

It is to be regretted that British filmmakers, much given in the 1920s and 30s to the production of colonial-themed epics like *Sanders of the River*, never got around to a film about or inspired by the Tutankhamen excavation. Clearly, the perspective they could have offered now seems like the most significant missing link in our cinematic picture of the subject; an authentic recreation of the attitudes prevailing of a sort that *The Mummy*, with its emphasis on fantasy, was able only to paint in the broadest strokes. Through its unimpeded integration within the family of the American horror film, the subject was allowed to become a comic strip from the first, and by the time British cinema did get around to it in 1959 it was strictly on the terms laid down by Hollywood. Nonetheless, it was inevitable that elements of the British experience, both past and present, would bleed into the tapestry, and it is these elements that are the most interesting thing about Hammer's version of *The Mummy* and its follow-ups.

Incredible though it seems that we had to wait until the dawn of the 1960s for a British take on the material, we could easily have been waiting yet longer, or waiting still. Hammer studios had, in fact, single-handedly revived the classical horror film from a state of terminal inactivity, after Hollywood had abandoned it to the ministrations of Abbott and Costello and diverted their serious energies to the new style of science fiction horror. With the exception of *Abbott and Costello Meet the Mummy* (1955), the only film that even came close to being a traditional mummy movie produced between Chaney's last and Hammer's first was *Pharaoh's Curse* in 1957.

But while the mummy movie was slumbering, Ancient Egypt itself made a spectacular revival in the cinema of the 1950s. The Cinemascope epics of that decade—a response to the crisis of mass television ownership—looked naturally to lavish historical and Biblical subjects to fill their daunting canvases and supply their casts of thousands. Thus DeMille made inevitable return to *The Ten Commandments* (1956), dispensed with the parallel modern story, and took twice as long to tell the remainder as he did to tell both parts in 1925. A widescreen and Technicolor banquet, the film plays like a visitation from another world, saw out the director's distinguished career in high style, and richly deserved its massive commercial success, but there were others on a similar scale. *The Egyptian* (1954) benefited enormously from the technical assistance of Elizabeth Titzel, at the time assistant curator of Egyptology at the Brooklyn Museum, later Executive Secretary of The American Research Center in Egypt. (She was still at work into her eighties, on exhibition catalogues and scholarly publications.) Meanwhile, *Valley of the Kings* (1954) mixed real Egyptian footage with California subterfuge, including valuable film record of the Abu Simbel temples before their relocation.

Most interesting of all, however, was *Land of the Pharaohs* (1955), an atypical collaboration between director Howard Hawks and William Faulkner. It is essentially two films, running parallel and never really intersecting except by continuity of characters. One half is typical melodrama, with Joan Collins as a duplicitous femme fatale conspiring to kill Khufu (Jack Hawkins) for his funerary treasure, decorated with massive panoramic shots of spectacular sets and locations, literally thousands of extras (many of them moonlighting members of the Egyptian army), huge herds of historically inaccurate camels, dancers, swordfights, tiger skin rugs, murders by snake, and people being thrown to alligators. The other half is the part that interested Hawks, and most interests us: Khufu's obsession with building the Great Pyramid, and how to design it in such a way as to proclaim his glory and defeat the attentions of tomb robbers.

Long stretches of the film are devoted to the construction of the monument, ingeniously shot at the site of the unfinished pyramid of Baka at Zawyet el'Aryan. This is one of a number of clever, vaguely ironic uses of real information and locations. In addition, in a truly superb shot, the laborers are shown hacking away at the unfinished obelisk at Aswan, as if in the act of successfully removing it for their use. And in the scene in which Khufu first inspects prospective plans for his tomb he indignantly rejects an exact copy of the interior of the actual Great Pyramid!

Standing in for Imhotep, James Robertson Justice's Vashtar concocts a cunning system whereby huge stones are lowered into place using dispersed sand, sealing the pyramid beyond the ingenuity of even the most resourceful tomb robber. Apparently Hawks himself designed the mechanism, and it is certainly ingenious, but its ingenuity stems from the possibly insupportable assumption that only an extraordinary explanation will suffice. The truth about the Pyramid may be that it is far less mysterious than we are inclined

Historical authenticity all but leaks from this promotional shot of Joan Collins in *Land of the Pharaohs* (1955).

(and keen) to believe, and accepting that in no way detracts from its majesty and architectural splendor. For some, nothing less than Atlanteans or green men from Mars will suffice. For many more, the assumption that it took hundreds of thousands of toiling men, tormented by heat and thirst and bitten by the lash, seems only obvious.

Our standard account of the construction stems from Herodotus, but he visited the site some two thousand years after construction, and received his information from people who knew little more about them than he did. (Speaking no Egyptian, he spoke only to communities of immigrant Greeks.) Much of what has been handed down to us, therefore, is hyperbole at best and often sheer nonsense. (He gets the dimensions of the building comprehensively wrong.) It is from Herodotus that we learn that Khufu employed slave labor in vast quantities: "The work went on in three monthly shifts, a hundred thousand men in one shift. It took ten years of this oppressive slave labor to build the track along which the blocks were hauled."

Our standard screen image, familiar from Hawks, DeMille and the rest, of agonized slaves straining to erect the massive stones, comes straight from these texts. The truth is that work of this order simply cannot be produced by men working against their will: it needs craftsmen who take pride in their work. The film hedges its bets here, showing a workforce that begins the job cheerfully and willingly, but has to be supplemented and enslaved as the backbreaking chore goes on, seemingly without end. It repeats Herodotus's assertion that the entire able workforce of the country was recruited to complete the unimaginably complex task.

It is unlikely that it was anything like that. An unskilled workforce makes the job longer, more difficult and less precise: much more likely that it was the work of dedicated, hard-working artisans carrying out a meticulously constructed plan. And in nothing like the numbers Herodotus would have us believe, either: more like two thousands than a hundred, and with every amenity on hand in the form of food, health care, and after-hours recreation. A collection of papyri discovered in 2013 cast further light on the process, detailing the food eaten by the laborers, and the logistics of moving the stones. As expected, they reveal a smoothly maintained bureaucracy, with no trace of enslavement or tyranny.[1]

The film's two plots come together only at the end, when sneaky Joan is tricked into being present inside the tomb as the sealing mechanism is tripped, and finds herself buried alive with the treasures for which she has schemed and murdered. It's a bleak moment of *grand guignol* that incorporates the aesthetics of the horror film almost as if by magnetic pull. The whole subject now had an almost unavoidable aura of the frightening and the supernatural. In that respect, it seemed to be leveling the ground for the revival of the mummy film proper, which, as stated, came not from Hollywood but from a small, independent British film studio on the banks of the river Thames.

Hammer horror films stand in relation to the Universal originals as so much later Egyptian art does to the earliest symbolic illustration found in early–Dynastic and Predynastic settlements: it can be striking, beautiful, majestic, even, on occasion, but its manifest merits do not include thematic or structural inspiration. They adhere to prototype, handed down from craftsman to craftsman, artist to artist, imagination to imagination. The Karloff film is unmediated: it is the instinctive brew of a variety of ingredients, chief among them the Egyptomania of the decade it caps. The Hammer films are purely cultural products, in that they draw their inspiration only from other, earlier cultural products. The chief difference between their initial batch of horrors and Universal's is that the latter (even *Frankenstein* and *Dracula*) were set in the then-present day. Hammer's adhere to a more literary conception of the gothic, handed on cinematically from the Gainsborough melodramas and the films of Tod Slaughter. Perversely, then, even their version of *The Mummy* is set in 1898, long before Tutmania, and largely in England, in that more parochial world where archaeology was a pastime for gentlemen, not a mass media spectacle.

Somewhat sadomasochistic poster art for *Land of the Pharaohs* (1955).

But while even the contemporary scenes of the 1932 film had a dream-like and unreal quality, at Hammer, the emphasis on action and mayhem overrides the distancing potential of its period dress. Rather than from *The Ring of Thoth* it seems to draw its atmospherics from the more overtly thrilling *Lot No. 249*. As such, in famous moments like the bravura scene in which Christopher Lee's mummy crashes through Peter Cushing's French windows and attempts to throttle him in his study, calmly breaking off the spear that Cushing thrusts through his gut, and especially in the nocturnal shots of the robust

Christopher Lee (left) takes one for the tomb in *The Mummy* (1959). Peter Cushing deals the blow.

and agile mummy stalking the twilit English countryside, we see the truest cinematic evocation of the atmosphere of Doyle's revenge story.

Plot-wise the film is a mix of material from the Universal sequels, with little or nothing derived from the Karloff film. For the most part it draws from the last three Chaney films, with the mummy attacking the defilers of his tomb on their own ground. For completeness, however, screenwriter Jimmy Sangster has added a sequence showing the excavation itself as a prologue, and (also in Universal tradition) Kharis's back story as a flashback. (Sangster's original script had intended to give Lee some appearances unwrapped in the manner of Karloff's Ardeth Bay, as George Pastell's supposed mute Egyptian servant, whom he then bizarrely re-wraps prior to sending him out on each murder mission. But it proved impractical, and Lee's time out of wraps, like most mummies before him, was limited solely to the flashback.)

At once the most interesting and the least successful part of the film, the ancient flashback is strikingly gaudy and garish and makes the error of mistaking detail for style (compare it with the vastly more effective but far less meticulous flashback sequences of the later *Blood from the Mummy's Tomb*). One could easily believe it the work of a separate director, or even spliced in from another movie entirely. In his book *A Heritage of Horror*, David Pirie makes the interesting observation that it "is actually more clear-cut and prosaic than the rest of the action. This is in absolute contrast to Universal, who filmed the flashbacks to Ancient Egypt in their version of *The Mummy* in a dreamy occult fashion before returning to 'reality.'" The ambitious sequence shows the funeral procession of the Princess Ananka making its way through the hills, her embalming and funerary ritual in considerable technical detail, and a mass-sacrifice, as well as the expected scenes of Kharis's attempts to bring her back to life and his subsequent apprehension and punishment. (Hammer's budgets were small and any such pageantry would have been beyond their resources had the film, as was their custom at this time, been shot entirely at their small Bray Studios, a partially converted riverside manor house. Luckily, they were able to secure use of a stage at Shepperton Studios, but it's still pinched and plainly studio-bound, most obviously in its attempts to recreate Egyptian exteriors.)

Though not without its quota of oddities (Karnak has for some reason become a god rather than a location), it is distinguished chiefly by both the accuracy and the sheer *quantity* of its replicated tomb artefacts, art and represented ritual (the sealing of the lips, the bath of natron). The artefacts are in many cases faithful copies of those from Tutankhamen's tomb. Clearly, both screenwriter Sangster and director Terence Fisher have handed the reins to their technical advisor, and their technical advisor has gone for a gallop. That advisor (as well as on *Curse of the Mummy's Tomb* and their 1965 version of *She*) was a mysterious individual by the name of Andrew Low. He's usually described as "the Egyptologist Andrew Low," but good luck finding reference to him anywhere other than books on horror films. You certainly won't find him in *Who Was Who In Egyptology?*, the reference source where, according to the British Museum, all Egyptologists go when they die. (In fact the British Museum hadn't heard of him *or* Tom Terriss.) So he appears to have been an expert of the self-appointed sort, and according to the memories of those who worked with him, an extremely characterful one, much given to scrutinizing the scripts and set dressings and then objecting to small details of them.

The big question, therefore, is how he came to Hammer's attention in the first place, but what is not in doubt is the fun and games he caused once he had. Wayne Kinsey in his book *Hammer Films: The Bray Studios Years* amusingly quotes Margaret Robinson, wife of Hammer's art director Bernard Robinson:

> A lot of things were sent away because Andrew was very angry.... Andrew said, "These will have to go back, Bernie, they've got the noses wrong. Those are Hittite, not Egyptian!" Bernard naturally didn't send them back, because who was going to notice—in a funeral procession with a sacred cow, a leopard and a lot of very nubile dancing girls—a Hittite nose on a small vase? Andrew Low was that sort of perfectionist. He was the advisory expert on Egyptology and he wanted everything to be exactly right.

The Hammer sequels, like Universal's, are essentially variations on the theme, but they differ in one important respect which is that they are not, technically speaking, sequels at all. Each is a self-contained narrative, with entirely different characters and—crucially—a different mummy every time. And in fact, *Curse of the Mummy's Tomb* (1964), though a somewhat sluggish whole, boasts a far more intriguing plotline than its predecessor. The Ancient backstory is not the usual one of the sealing of the tomb that will then be opened in the film proper, but rather a mythical story (inspired by Osiris and Set) of two brothers, one of whom murders the other. It is the dead brother who becomes the film's (rather well-designed) murdering mummy, but in a twist few will see coming, Terence Morgan's suspiciously solicitous expert Adam Beauchamp is revealed not merely to be the villain we presumed but also the murdering brother, cursed to wander the earth in eternal life for his crime.

Jeanne Roland on the receiving end of the *Curse of the Mummy's Tomb* (1964).

Curse has the same flashback issues as its predecessor: unconvincing, overlit and theatrical, with the atmosphere of déjà vu compounded by its liberal reuse of the same props—and even music score—as the first film. The pacing works against it too: individual scenes are interesting and well done, but it meanders fatally, and over fifty minutes are gone before the Mummy appears as an ambulatory threat. Again, it pulls itself together for a lively climax, with both mummy and villain crushed under falling masonry in the London sewers.²

The Mummy's Shroud (1967) is set in 1920, so we're edging pretty close to the age of Tutmania this time. It also incorporates something of the spiritualist element informing the Tutankhamen curse myth, with Maggie Kimberly as a member of the expedition able

Prem the mummy (Eddie Powell) abducts Maggie Kimberly in a nonexistent shot from *The Mummy's Shroud* (1967) designed purely to get the punters in their seats.

to foresee the future, and the desperate peril that is about to engulf them. (Every expedition should have one.) Audiences lured to the film by the promotional stills of her in her underwear as the mummy looms over her went home disappointed, however.

Though in essence the mixture as before, it somewhat improves on its predecessors in terms of its pace and vigor: the Ancient backstory, though no more convincingly mounted, is at least dealt with briskly before the opening credits, and devilish thought has gone into spicing up the death scenes, which are ingeniously devised and rousingly staged by director John Gilling. The Egyptian exteriors may be all too clearly British but at least they *are* exteriors, and the climax (in which the mummy, chasing after the hero and heroine with an axe, stops and literally tears itself to pieces when Maggie reads aloud an incantation from an ancient scroll) is, as usual, stirringly realized.

To say that Hammer's inspiration came solely from earlier cultural models does not, of course, mean that in their construction they are not alert to wider issues, or do not reflect the tensions and preoccupations of their own times. Indeed, it would be bizarre if they did not. In that respect the most interesting scene in the first film is one that comes late in the movie, where Cushing's archaeologist visits the home of George Pastell's murderous high priest in the hope of making him show his true colors. Instead, he credibly asserts his right to an alternative belief system, with all its attendant codes and consequences:

> You have scratched only the surface, and you know nothing. You assume the right to disturb the everlasting peace of the gods. You pry and meddle, with unclean hands and eyes. Profanity, blasphemy, religious desecration—all of these, you are guilty of. But the powers with which you have meddled do not rest easy. I *think* you will not go unpunished.

It may feel like padding, in a film far from short of that commodity, but to contemporary audiences it may well have had a definitive if somewhat subliminal resonance. Relations between Britain and Egypt had changed greatly since the days of Carter and the Protectorate. The Nasser-led revolution of 1952 had ended the rule of King Faruq and with it went all guarantee of British influence over the region following the installation of President Muhammad Naguib. That the new nationalism would embrace Egypt's past as surely as its present was shown by the immediate passing of "Law No. 215," which set down a strict body of rules and regulations regarding access to and rights regarding the nation's antiquities:

1. Antiquities are defined as all movable and immovable objects, which are produced by the arts, sciences, literatures, customs, religions, etc. from prehistoric times to the reign of Ismail. Also included are any movable or immovable objects produced by foreign civilizations that were at one time related to Egypt (i.e., Greek, Ptolemaic, Roman, Libyan, Persian, etc.) that are found within Egypt's borders. Any movable or immovable object declared to be an antiquity.
2. All antiquities, either known or concealed, ultimately belong to the State, and are required to be registered on an official inventory. Modification, displacement or demolition of classified antiquities is prohibited. The State maintains the right to expropriate any antiquity, or land containing antiquities. Discovery of antiquities should be reported immediately to the nearest administrative official; the State may acquire any such antiquity for national collections, and the displaying of such antiquity.
3. A permit is legally required for all field research, the conditions of which are set at the time of granting of the permit. All foreign nationals are required to submit a security declaration form to the Ministry of Culture Security Office, via the SCA.
4. Exportation of cultural property (including environmental and biological samples) is strictly prohibited without a permit, which must be obtained 30 days prior to the intended date of

export. Movement of antiquities within the country must be approved 15 days prior to their transportation.
5. Dealers in antiquities must be licensed, and must maintain a daily register of transactions. Antiquities offered for sale must be authorised by the museums in advance.
6. The Supreme Council of Antiquities under the auspice of the Ministry of Culture, are responsible for the restoration and preservation of Egypt's cultural heritage.

With Nasser becoming the second President in 1956, new laws permitted the first national touring shows of selected treasures, and the first tour of Tutankhamen artefacts drew capacity crowds around the world in 1961–63. A further gain to Egypt was the fact that such tours reinforced the understanding that these treasures would now be available outside their home nation only briefly and occasionally. This established Egypt as a leading tourist destination, and the country has relied on tourism to support its economy ever since.

The source of the British Protectorate had been the Suez Canal, built in partnership with France in the 1860s. To offset the massive debt to European banks incurred in its construction, Egypt sold its share to Britain in 1875. The Canal was therefore, in that sense, the fragile guarantor of Britain's legal right to influence in the region, and without it the story of Tutankhamen and the twentieth century would have been very different (if, indeed, there would have been any kind of story at all).

In 1956, the Canal once again became news. On July 26, Nasser gave a speech railing against imperialism before a massive and enthusiastic crowd. As part of his speech he spoke at length on the subject of the Canal, and went on to describe its construction a hundred years before in seemingly unnecessary detail. Bizarrely, it appeared, he contrived to mention the name of Ferdinand de Lesseps, the French engineer who had constructed the canal, over a dozen times. In fact, "de Lesseps" was a coded signal, instructing his army to begin the seizure and nationalization of the Canal. The Suez Crisis had begun. Within a few months, British Prime Minister Anthony Eden would be forced to resign as the result of a botched attempt to regain control that decisively ended a century of British and French paternalism, and added an anti-climactic full stop to the British Empire entire.

For many viewers, then, this would have been the unspoken context behind Cushing's encounter with Pastell which, set in 1898 or not, bristles with a very contemporary unease and resentment. Pastell is a very different kind of Egyptian villain from the wild-eyed savages and secret cabal of necromancers that typified Universal's fairy-tale saga. He is a modern man, unmistakably so for all his capitulation to the ancient mysteries; articulate, personable, resolute and deadly. Cushing's attempts to goad him are, nominally at least, conducted with the specific aim of assessing the extent of his malevolence, but they play as a much more general enactment of the struggle between a waning colonial perspective and a newly empowered nationalist one. Cushing, limping and immersed in the past, is thus cast in the uneasy contours of Eden, while Pastell, confident and implacable, is Nasser.

It will be remembered that in the original film Karloff's mummy actually leads the British expedition to the tomb of Ankhesenamen for his own benefit, and he only threatens those who stand between him and his entirely personal goal of achieving eternal union with her. (Further, the only person he actually murders is an Egyptian guard in the Cairo Museum.) The wider questions of nationalism versus paternalism are not touched upon at all. Even in the later Universal films, the battle lines are essentially those

George Pastell reads from the scroll as Christopher Lee rises from the swamp in *The Mummy* (1959).

of modern indifference and ancient reverence, only coincidentally assembling themselves on nationalist lines.

Come Suez, this is no longer the case. Though *Pharaoh's Curse* turns up as promptly as 1957, already it's all change. The focus remains on an expedition releasing supernatural horrors from the tomb, but the first set of characters we see are military. The British army, beset by violent "native uprisings" accompanied by mutilation murders, has been tasked with locating and safeguarding an Anglo-American expedition team in the Valley of the Kings. Though the film is set in 1902, the commanding officer explaining the mission makes this new, post–Suez focus more than explicit:

> This (expedition) went out there without Egyptian approval. Just let that mob out there get the idea for one minute we're digging up their ancient kings' graves, tampering with their religious beliefs, their superstitions ... and the fanatics that started this riot would soon spread it into a national situation. All they want is a chance to throw us out and bury British rule.

And so in the Hammer films the specificity of the mummy's revenge starts to feel more like a symbolic gesture on behalf of Egypt itself, the killings not mere murders but rather revolutionary assassinations. *Curse of the Mummy's Tomb* opens with the heroine's father, staked out between two posts, having his hand severed by a gang of Egyptians on horseback, as a warning to the British archaeologists to keep away. Though still set well before Carter's discovery the act of desecration this time is not merely colonial but also commercial, with the violation of the discovery compounded by the decision to roadshow the finds in a crassly sensational public exhibition. This is at the instigation of American showman Alexander King (played for all the character is worth and more by the great Fred Clark), who induces the team to turn down the Cairo Museum's offer of seventy thousand pounds for the contents of the tomb:

> You remember when we opened the tomb? I was standing right beside you. I was as excited as a kid with a double sarsaparilla. You told me we made a great discovery, for the good of all mankind. Well, who is in a better position to do that good—you or me? You'll put it in a stuffy museum in a one-camel town, where nobody will see it except a few tourists on a wet afternoon. I can show it to the world. If people want to be educated, I'll educate them—at ten cents a time!

Unsurprisingly, then, King is the first to meet his end at the hands of the walking mummy, which (until the unexpected twist ending) appears to be acting entirely without instruction. As such, the film creates the impression that the mummy is standing as proxy for his entire violated nation, rather than a particular tomb, or Queen. George Pastell is again cast as surly intermediary between the interests of the British archaeologists and those of Egypt, but this time without villainous intent (he is not connected in any way with the mummy's revival or killing spree), and the Egypt on whose behalf he pleads is as much the contemporary as the ancient one. When the expedition's leader accuses him of deliberately sabotaging their interests in the tomb so as to claim the treasures for Cairo he responds: "How dare you speak such accusations! My government and I have given you every possible co-operation."

In Hammer's first mummy film there is no sense at all of Egyptian government involvement: the team seemed to be operating in a complete wilderness. This idea of the mummy as agent of Arab nationalism continues into *The Mummy's Shroud*. Here the Egyptian authorities are presented as plainly superior to the British expeditionary team. In particular the integrity of the Egyptian police Inspector is contrasted starkly with the expedition's cruel and ignorant financier Sir Basil Waldon, whose presumption of native corruptibility is swiftly rebuffed when he attempts to offer him a bribe. While the entire British team that comprises the Mummy's victims and intended victims in the 1959 film are decent, honorable and upright, the sequels deliberately pepper the list with characters that, if not strictly speaking deserving of their grim fate, nonetheless in some sense have it coming. Inevitably—given the nature of their foe—it is their disrespect for the tombs, the dead, the old religion and the country's right to its own history that is their undoing. These are the very crimes that Pastell accuses Cushing of in the first film: it is as if the sequels are going out of their way to vindicate, if only partially, the argument they had originally set up solely to overrule.

No more could the graves of Egypt be violated and their relics transported around the world with impunity. Now it was an outrage committed not only against the Ancient Egyptians, but the modern ones too. The isolated, subjugated menace of Conan Doyle's lot number 249 had been replaced by a concerted, globalist vengeance on behalf of Egypt's law number 215.

8

In Many Forms, Shall We Return

> In the statement it was plainly set forth that the hatred of the priests was, she knew, stored up for her, and that they would after her death try to suppress her name. This was a terrible revenge, I may tell you, in Egyptian mythology; for without a name no one can after death be introduced to the gods, or have prayers said for him. Therefore, she had intended her resurrection to be after a long time and in a more northern land, under the constellation whose seven stars had ruled her birth.—Bram Stoker, *The Jewel of Seven Stars*

The Jewel of Seven Stars (almost invariably mistitled "Jewel of the Seven Stars" in reference sources, film credits and even reprints of the book itself) opens with the discovery by heroine Margaret Trelawny of her Egyptologist father, wounded and seemingly unconscious in his room, the apparent victim of a violent robbery. It soon transpires that the assault has been a supernatural one, and the wounding is ultimately revealed as the work of a mummified cat, possessed of the spirit of Tera, an Ancient Egyptian queen whose name had for some reason been entirely erased from the dynastic record after her death. Trelawny is engaged in a scheme to resurrect Tera, whose mummy he also has in his collection, and whose spirit is waiting to be reborn in Margaret's body. The novel ends with his attempt to put this plan into action.

As well as a lively entertainment, mixing elements of horror, fantasy and detective story, Bram Stoker's novel makes for one of the most interesting jigsaw puzzles in all Egypt-inspired popular culture, both in terms of its influence elsewhere and of the influences upon which it draws. The latter begin many years before it was published or even embarked upon, at the house of Sir William Wilde, the less-known but vastly more accomplished father of playwright Oscar.[1] A fine example of the Victorian polymath, Wilde was many things, including a pioneering surgeon, and an eclectic acquirer of curiosities, who had travelled to Egypt in 1838 and seen what would become the London Cleopatra Needle while it was still lying half-buried in the sand. The following year he published an article in the *Dublin University Magazine* urging the government to transport it to London. (He died in 1876, and so never saw his hopes fulfilled.)

Stoker made Wilde's acquaintance in the early 1870s, when he was theater critic of the *Dublin Evening Mail*. The Wildes would hold literary soirees at their home in Merrion Square, and Stoker was an enthusiastic attendee. Wilde, an expert on folklore as well as archaeology, would sometimes give accounts of the strange myths and legends of Egypt, and show off his collection, which included a number of embalmed ibises and a mummy that he had found outside a tomb at Saqqara. He claimed to have spent the night in a tomb, and been kept awake by ethereal whispers. Enraptured, Stoker made a mental note to build a story based on the idea of an Egyptologist haunted by the relics he had brought back to England with him. It would be some time before he got around to it, however—in between came *Dracula*—and *The Jewel of Seven Stars* did not in fact appear until 1903.

Though the novel predates Carter's great find, there is the possibility it may have family connections with one of his earlier ones. The same year the book appeared, Carter had discovered a tomb in the Valley of the Kings that contained two female mummies and an unoccupied sarcophagus. The tomb had been built, for her own use, by Hatshepsut, an Eighteenth Dynasty pharaoh and the first woman to exercise long-term rule over Egypt as a full-blown king, rather than as interim ruler or regent.[2] Though it has been asserted that one of the mummies Carter found was indeed Hatshepsut's,[3] there are also good reasons for thinking that it is not and that, for some reason, she never used the tomb.[4] But the really important link between Hatshepsut and Stoker's fictional Tera is that deliberate efforts had likewise been made, some time after the former's death, to remove her identity and even her existence.

Jean-François Champollion, the decipherer of hieroglyphs, had noted in the nineteenth century a curiosity regarding the texts in the Deir el-Bahri temple: "If I felt somewhat surprised at seeing here, as elsewhere throughout the temple, the renowned Moeris adorned with all the insignia of royalty, giving place to this Amenenthe, for whose name we may search the royal lists in vain, still more astonished was I to find upon reading the inscriptions that wherever they referred to this bearded king in the usual dress of the Pharaohs, nouns and verbs were in the feminine, as though a queen were in question."[5] Clearly, there was courtly intrigue to be uncovered here, but of what sort?

The facts were that Hatshepsut had come to the throne around 1478 BC, and had co-ruled with her nephew Thutmose III. She pre-deceased him in 1458 BC, and at some point towards the end of his reign a concerted and often elaborate effort was made to erase her name and history from the dynastic records. Like the puritan iconoclasts of England, a

Bram Stoker takes a well-earned break from writing spooky books.

sinister band of bashers and defacers toured the temples and monuments, chiseling away her name, cutting out her image, and altering pronouns to melt away her status as a female ruler. Statues were removed and destroyed, scattered, buried, or hidden within larger structures.

The vandalism worked: Manetho spoke only vaguely of a female king called Amensis, now presumed to have been Hatshepsut. The mystery greatly excited Egyptologists, whose competing theories were often pugilistically advanced. It was first presumed that the defacements were vengeful, and suggestive of violent animosity on the part of Thutmose. Later theorists, noting that a gap of two decades separate Hatshepsut's death and the beginning of the removals, usually favor a more pragmatic and constitutional explanation: that rather than proof of a personal vendetta (which all evidence seems to point away from having existed) it was simply a matter of tidying up the record, restoring the notion of male supremacy and thus helping prevent such anomalous circumstances re-occurring. On the other hand (or possibly even a third one) John Romer makes the following intriguing observation in *Romer's Egypt*:

> Although the figures of Hatshepsut had been carefully hacked from the walls of mortuary temple at Deir el Bahari, the other figures in the scenes, such as the attendant gods, were not attacked. In many instances the mutilation was made precisely along the outlines of Hatshepsut's figures without any effort being made to disguise the fact that her figure had originally been carved on the wall. The figures, then, have been publicly erased but they still exist as negative scratched out images, and so we may still read the queen's mutilated texts and see her chiselled-out figure on the temple walls. The erasures are, therefore, of a magical nature: the physical removal of an image that held the presence of a person and *not* an attempt to erase Hatshepsut's political presence or to change history.

Given that defacement of the images of the dead was no trivial matter—rather it could actually impede the spirit in its afterlife—it was inevitable at first to presume that there was some great scandal or mystery to be unearthed here. Stoker, who may have heard of the story during his visits to William Wilde, would surely have had his imagination excited by such speculation. And indeed, the similarities between this Victorian conception of Hatshepsut and Stoker's Tera seem too overt to be unintended:

> Then they told me that a great sorcerer in ancient days—"millions of millions of years" was the term they used—a king or a queen, they could not say which, was buried there. They could not give the name, persisting to the last that there was no name; and that anyone who should name it would waste away in life so that at death nothing of him would remain to be raised again in another world.

Even Manetho's uncertainty is evoked:

> See how the priests of her time, and those after it, tried to wipe out her name from the face of the earth, and put a curse over the very door of her tomb so that none might ever discover the lost name. Ay, and they succeeded so well that even Manetho, the historian of the Egyptian kings, writing in the tenth century before Christ, with all the lore of the priesthood for forty centuries behind him, and with possibility of access to every existing record, could not even find her name.

Stoker also makes reference to Flinders Petrie and Wallis Budge, and has Tera, like Hatshepsut, construct a tomb for herself in the side of a cliff-face. And given his usual fastidious research into history, myth and custom, it comes as no surprise to find the mummy's severed hand among Stoker's relics:

> Within, on a cushion of cloth of gold as fine as silk, and with the peculiar softness of old gold, rested a mummy hand, so perfect that it startled one to see it. A woman's hand, fine and long, with

slim tapering fingers and nearly as perfect as when it was given to the embalmer thousands of years before.

In the embalming it had lost nothing of its beautiful shape; even the wrist seemed to maintain its pliability as the gentle curve lay on the cushion. The skin was of a rich creamy or old ivory colour; a dusky fair skin which suggested heat, but heat in shadow. The great peculiarity of it, as a hand, was that it had in all seven fingers, there being two middle and two index fingers. The upper end of the wrist was jagged, as though it had been broken off, and was stained with a red-brown stain.

We have already noted in an earlier chapter the preponderance of mummy's hands in Egypt-inspired popular culture; it should also be noted that the hand was of symbolic importance to the Egyptians themselves. In a curious incestuous creation myth, Egypt's prototype God Atum procreated with his own hand in order to be born himself and thus begin the creation of subsequent Egyptian Gods. (Kara Cooney notes that the Egyptian word for hand, djeret, is feminine, thus Atum might be said to have made union with the feminine part of his body.) That the hand retained symbolic importance as a seat of generative power may likewise be indicated by the Egyptian tendency to sever the hands of their dead enemies and retain them as trophies. (As an incentive scheme during the reigns of Ahmose I and Amenhotep I, warriors would receive gold in exchange for the hands they accumulated, "which they sometimes gruesomely displayed in strings around their necks," again according to Cooney.)

And if all of this is taking you back to our old friend Cheiro and his prophesying mummy's hand—well, perhaps it should. Of his believability we were already decided: I think it's fair to speculate now as to some of his preferred reading matter, too. Here, after all, is the man himself documenting his own experience in 1924:

The next day I felt the hand, and the flesh had begun to be quite soft, as in life. Three weeks after that, one morning, to my wonderment, I saw little red drops along the knuckles. I touched them, and they made red smears. That was in 1920. In May, 1921, the hand appeared red; in August, 1922, the hand was again soft, and the blood was showing. I feared that nobody would believe it, so I obtained sworn depositions, taken before a notary, of an engineer and a chemist who both saw the hand in this condition.[6]

While it seems fairly obvious that Cheiro, at least, had Stoker's novel on his bedside table, gauging the extent of the work's influence in a more general sense is not easy. It's a novel that not many people seem to have read, or even heard of (obscure indeed in comparison with *Dracula*), and yet it has been adapted for the screen no fewer than four times—as three movies: Hammer's *Blood from the Mummy's Tomb* in 1972, the big-budget Charlton Heston movie *The Awakening* in 1980 and *Bram Stoker's Legend of the Mummy* in 1997,[7] plus *Curse of the Mummy*, a highly regarded British TV adaptation in 1970.[8]

But just as importantly, it brings something new and hugely influential to the kit bag of motifs from which the later Egypt-inspired popular culture draws. This is the concept of reincarnation, wherein the spirits or souls of the Egyptian dead enter the bodies of others and take possession of them. The idea of the free transmutation of souls has no natural home amidst the complicated relations between undying spirit and mortal vessel in Egyptian funerary myth (where the original body, preserved through mummification, retains its function as repository of the deathless subject). Again, like the vengeful mummy itself, arrested in some transitory point between death and rebirth, the idea is a modern convenience: one of the means by which the past and the present interrelate in mummy fiction.

In the movies, the theme took root early. Francis X. Bushman played an Egyptologist who realizes he loved an Egyptian princess in a past life in *When Soul Meets Soul* (1913), while Olga Petrova gets a second chance at love with her shepherd boyfriend in *The Undying Flame* (1917). Its defining formulation is of course to be found in the 1932 version of *The Mummy*, where Karloff's undead courtier revives to find his beloved queen enjoying the latest of several earthly reincarnations among the Western infidels of Jazz Age Cairo. (An elaborate flashback sequence, shot but deleted from the release print, would have shown the various women of history through which her soul had passed.) This is all very different from *The Ring of Thoth*, the Conan Doyle story that inspired it, where (it will be remembered) the "mummy" is not revived but rather has never died (via a process which he stresses is not supernatural), and his ancient love is very much dead and un-reincarnated, remaining so throughout. (His only wish is to join her in death.)

So where the story remains true to the spirit of the real ancient beliefs, the movie completely reinvents them. But it set in stone the convention that the Mummy, as well as vengefully guarding tombs and killing interlopers, should also be mooning over some lost love who, frequently, he encounters in some modern guise, reincarnated, and tormented by half-memories of her earlier self. Kharis, the later Universal mummy, is essentially motivated by his devotion to the Princess Ananka, who by the time of 1944's *The Mummy's Ghost* is found to have been reincarnated in wartime America. (Oddly, when Hammer adapted strands from various of the Kharis movies into their 1959 version of *The Mummy* they retained only half of the idea: though Yvonne Furneaux's heroine is so exact a lookalike of Ananka that she is able to convince Kharis to obey her command, the resemblance is never presumed to be anything more than an extraordinary coincidence.)

Stoker's use of the cat as vessel for the transition of spirits also seems to have bled into the common store. In the independent production *Pharaoh's Curse* (1957) the malign spirit of an Ancient Egyptian priest enters and possesses the body of a modern Egyptian, whose sister is revealed independently to be the reincarnation of the Egyptian cat goddess Bastet. The same twist concludes a lively TV movie, *The Cat Creature* (1972), from the pen of Robert Bloch.

Several writers have noted that John Balderston may have introduced reincarnation into the Karloff script as a carry-over from H. Rider Haggard's novel *She*, a screenplay of which he was working on at the same time as he was writing *The Mummy*. But a reading of *The Jewel of Seven Stars* will show that not only was this a notion that had been pre-empted by Stoker, he had even gone so far as to *anticipate the incompatibility* of the idea with its source, and dealt with it via the reconciliation of Buddhist and Egyptian dogma:

> "Her 'astral body'? What is that, Father? What does that mean?" There was a keenness in Margaret's voice as she asked the question which surprised me a little; but Trelawny smiled a sort of indulgent parental smile, which came through his grim solemnity like sunshine through a rifted cloud, as he spoke: "The astral body, which is a part of Buddhist belief, long subsequent to the time I speak of, and which is an accepted fact of modern mysticism, had its rise in Ancient Egypt; at least, so far as we know. It is that the gifted individual can at will, quick as thought itself, transfer his body whithersoever he chooses, by the dissolution and reincarnation of particles. In the ancient belief there were several parts of a human being. You may as well know them; so that you will understand matters relative to them or dependent on them as they occur.
>
> "First there is the 'Ka,' or 'Double,' which, as Doctor Budge explains, may be defined as 'an abstract individuality of personality' which was imbued with all the characteristic attributes of the individual it represented, and possessed an absolutely independent existence. It was free to move from place to place on earth at will; and it could enter into heaven and hold converse with the gods.

Then there was the 'Ba,' or 'soul,' which dwelt in the 'Ka,' and had the power of becoming corporeal or incorporeal at will; 'it had both substance and form.... It had power to leave the tomb.... It could revisit the body in the tomb ... and could reincarnate it and hold converse with it.' Again there was the 'Khu,' the 'spiritual intelligence,' or spirit. It took the form of 'a shining, luminous, intangible shape of the body.'... Then, again, there was the 'Sekhem,' or 'power' of a man, his strength or vital force personified. These were the 'Khaibit,' or 'shadow,' the 'Ren,' or 'name,' the 'Khat,' or 'physical body,' and 'Ab,' the 'heart,' in which life was seated, went to the full making up of a man.

"Thus you will see, that if this division of functions, spiritual and bodily, ethereal and corporeal, ideal and actual, be accepted as exact, there are all the possibilities and capabilities of corporeal transference, guided always by an unimprisonable will or intelligence."

Yvonne Furneaux as Ananka in *The Mummy* (1959).

Another coincidence: there is a real life story that also seems to parallel aspects of Stoker's tale of Margaret and Tera, which began just a few years after the novel first appeared.[9] In 1907, a three-year-old girl named Dorothy Eady was pronounced dead after a fall down the stairs at her family home in London. Confounding all, however, she revived, and within an hour was behaving as though nothing had happened. But as the days and weeks drew on it became apparent that something had: she would wake in an agitated state from vivid dreams of strange buildings in strange lands, tearfully imploring her parents to allow her to "go home." Where "home" might be was revealed a year later, when on a visit to the British museum she rushed to embrace the Egyptian statues, kissed their feet, and proclaimed them her long-lost kin. (E. A. Wallis Budge, the author of *Egyptian Magic* mentioned by name in the passage from Stoker quoted above, was so impressed by her fervor he volunteered to teach her how to read hieroglyphs.) At age seven she saw a photo of the Seti I temple at Abydos and said, "That is where I used to live."

From then on, Dorothy's course was set. In her twenties she married an Egyptian, moved to Cairo, had a son whom she called Seti, and changed her own name to Omm Seti ("mother of Seti"). Eventually, she said, Seti made himself apparent to her in dreams and visions, and confirmed her suspicions that she had lived in Egypt three thousand years earlier. Seti had been a good man with whom she fell in love: after becoming pregnant she had chosen to take her own life rather than embroil him in scandal. Consumed with guilt about what had happened, Seti's spirit assured her that this time round he would not allow her to leave him. This was unsurprisingly one revelation too many for Dorothy's husband who, feeling himself unable to compete for her affections with a dead and lovesick Pharaoh, promptly left her and gained custody of their son. However unstable she may have already been, this was clearly a major turning point for Eady, who now found herself without any ties to her real homeland or to the age in which she really lived: accordingly, "Omm Seti" melted entirely into the ancient past. After the liberation of the Suez Canal in 1956, the Egyptian Antiquities Organisation recognized her years of devotion to the past by giving her managerial responsibility of the Seti temple at Abydos—the "home" she had seen and dedicated her life to returning to after her near-fatal accident at the age of three. Here she remained until her death in 1981, communing with the spirits and—the story goes—using her privileged access to their counsel to locate a long-lost garden in which she remembered playing as a girl in her first life.

Fascinating film footage of Dorothy Eady can be found in the National Geographic film *Egypt: Quest for Eternity* (1982). (This documentary also includes some great film of the Abu Simbel temple being dismantled and re-assembled following the creation of the Aswan dam.) It's strange indeed to see Eady in the flesh after reading her story, because she seems so disconcertingly normal. Shown celebrating her 77th birthday, translating hieroglyphs and describing the offerings she still brings to the temple on ceremonial occasions, her 1920s English accent intact, she is amusing, likeable and impressive. The documentary does not mention her reincarnation claims, and it is difficult to square the woman we see in the film with the one described above. The program tells us that she died three days after recording her scenes, and was buried at Abydos.

Directed by Seth Holt from a script by Christopher Wicking, *Blood from the Mummy's Tomb* updates Stoker's story to the 1970s, and beautifully restages it as a complex, interweaved narrative content only to half-explain its premises and development. (It may be the last truly great Hammer horror film, as well as surely the best by a mile of their mummy films.) Its complicated structure alternates between dream and reality, the perspectives of the sane and the insane, and the vantage points of three linked time streams: the present, the discovery of the tomb twenty years prior, and the ancient past. The ancient flashbacks, in stark contrast to the overlit, studio-and-sandpit efforts of Hammer's earlier movies, are shot eerily and effectively at night. Holt achieves a texture unseen in mummy cinema since Karloff, and the film's visual style is at all times striking. Many scenes have a poetic, dreamlike power rare in Hammer, or for that matter in British cinema generally. The film's star, Valerie Leon (usually eye candy in British comedies but here very effective, in her only lead, as both Margaret and Tera), singles out in particular a "wonderful, moody scene when I am walking into the cellar as Margaret, with my hair blowing, till I come to Tera's coffin and gaze upon my own image,"[10] and the leisurely, wordless sequence is indeed a tour de force, making otherworldly use of lighting, angles and slow motion. In the close-ups as Leon descends the stairs, a handheld camera gazes up at her face from under her chin: a distinctly unflattering prospect for most of us but not, as it turned out, for Leon, as camera operator Neil Binney recalled: "Normally for a perfect close-up you try to keep the camera at eye level or a bit higher, but I remember you could photograph her from any angle, looking right up her nose, and she would still be absolutely beautiful."[11]

As already noted, Holt dropped dead before completion of the film, the last of a short series of tragedies that would acquire the film a reputation as cursed. This was of course only suggested later: obviously its cast and crew did not literally think themselves risking their lives by participating. But the film's potent atmosphere was still palpable on set, according to Leon:

> It's only in retrospect one says it was jinxed, but to do a day's filming and then have Peter Cushing leave the film due to his wife's illness was a bitter blow, and then a week before completion of the movie to have the director die was quite terrible. Looking back, I guess it was all quite eerie. Also full of atmosphere. I really don't like horror films, or mummy films, and I hated it when I was lying in the sarcophagus and the lid was put on. It was really spooky lying in the dark before the lid was lifted.

Some commentators have detected an incestuous tinge to the relationship between Margaret and her father, oddly renamed Julian Fuchs, in the film. It's possible this may have been a deliberate interpolation from Wicking, who must have noted the regularity with which incestuous union features not only in Egypt's dynastic chronology but also in their deistic and creation myths. Having said that, there is nothing overt in the dialogue or narrative construction, so it might just as easily been something that Andrew Keir (hurriedly brought in to play Fuchs after Cushing's withdrawal) brought to the role. The other possibility, that it was an element Seth Holt was keen to tease from the margins of the script, can sadly no longer be tested, though it would be extremely interesting for this reason (as well as the obvious hundred others) to see the raw footage of Cushing in the scene where Fuchs first gives Tera the sacred ring, that being the only work he completed before leaving the film. (Though there are definite hints of this dynamic in Stoker—Trelawny's obsession with Tera transcends all other bonds and boundaries—it is developed still further in *The Awakening*, in which the Trelawny/Fuchs character—here played by Charlton Heston and for some reason now called Corbeck, the name of a secondary character in Stoker and the earlier film—receives a passionate kiss from his possessed daughter.)

Wicking draws on Stoker, Hatshepsut and a century of Egyptomania in popular culture

Margaret meets Tera: Valerie Leon in a memorable scene from *Blood from the Mummy's Tomb* (1972).

to produce a screenplay that abounds with references and allusions. He has the archaeologists discover the following message in Tera's tomb: "She who is buried here shall henceforth have no name, shall cease to exist in the minds of man as she has ceased to exist in life." The flashbacks to Tera's history are presented as Margaret's nightmares, suggesting that Tera is contacting her in her dream state, a notion that carries a distinct echo of Dorothy Eady. A sequence in which the member of the expedition who has retained the tomb's Bastet statue is symbolically clawed, as if by a cat, recalls both the wounding of Trelawny in the original novel and one of the essays in Weigall's 1923 book on Tutankhamen, in which he suggests he too had been clawed by a mummified cat that burst from its bandages and fled. A hint too, perhaps, of the temple of Pakhet, built by Hatshepsut, in which mummified cats, some brought considerable distances, were found in vast numbers.

Wicking, a keenly (indeed sometimes excessively) literate and reflective screenwriter, would have been alert to all these resonances. Though he gives Tera only the customary quota of digits, he makes far greater play with the hand than does Stoker, in deference, presumably, to its ubiquity in many other variations on the theme. The film's hand is *alive*: first seen being grimly hacked from Tera's wrist and thrown to jackals, it becomes the symbolic agent of her revenge, crawling self-articulated from the tomb, and later, squirming in its box. (The severing of Tera's hand serves as the ultimate demonstration that her power has been taken from her. Physically incomplete, she is denied relevance both in this world and the next.)

The curse's victims in the film all die bloodily with their throats torn. No clear explanation is given, though the idea derives from the wounding of Trelawny which is ultimately attributed to the cat familiar. Here, however, the mutilation is presumably the symbolic work of the hand; a gorier variation on this passage from Stoker:

> He had evidently been strangled for on looking, I found on his throat the red marks where fingers had been pressed. There seemed so many of these marks that I counted them. There were seven; and all parallel, except the thumb mark, as though made with one hand. This thrilled me, as I thought of the mummy hand with the seven fingers.

In general, the film boasts an attention to detail and authenticity that is the more impressive for being unobtrusive, even if it did not quite extend to the supposedly ancient phrases mumbled by Margaret as she tosses and turns in bed. Leon recalls: "I do remember Seth asking me to mutter some Egyptian words when I was tossing and turning in bed and I said, 'How can I? I don't know any!' And he said, 'Just say 'knickers'! So I did, and this became 'knick-*airs*, knick-*airs*...'!"[12]

9

An Egyptian Feast

> The tomb of an Egyptian queen who lived 2,000 years before King Tutankhamen provided evidence today that 23 young servants had been sacrificed and buried with the queen to care for her in the land of the dead. Walter B. Emery, English archaeologist who made the discovery recently for the Egyptian antiquities department at Sakkara, overlooking the Nile, believes the servants were poisoned.—*Chicago Tribune*, December 30, 1946

Blood, above all else, is the defining visual element of the second cycle of classic horror films, inaugurated by Hammer's *Curse of Frankenstein* in 1957. This more explicitly violent turn that horror cinema took in the second half of the twentieth century inevitably presented the mummy sub-genre with a set of challenges that asked significant questions about historical and cultural license.

The Hammer films, though far from extreme in any modern sense, made a selling point of their willingness to show gruesome imagery in general and blood in particular. Their first film seized the opportunity to make a set-piece of the tongue-pulling that had been only alluded to in the Universal canon, and to include a scene in which, as part of the funeral ceremony of the Princess Ananka, a row of handmaidens are ritually beheaded.[1] For the sequels, more invention was called for. George Pastell, who only had his spine snapped in the first film, gets his head crushed underfoot in *Curse of the Mummy's Tomb*. In *The Mummy's Shroud* one victim has his skull pulped between the mummy's superhuman hands; another is pushed to the floor and drenched with acid; still another is flung from an upper story window and lands in an ornamental pond into which he bleeds picturesquely; in the finale the mummy comes after the hero and heroine swinging an axe. In *Blood from the Mummy's Tomb* an ancient curse manifests itself in the present day by ripping open the throats of its victims.

The head crushings in particular seemed to catch on, and are much in evidence in *Vengeance of the Mummy* (1973), the inevitable contribution to the subgenre by barrel-chested Paul Naschy, the imposing but somewhat comical auteur of scores of Spanish horror movies. In addition, the film begins (in a fairly bargain basement ancient prologue) with Amenhotep (it doesn't specify which one) presiding over a series of torture killings staged for his jaded amusement, like the Sadean decadents of Pasolini's *Salo*.

But even such excesses as are to be found in *Dawn of the Mummy* (1981), an eccentric marriage of the standard mummy narrative and the aesthetics and priorities of Lucio Fulci's *Zombie Flesh Eaters*, play as light relief compared to *Blood Feast* (1963). Released in the same year as the Elizabeth Taylor version of *Cleopatra*, and made for a total bill less than the cost of Taylor's mid-morning martinis, it's a film that shouldn't by rights detain us for a second. But generation upon subsequent generation of film fans all seem to reach the same conclusion: that there's something truly compelling about it, despite what appear to be deliberate efforts to be as inept and uninvolving as it possibly can.

Herschell Gordon Lewis, its director and (uncredited) writer, was a former literature teacher, and an extremely sophisticated and erudite individual who, as a filmmaker, took perverse delight in discovering just how low the lowest common denominator of the American cinemagoing audience would be happy to stoop. His motives were largely mercenary—as a low-to-no budget independent filmmaker he needed to find the kind of formulae that the drive-in and grindhouse audiences would most instinctively respond to. But the genuine glee he took in it all, happily confessed to in the interviews that accompanied his elevation in the 1980s to the status of cult auteur, is obvious in his work.

The film's title sequence shows a photograph of the Sphinx, over which the words "Blood Feast" are formed by the patterns of spurting blood. This is in acknowledgment of the film's inspiration: a garish fiber glass sphinx that had been erected in the grounds of Miami's Suez Motel, of which Lewis and his location crews had long been habitués when shooting on location, owing mainly to the inexpensiveness of the rooms. Having hit on the idea of gore cinema with his business partner, producer David F. Friedman (the market for "nudie-cuties" having been judged on the wane), Lewis was then left with the need to invent some kind of scenario to encompass the set-piece scenes of murder, mutilation and dismemberment he had in mind for his new epic. And there, right before him, was the motel sphinx. "The sphinx and I exchanged a meaningful glance," Lewis told a 1986 TV documentary, "and *Blood Feast* was born."

Blood Feast, plainly, is not a film to be taken seriously. The plot makes no sense of any sort, characters behave in ridiculous ways, and it has often been noted that the acting is,

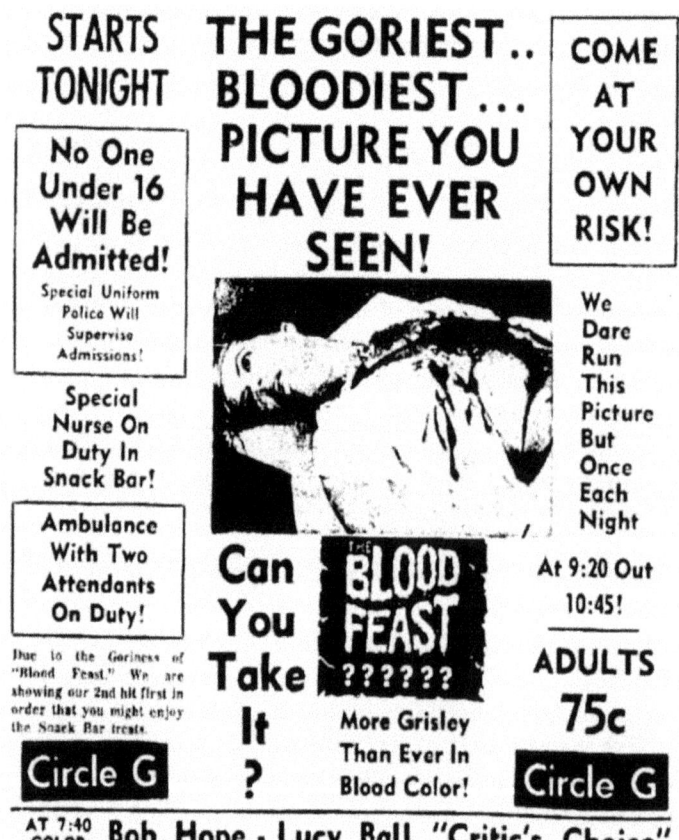

Blood Feast (1963) set new standards in tastelessness but was not without a sense of humor.

strangely, of a standard somewhat lower than one would expect if the players had simply been chosen at random from amongst the general population. Its sole *raison d'etre*—a half dozen scenes of graphic murder presented with little realism but more blood and offal than any film before and the majority since—was deemed (and proved) so potent a lure that verisimilitude or professionalism on any level were an unnecessary waste of the production's time and expenditure.

The plot, basically, is as follows. The police are investigating a series of savage mutilation murders, in which parts of the bodies are taken away. (After one unfortunate woman's legs are cut off, we see a newspaper with the headline: LEGS CUT OFF!) The crimes are shown to be the work of one Fuad Ramses, a deranged Egyptian caterer with an exaggerated limp and painted grey eyebrows that come and go from scene to scene. Ramses is preparing a cannibalistic "blood feast'—"an authentic dinner such as might have been served in Ancient Egypt"—either as an offering to the goddess Ishtar or, possibly—he seems not entirely certain himself—as part of an occult ceremony to "revive" her (as if goddesses need reviving). The statue to which he offers his incantations and pledges is a department store mannequin sprayed gold. Ramses has two side-lines: he runs an exotic delicatessen, the shelves of which are stacked high with massive quantities of cute-looking boxed and canned items, and he is the author of a book entitled "Ancient Weird Religious Rites" (for which he occasionally takes telephone orders at the deli, and from whose purchasers he ungratefully selects his victims). When not selling boxes of crackers he is usually to be found torturing and cooking girls in the kitchen-cum-shrine room cunningly concealed behind a curtain to the right of the cash desk.

A jaunty society matron enters to ask if he is willing to make a special dinner for her daughter Suzette's 21st birthday. The perverse delight he seems to take in choosing his subjects from among the ranks of those most likely to send the police straight to him continues as Lewis cuts to a massive close-up of his eyes and he intones the film's most quoted line of dialogue: "Have you ever had … *an Egyptian feast?*" Mrs. Freemont could not be more delighted at the idea: "My daughter Suzette is a student of Egyptian culture!" Sight unseen, Suzette (*Playboy* playmate Connie Mason) is then added to his prospective list of ingredients, and in classic Ramses style he decides to slaughter her at a public event for which he has been contracted by name to do the catering. He does succeed in getting her alone in the kitchen, where she obligingly lies on the table and closes her eyes, but when she opens them again and screams as he raises his knife—exactly as all his other victims did—he inexplicably panics and flees. The police show up and chase him across open ground, but he manages to easily outpace them, despite the limp, which migrates from one leg to the other and back again. He then accidentally falls into the back of a garbage truck and dies. The End.

The film was a sensational success with audiences and, if your stomach is strong enough and your sense of the bizarre tuned to its approximate wavelength, you may well find that there is something about the film that, for all its amateurishness and absurdity, keeps you gripped from first frame to last. Lewis's films have something very definite going for them though, God knows, it's hard to put your finger on precisely what, and you may end up feeling guilty for having enjoyed them so much.

It is unlikely that Lewis drew influence from any channel. That the film's most famous scene should be a tongue-pulling feels like a riff on Tom Tyler's fate in *The Mummy's Hand* or Christopher Lee's in *The Mummy*, and the killer's ridiculous gammy leg could almost be a sly nod to Kharis himself. These echoes, however, are more likely strictly coincidental. Entertain no hope, therefore, that any degree of research or even thought has gone into the Egyptological underpinnings of the idea: the fact that the goddess is called Ishtar should be all the tip-off we need in that regard.

The key non-gore scene in the movie is a lecture supposedly given by a respected Egyptologist (in reality an old friend of the producer's called Ray Golden who, Lewis recalled, had to shoot his scene thirty-six times before he stopped saying "indentify" instead of "identify"). Here is his explanation of the cult of Ishtar:

> Rameses the First and Rameses the Second were pharaohs. It was Rameses the Second whose soldiers were drowned in the Red Sea while chasing Moses and the Israelites. Now, our mutual interest in the cults of Ancient Egypt takes us tonight to the cult of Ishtar, a goddess who was worshipped by the early Egyptian and Assyrian peoples more than five thousand years ago. The worship of Ishtar, or "the mother of the veiled darkness" as she was sometimes called, was one of the most bloodthirsty religions ever known. Though she was worshipped as the goddess of love and beauty, such as Venus or Aphrodite of the Greek and Roman civilisations, hers was an evil love that thrived on violence. The festival of Ishtar was celebrated at the beginning of spring, when life again was given to the land from the swollen body of the Nile River. The temple of Ishtar stood high on the hill overlooking the city of Antioch. The goddess was served by twenty beautiful young virgin girls. Shamus was Ishtar's high priest, and lover. He was worshipped as a lesser god by the men of the city. On the eve of the feast of Ishtar the people of the city crowded around the temple. Here, for six wild days and nights, the young priestesses would mingle with the men of the city, and lust would reign over the land. On the seventh day, the crowd would gather at the temple for the great feast: a blood feast, that would give the goddess to the people. The young priestesses would be slaughtered on the great altar. Their blood would be caught in silver bowls as it ran from their bodies. Then, certain organs and limbs would be removed and prepared as dishes to serve the people. As the last morsel of this horrible feast was eaten, the high priestess would show herself rising from the tomb, a living incarnation of Ishtar. Ishtar, arisen in flesh and blood, had become part of the people. This custom of the blood feast existed for more than four hundred years, and was finally abolished by Amenhotep, the second of the 15th Dynasty. It is said that even today there are still followers of this gruesome goddess, however it has never been proven. And this concludes my lecture on Ancient Egyptian cults. I hope to see you all here again next week.

As the above suggests, the film's incorporation of real historical references seems deliberately rather than carelessly inaccurate. The suggestion that the feast was abolished in the 15th Dynasty by one of the Amenhoteps, moonlighting from the 18th, could pass for mere gibberish, but there is a touch of knowing mischief in the incorporation of Ishtar and Antioch, and in the meaninglessness of the lecture even on its own terms. (Oddly, the narrator doesn't appear to say "indentify" *or* "identify," but he does refer to Rameses as "Ramsay" at one stage.)

Clearly, then, there is nothing to take the least bit seriously here. Nonetheless, while not in itself leading us anywhere further than its own ever-decreasing Dantean circles, contemplation of *Blood Feast* does raise a couple of very important issues that take us right back to the question with which this book began: does this insistent portrayal of their culture as sinister, which finds its ultimate outlet in this film, represent a serious libel of the ancients? Or may it perhaps open doors on hidden parts of their existence that we might prefer to keep closed?

The Egypt left to posterity by its art and literature is of a nation state in which everything is neat and tidy, and under control. There is an uncontained, visceral force to the sight of incontinently shed blood that seems at odds with this aesthetic. The thought of the embalmers, for instance, red to the elbows as they remove the internal organs of the deceased, is almost impossible to reconcile with a public culture that rebelled at ugliness

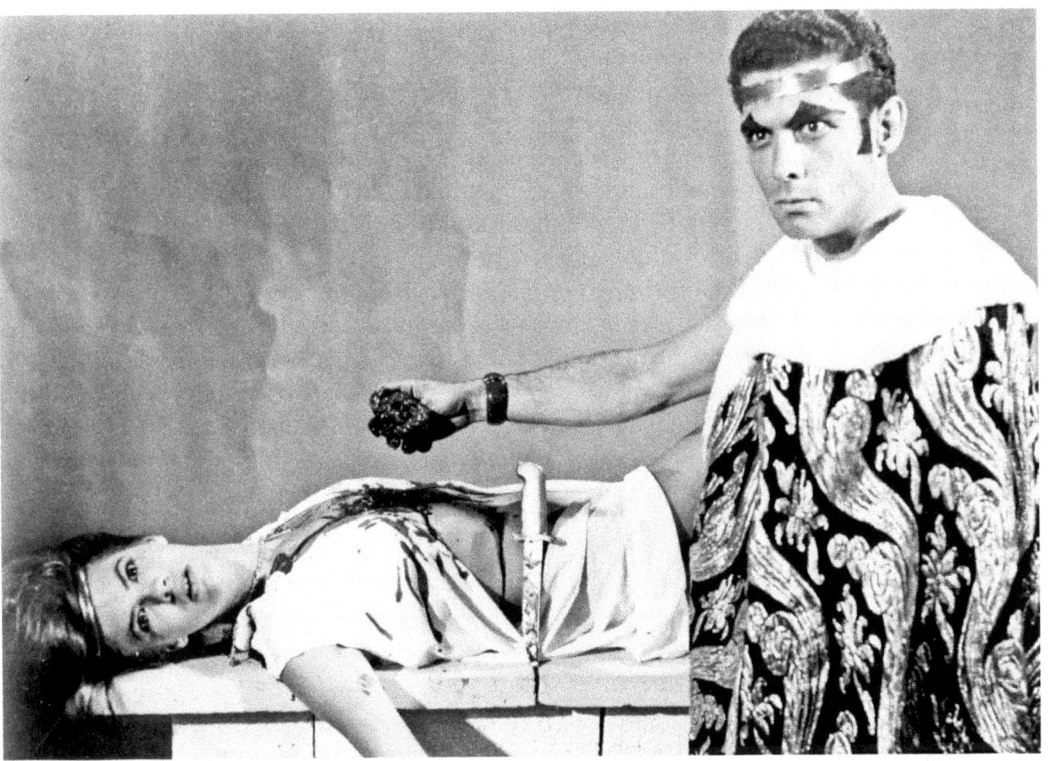

The cannibalistic feast of Ishtar, served buffet-style, in *Blood Feast* (1963).

and disorder. When just these images were included in *Dawn of the Mummy* they seemed as gratuitous as anything else in the film, yet they are almost certainly historically accurate. How far can we say the same of the other attempts to reimagine the ancients as a race of blood drinkers, cannibals and ghouls?

We'll start at the most restrained point, with the sacrifices of the servants seen in Hammer's first take on *The Mummy*, and which also feature in *Land of the Pharaohs* (1955). The custom, though not an invented one, is at least anachronistic in the eras in which these films are set. Human sacrifice was indeed carried out in First Dynasty burials, as Walter Emery saw in the tomb of Queen Merneith in 1946. (Even allowing for the leap in dynasties, however, the Hammer film, at least, with its line of beautiful temple maidens being messily hacked to death right there in the burial chamber, seems a somewhat excessive capitulation to the aesthetics of De Sade.) The tombs of the Royal Cemetery at Abydos contain numerous "subsidiary graves" containing young servants, seemingly killed en masse at the time of the burial. Poisoning remains a possibility, while evidence of dried blood on their teeth also hints at strangulation.

But though widespread, these mass-sacrifices are confined entirely to the First Dynasty. By the Third Dynasty, the age of the pyramid builders, the practice had died out entirely. Sadly, the Second Dynasty, which surely holds the key to this transition, is the most frustratingly undocumented chapter in the whole of Egyptian dynastic history: explanations for this vary from exciting intimations of conflict, sacking and usurpation, sadly unsupported by archaeological evidence, to the less stirring but more plausible role played by the decision of Second Dynasty pharaohs to relocate the royal burial ground from Abydos to Saqqara. (The latter was then all but completely destroyed by later construction, taking a dynasty's worth of history with it.)

So why did they stop? Most likely it was an example of that process by which custom becomes ritual, and thence journeys from ritual practice to ritual symbolism. Servants *are* still interred in the tombs of later dynastic kings—but in the form of art. This is exactly analogous to food offerings, which begin as real (and replenished) feasts, but are eventually offered symbolically in offerings painted on the tomb walls. The same applies to the pharaoh's chariot, furniture, and retainers.

Surely, though, we can entirely rule out cannibalism? Yes, it's probable that we can— but the issue *has* been raised. A recurring feature of gravesites in the pre–Dynastic period is the presence of partially dismembered bodies. At first the disarray was attributed to damage enacted at a later date, most likely the despoliation of the tomb robbers. But it soon became apparent that this could not be the case. Many of these bodies were in entirely sealed tomb enclosures. In some cases, the missing heads and limbs had been carefully replaced with pottery and other funerary items. Dismemberment has even been discovered within the bandages of some wrapped mummies.

Petrie had found a great many of these dismembered bodies when excavating at Naqada in 1895, and had speculated that in at least some of the cases (where body parts were not merely detached but also missing), the bodies may have been cut up so that the

Kharis (Christopher Lee) prepares the handmaidens for sacrifice in *The Mummy* (1959).

flesh could be consumed. This may have been as a means of acquiring the virtues and characteristics of the deceased: some funerary texts tell of the dead king devouring the gods so as to assume their powers. Petrie suggested that some of the excavated bones may have been gnawed, and also divested of their marrows. More recent scholarship has cast considerable doubt on these conclusions, however.[2]

But even if Petrie was wrong and there was no cannibalism, what of blood feasts in a wider sense? Disquieting food for thought on that matter was offered when archaeologists discovered a walled court at Hierakonpolis in 1985.[3] The oval shaped courtyard, around 100 feet in length and with a sloping floor, had been built in pre–Dynastic times, and had remained in use for several centuries. It was clear from the large numbers of accumulated bones, as well as a cache of razor-sharp flint knives, that huge numbers of animals of all kinds had been butchered in this enclosure. Two things distinguished this space from any workaday slaughterhouse, however. First, the accumulated bones of the dispatched creatures revealed that many were in infancy: a bizarrely wasteful use of livestock if this were a strictly utilitarian activity. Second, archaeologist Michael Hoffman uncovered at one end of the court the remnants of a structure that was oddly familiar from the imagery of later pharaonic Egypt: a dais supported on an enormous pole, on which the king would sit as presentation is made to him below.

The implication, clearly, is that the killings were *watched*, whether as a kind of tithe ceremony in which livestock owners presented the king with a representative offering before his eyes or simply the enactment of death as spectator sport, it is impossible to say with any certainty. And did a blood feast follow? It is sensible to suppose so. Any budding Fuad Ramses should of course be assured that this was definitely a non-human slaughter, and the majority who discern absolute moral significance in the distinction will doubtless be much comforted by that. But with the vast array of slaughtered animals, from lambs and hares to crocodiles and fish six feet in length, and with that sloping floor indicating that the scene would have been literally awash with blood, the images evoked certainly remain grotesque ones. And there's still more to come.

The Narmer Palette is generally considered the earliest great artefact of Ancient Egypt. Narmer was the first pharaoh, who supposedly united the two kingdoms of Upper and Lower Egypt. The palette was discovered at Hierakonpolis in 1897 by two British archaeologists, James Quibell and Frederick Green. Its key image is one that, in its essentials, appears repeatedly in later pharaonic illustration. It shows the ruler holding a vanquished prisoner by the hair, and raising above him a ceremonial mace, of a sort found in vast numbers in Egyptian tombs, prior to bringing it down upon the victim's head and bashing out his brains. The hieroglyphic symbol of the tadpole underneath it seems likely to indicate that this particular slaying is but one of ten thousand similar carried out by Narmer. It is not an image of the battlefield: the victim is captive and bound. It is an execution, and it appears to be a demonstration of might.

It is hard to come up with explanations that make it any less chilling than it appears at first glance, though one could argue, perhaps, that there is simply no a priori imperative to read this or any Egyptian art as a literal representation of reality, a "snapshot," as it were. It could be that the image is entirely symbolic. It could merely be designed to indicate that he was a great conqueror. Or it might be a representational symbol of his authority, indicating the totality of his power over his people, with no basis in reality at all. But recent excavation in the cemeteries of Hierakonpolis suggests otherwise. As well as the expected dismemberment in many of these graves, archaeologists uncovered evidence of large numbers of bodies that had seemingly had their skulls smashed, exactly in the manner of the unfortunates depicted on the Narmer palette and elsewhere. Many had been decapitated, and a series of cuts visible on the skulls suggested they had also been scalped.

So were these prisoners of war, conquered insurgents? Recent writers have taken issue with what they deem the unsupported assumptions of European "grand narrative" history—all kings and wars and empires, and civilizations that rise and fall—and have rightly pointed out that there is very little evidence that warfare or conquest played any part in the establishment of pharaonic Egypt. Even the basic idea of the two kingdoms

The king smites his enemies: a detail from the Narmer Palette.

is widely challenged. The age span of the victims, and the inclusion of women among them, further argues against these being the bodies of captured warriors. But without the slender justification of warfare, just how *do* we account for these hideous relics? If not prisoners of war, who are these people being ceremonially slaughtered in public spaces? How were they chosen, and from where?

As John Romer records in his *History of Ancient Egypt*:

> The people who were bludgeoned to death had been struck by objects directed with such force that some of the skulls had shattered like teacups. Others, however, had survived just such attacks; one girl, for example, had suffered a brutal crack to the head as a child and her skull had almost healed before she died in early adulthood. Five other people, though, had each been killed with one swift blow; one of these, a woman in her late thirties, had already sustained a broken arm, while a younger man, who had earlier suffered fractures of a rib and wrist and who also had a well-healed depression in his skull from an earlier blow, had finally succumbed to a hit so powerful that it had sent fragments of his skull deep into his brain, from where a palaeopathologist would eventually retrieve them.

This weird evidence of repeated assaults, with wounds given time to heal when not fatal, seems to evoke the grimly fatuous logic of the corrida, where "brave" bulls may be occasionally rewarded with freedom, and "cowardly" ones subjected to righteously administered "punishment." It suggests a ceremonial rather than retributive quality to the scenes, depicted widely in Egyptian illustration, in which helpless figures are stabbed, bludgeoned, scalped and dismembered, and publicly displayed. Descriptive plaques found at Abydos, Naqada and several other sites tell the same grim story: that in many places and over a prolonged period of time, regular demonstration was made of the ordered, systematic murder and mutilation of Egyptians, by Egyptians. And in the most overt echo of *Blood Feast*, the images further tell us that their blood was caught in overflowing bowls "as it ran from their bodies."

Archaeologists tend to be remarkably laid back about this sort of thing. Sacrifice and ritual murder usually make them switch into what I call their "what we must understand" mode. It's very easy to dismiss such behavior as barbaric, primitive savagery, they will tell us, but *what we must understand* is that this was a complex social/political/religious gesture of deep symbolic/ceremonial/religious importance, and it is a kind of chauvinism to project our values onto them. And this usually after pedantically cautioning us against underrating the sophistication, intelligence and rationality of ancient peoples, or making the mistake of viewing their bizarre cosmologies as anything other than the ordinary and sensible structure by which they lived lives, in a relative sense, no different from our own. Personally, I'm more comfortable endorsing the sentiments of Nicholas Humphrey, who in his influential lecture *What Shall We Tell the Children?* observes:

> In 1995, in the high mountains of Peru, some climbers came across the frozen mummified body of a young Inca girl. She was dressed as a princess. She was thirteen years old. About five hundred years ago, this little girl had, it seems, been taken alive up the mountain by a party of priests, and then ritually killed—a sacrifice to the mountain's Gods in the hope that they would look kindly on the people below. The discovery was ... made the subject of a documentary film shown on American television.... [Viewers were] invited to marvel at the spiritual commitment of the Inca priests and to share with the girl on her last journey her pride and excitement at having been selected for the signal honor of being sacrificed. The message of the TV program was in effect that the practice of human sacrifice was in its own way a glorious cultural invention—another jewel in the crown of multiculturalism, if you like.
>
> But, how dare anyone suggest this? How dare they invite us—in our sitting rooms, watching television—to feel uplifted by contemplating an act of ritual murder: the murder of a dependent child

by a group of stupid, puffed-up, superstitious, ignorant old men? How dare they invite us to find good for ourselves in contemplating an immoral action against someone else?[4]

The evidence that such extraordinarily brutal ceremonies may have been a routine part of later Predynastic and early Dynastic society, and especially that they may have been enacted before passive spectators, brings a fetid whiff of the Roman arena into the world of Egyptian culture. And with it, a little too close to reality for comfort, it brings the specter of Fuad Ramses.

10

The Pharaoh's Razor Blade

> The grandest jackpot ever hit is again causing a sensation in this country.... The fabled hoard—2,500 dazzling objects crammed helter-skelter in the small, four-room tomb—has sparked an Egyptian revival reminiscent of the 1920s.—*Chicago Tribune*, December 21, 1976

Tutankhamen rose from the tomb to transfix the world twice.

Though nothing would ever rival the extraordinary effects of his first appearance in the 1920s, the reception awarded the boy king in the 1970s certainly qualified as one of the more spectacular showbiz comebacks. His world tour, *The Treasures of Tutankhamun*, lasted between 1972 and 1981, but the stop-off that really caught the headlines was his visit to several American cities between 1976 and 1979. In the interests of international relations, Richard Nixon had become the first U.S. President to visit Egypt since World War II, and successfully made the case to President Sadat for bringing Tutankhamen's treasures to their cultural second home, even managing to snub the Kremlin by arranging for the show to include more exhibits *and* more city stops than on the tour's Russian leg.

Ticket receipts and general interest left little doubt that the exhibition would be a massive hit, but it was soon obvious that this was something still more: it was Tutmania all over again. Seven thousand people a day filled Washington's National Gallery of Art, and in New York, all 1.3 million available tickets were snapped up within one week of their going on sale. At other venues the queues began at dawn, and wrapped around the buildings. Celebrities flocked to pay homage, and thus Tutankhamen met Cleopatra, or at least Elizabeth Taylor. Kids bought sleeping bags shaped like sarcophagi; illicit vendors outside the venues sold unauthorized women's T-shirts reading "Get Your Hands Off My Tuts."

As itemized by the *Montreal Gazette*:

> More than $15 million has been grossed so far on the sale of the "official" Tut product line. Posters, post cards and reproductions of objects in the exhibition, all sanctioned by Egyptian authorities and New York's Metropolitan Museum of Art. Millions more have been taken in on pirated items and spinoffs. There are Tut sheets, Tut towels, Tut swizzle sticks and Tut tea cosies. Hairdressers are offering Tut cuts. What is this mummy madness? When will it end?[1]

The *Chicago Tribune* added that a New York perfumier "using what he claims to be Egyptological research" has created a new fragrance called "Blue Lotus of the Nile" "based on ingredients found in the tomb." No reports of a curse this time, however: "It seems that

Tut has mended his ways," observed Kenneth Donahue, director of the Los Angeles County Museum of Art.[2]

What was it, beyond the treasures themselves, which conveyed itself so powerfully at this time? There's no question that a large part of the phenomenon was just what it seemed: the widespread, insatiable curiosity to see those "wonderful things" for maybe the only time before they were spirited back to Cairo. If there was anything, demographically speaking, uniting the crowds that ringed the museums showing the exhibition, it was their sheer disparateness: everybody caught the bug.

One contingent is especially worth noting, however, because it was one that we might not necessarily have expected to be a major constituent of the whole, that being the young, the hip and the turned on. In part, the cool set had been engaged by the accidental popularity of a silly "King Tut" song-cum-skit on the TV comedy series *Saturday Night Live*, delivered by Steve Martin, arch proponent of the "pull a face" school of humor. But more powerfully, Ancient Egyptian cosmology and aesthetics were now making potent appeal to a post-sixties generation made uneasy by their partial re-embrace of consumerism, and feeling the need to re-affirm (and conspicuously wear) their spiritual values as riposte. Thus the Tutankhamen exhibition, in every obvious sense a triumph of capitalism, became at the same time a magnet for an off-the-peg mysticism that automatically equated antiquity with purity and wisdom. It was very old wine in a slightly new bottle but even so, a giant paradox remained. Yes, it was all wonderfully ancient, esoteric, non–Western and woo-woo spooky. But at the same time, this was the vast, unearned wealth of a king, the grotesque spoils of institutionalized social inequality. Wasn't it?

In an attempt to sidestep the issue, a new Tutankhamen was created. No autocrat or tyrant, he was suddenly a teenage free spirit, trapped in archaic systems of succession and title. A victim too. Cue the glorious 1976 disco number *Tutankhamen, King of the Nile*, in which composer and singer Riccardo Wolf croons: "He was rich but he weren't never free, and I wondered if he was what he wanted to be."[3] This was a king ready to tune in and drop out, as the chorus concluded: "Tutankhamen weren't no regular guy—he could send you on a trip without you sayin' goodbye." It was all a long way from *Old King Tut Was a Wise Old Nut*.

The symbol of this "new" Ancient Egypt, above all else, was the pyramid, re-invented with a Californian accent as a timeless repository of wisdom and power, as well as some seriously heavy vibes. We have already noted the long tradition of presuming, virtually on instinct, that the Pyramids must be fundamentally mysterious in their meaning, and in the manner in which they were built, since the former must lie beyond human understanding, the latter beyond human capabilities. Neither is true, as we have seen, but the need for mystery persists, and results on the one hand in a strain of redundant speculative ingenuity (such as we saw in the film *Land of the Pharaohs*) and on the other in an explosion of all-out insanity that characterized the 1970s as one of the great ages of human gullibility.

The association of Egypt with outer space would manifest itself most pointedly in popular culture in the next couple of decades, when *The Orion Mystery* and other such books positing that the Sphinx was thousands of years older than claimed, and the Pyramids a star map of the constellation of Orion, fed into such cinematic variations as *Stargate* (1994). But such ideas were very much born in this second Tutmania wave, and the effects instantly filtered into such as *Pyramids of Mars* (1975), a four-part installment of the popular British science fiction TV program *Doctor Who*, in which our hero battles robot mummies and discovers that Egyptian civilization owes its genius to an alien race called the Osirians.

The key figure behind this off-shoot of the earlier Egyptian spiritualist movement was bestselling Swiss author Erich von Daniken, the "high priest of the improbable," as Colin Wilson put it, "who, in explaining how the pyramids were built by visitors from outer space, managed to multiply the weight of the Great Pyramid by five."[4] But the decade above all else would be defined by an even stranger manifestation of the wider cult, and one with still earlier roots.

In the 1930s, a French pendulum dowser and ironmonger called Antoine Bovis made a replica of the Khufu pyramid from cardboard and for some reason convinced himself that it had the power to preserve food. This he attributed to some mysterious consequence of its dimensions and orientation:

> I have measured exactly with a Biomètre the radiations of the 4 sides and I have found positive 215° at the North, negative 215° at the South, dual-positive 240° at the East, and at the West negative 75° only (notice that this negative 75° reading at the west of the pyramid corresponds to the most harmful waves that we know of). Then I measured the radiations inside the monument at around a third of its height, where the so-called Royal Chamber is located, and I found a result of positive 2000°. A new supposition: since with the help of our positive 2000° magnetic plates we can mummify small animals, could the pyramid have the same property? I tried, and as you can observe with the small fish and the little piece of meat still hanging, I succeeded totally.[5]

One will notice, however, that he did *not* claim that his pyramid sharpened razor blades. That revelation had to wait until 1949, and for an enterprising Czech called Karel Drbal, who had been sufficiently impressed by Bovis's work to try some experiments of his own. Going one further than Bovis, not only did he make his own cardboard pyramids to prove his assertions, he also patented and sold them, under the name "Pharaoh's Shaving Device." Describing the device in his patent application as "a method of keeping razor blades and straight razors sharp without an auxiliary source of energy," Drbal was keen to stress that there was "no magic involved in the functioning of the razor-blade pyramid." Rather (as Robert M. Schoch and Robert Aquinas McNally explain in their book *Pyramid Quest: Secrets of the Great Pyramid and the Dawn of Civilization*) it was simply that "the pyramid affected the microscopic structure of materials both living and dead, reorienting the steel to its original state and preventing the growth of microorganisms ... because the cavity of the pyramid resonated with cosmic microwaves concentrated by the earth's magnetic field."

Well, yes, when you put it like that...

How, then, did these two obscure cranks inspire a worldwide cult in the 1970s? The answer is via authors Sheila Ostrander and Lynn Schroeder, who encountered the Pharaoh's Shaving Device first-hand on a 1968 visit to Czechoslovakia, and then introduced the wonderful claims of both Drbal and Bovis to Anglophone audiences in their 1970 book *Psychic Discoveries Behind the Iron Curtain*. In it, they coined a new phrase to describe the phenomenon: Pyramid Power.

Pyramid Power, as a concept, immediately exploded. Pyramids, it seemed, could enhance creativity, spirituality, intelligence, even sexual virility. Charles W. Williams, president of the American Society of Dowsers, claimed in 1973 that "the pyramid is able to give relief for arthritis, bursitis, headaches and other ailments. Placing a cardboard pyramid over the location of the trouble, having one base facing the north—the magnetic pole—and keeping it there for twenty minutes or so is of great benefit. If that method isn't feasible, place the pyramid under the bed for the night."[6] And if that's not feasible, go to sleep thinking about pyramids jumping over a gate.

Two separate books appeared with *Pyramid Power* as the title, one by Max Toth and Greg Nielsen, and the other by Dr. G. Patrick Flanagan, who tried to sue Max Toth and Greg Nielsen. Toth explained to the *Evening Independent* that "Pyramid Power is a resonating cavity of frequencies. The base of the pyramid collects the frequency of vibrations coming up from the earth and the four sides of the pyramid collect frequencies zipping in from outer space."[7] When not collecting frequencies zipping in from outer space, Toth also sold cardboard pyramids by mail order which, he said, "work 90% of the time if they're set up properly."[8] Another supplier was Shelly Siegel of Santa Monica who got into the business purely on the grounds that it was a sound investment, and duly made a fortune. "It's blowing my mind," Siegel told the *Lakeland Ledger*. "A segment of the population is always a little screwy."[9]

In 1977, Jim Onan, the owner of a concrete business in Illinois, built a gold-plated ⅑th scale replica of Khufu's Pyramid and lived in it with his family, harnessing its energy to grow miraculous plants and vegetables. It became a national tourist stop, and the boxer Muhammad Ali tried to buy it and turn it into a gym. In 1975, the coach of the Toronto Maple Leafs, a Canadian ice hockey team, made the players stand under a plastic model pyramid before every game. "I took the six sticks I was going to use in the game and put them under the pyramid," player Daryl Stittler told the *St Petersburg Times*. "Then I stood under the pyramid. You're supposed to stand under the pyramid for four minutes—not any more, not any less—to get its vibrations. A lot of guys on our team saw what I was doing and soon each guy was standing under the pyramid. I still get vibrations from this stick."[10]

American baseball team the Kansas City Royals did the same in 1977, and found the results similarly beneficial.[11] The ever-reliable Erich von Daniken asserted that he used a pyramid to turn table wine into a *grand cru*. (I'm trying that tonight.) James Coburn liked to meditate in a pyramid-shaped tent, and Gloria Swanson told the press she slept with a pyramid under her bed because it "makes every cell in my body tingle."[12] (The tents, along with pyramid-shaped hats, are both still widely available from quack New Age outlets.) Meanwhile, killjoys from the Stanford Research Institute decided to test the theories right at the source, and put various perishable items inside the Great Pyramid itself and made the extraordinary discovery that they decayed at exactly the same rate as they would anywhere else. Spooky!

The cinematic manifestations of this second wave of Tutmania were fewer in number than those of the first, but fully as eccentric. In the first place we had the TV movie *The Curse of King Tutankhamun's Tomb* (1980), a.k.a. *The Curse of King Tut's Tomb*, a co-production between British HTV West and American Columbia Pictures Television that plays like exactly that. Like the later, similar *Jack the Ripper* (1988), a collaboration between Thames and Lorimar, it's almost as if two separate films have collided. A nicely detailed (if largely fanciful) account of the discovery of Tutankhamun's tomb frequently gives way to a nutty *Boys' Own* adventure subplot featuring Raymond Burr as devilish Egyptian villain "Jonash Sebastian," stirring up political intrigue and intent on securing the treasures for himself, his bulk clad bizarrely in a massive wraparound garment and loose, floppy turban that changes color from scene to scene, like a symbolic game in a Peter Greenaway movie. One minute it's a fiery red, then deep midnight blue, and boot-polished and bellowing all the while, he seems to have strayed in from a Hanna Barbera cartoon.

Harry Andrews and Robin Ellis are good as Carnarvon and Carter, the latter stepping in at the eleventh hour to replace an injured Ian McShane. The scenes in England, the preliminaries of the planning and digging, the thrill of the accidental discovery when all seemed hopeless, and then the tension and wonder of the discovery are all conveyed nicely. Excellent use is made of real locations, and atmosphere is well sustained. But given the sensational potential of the established story, already so dependent on wild conjecture and exaggeration, why anyone felt the need to go further even than the original journalists, and create entirely new characters and events out of whole cloth, is hard to imagine. We have an international conspiracy of occultists, exploding airplanes, berserk clairvoyants rasping out coded warnings, and a top-billed Eva Marie Saint contributing almost nothing to the plot as a sympathetic journalist, grafted in seemingly only to provide a little fictitious love interest which then, even more oddly, comes to nothing. A sober, National Geographic–style commentary in the reassuring tones of Paul Scofield is ladled over all, and the results are curious if never less than engaging.

Angharad Rees as Lady Evelyn Herbert in *The Curse of King Tut's Tomb* (1980).

The Awakening (1980), meanwhile, was a big budget horror spectacular, replaying *The Jewel of Seven Stars* in the mode of *The Omen*, with Charlton Heston in the lead. Reference sources all but unanimously record it as a soporific disaster. But while it must ultimately be counted a failure, it is full of exceptional things. For one thing it's exquisitely made—perhaps the most beautiful of all Egyptian horror movies—with stunning location photography by Jack Cardiff (wisely redrafted after similarly gorgeous work on 1978's *Death on the Nile*) and a haunting and magnificent music score—the best of any film in this book—by Claude Bolling. As a failure, then, it is a heroic one: no other horror movie so convincingly recreates the opening of a tomb, nor so keenly captures the flavor of Egypt, its landscape, its tombs, its light and shade, and the aural and visual texture of its days and nights. It seems to have a perfume lingering around it, a heady incense. It also has a general air of conviction, and the Egyptological elements are filtered in with intelligence. (The Hatshepsut analogies are again deliberately played up, as we see images of the Queen's face chiseled out of ancient reliefs in a manner exactly analogous to the defacement of the Hatshepsut monuments, though Tera has strangely become Kara here.)

In its better, quieter stretches the film is stunningly dreamlike, and visually and atmospherically effective to a degree achieved by no film since the Karloff original. Sadly, in deference to the times and in ill-advised imitation of *The Omen*, it continually punctuates its hypnotic mood with a string of unimaginatively nasty set-piece deaths that both subvert its finer intentions and fail in their own efforts to give the film the energy of a rattling horror suspense film in the contemporary manner. As a result the film's better portions are made to feel like thumb-twiddling, and the excellent finale is left looking absurdly anti-climactic. Few films cry out so plaintively for a return to the original materials and a complete re-edit: were it possible, a masterpiece may yet be found hiding.

Set to be the real blockbuster of this second wave was *Sphinx* (1981), from the 1979 novel by Robin Cook. (Oddly, neither film nor book has anything to do with the sphinx.) Cook produced a very enjoyable page-turning thriller, set in the murky world of the antiquities black market, full of romance, peril, plot twists and local color, building to a suspenseful finale in which the heroine, American Egyptologist Erica Baron, narrowly survives being entombed alive by a murderous team of tomb robbers. As such it proved a bestseller, and it was inevitable that (like *Coma*, the author's previous hit) it would make its way to the screen. "I think the whole thing is absolutely fascinating, this film, this place, everything," lead actress Lesley-Anne Down told *Photoplay*. "It's not about soppy mummies leaping out of sarcophagi. You don't have anybody coming to life 4,000 years after they've died. It's about a girl of today who's on holiday and gets into all kinds of trouble—and I can tell you from my bit of knowledge and experience of Egypt, it could easily have happened."

With yet more exquisite photography of authentic Egyptian locations (both under and above ground), sex, murder and a few touches of horror, this was surely the ultimate King Tut movie experience that had been threatened since 1923? (The film was budgeted at £6,000,000—lavish for the time, though an enticing set report from *Photoplay* magazine noted sagely that for a film shot in Egypt this was "actually reasonable enough when

Stephanie Zimbalist and Charlton Heston in *The Awakening* (1980).

Dr. Erica Baron (Lesley-Anne Down) in trouble again in *Sphinx* (1981).

you remember the schedule and logistics involved. A screwdriver vodka-orange in the bar, for instance, was being charged at £2 with five separate taxes and service charges added."[13]) Sadly, on release the cinematic curse of the Pharaohs struck again. The film, launched on a wave of publicity, emerged to terrible reviews and matching box-office, re-asserting the pattern of the 1923 projects—excitement before release, indifference after.

Looking at the film today, it is in several respects easy to see why it didn't meet expectations. Rightly thinking it an essential part of the package, the film lingers on its travelogue visuals, which are unquestionably beautiful, and as in so many of the announced 1923 projects, were touted beforehand as the production's principal come-on. (And the detail is certainly a feast: virtually everything we see is the real deal, from the interiors of the Luxor Winter Palace Hotel to the Cairo Museum to the Tutankhamen tomb itself.) Even in a two-hour thriller, however, this inevitably means that the plot is advanced somewhat breathlessly to make room for the pictorial splendor, and the effect is a little like being on a package tour: lots of traveling to get to places one must then rush through to keep to the schedule. The screenplay sticks to the basic trajectory of the novel, but attempts to straighten its labyrinthine course somewhat, inadvertently leaving several of the subsequently retained episodes obscurely motivated and hard to make sense of. (It's much more fun to watch after you've read the book than before.)

There is also a degree of confusion surrounding the characterization of the lead character. The book's Dr. Erica Baron is clever and resourceful, while at the same time a conventional romantic heroine. ("You keep forgetting that besides being a woman I'm an Egyptologist," she tells her whiney boyfriend Richard.) The film is not sure how to present her, perhaps from awareness that the very idea that a mainstream adventure story should have, for no particular reason, a fiercely independent woman for its hero was distinctly unusual—even more so then than it would be now. (Indeed, director Franklin J. Schaffner, late of *Patton* and *Planet of the Apes*, said it was the first thing that attracted him to the project.) If anything, the script makes the character still more independent, by removing entirely the character of the boyfriend, and giving her a couple of feisty speeches (not to be found in the book) about how her being a woman has stood in the way of her receiving her professional due as an Egyptologist. (While her boyfriend in the novel is a clod who thinks Egyptology is a silly hobby Erica needs to grow out of, the film gives her an unseen fellow Egyptologist ex-boyfriend who, it seems, stole the professional lead on her.)

But having first established her autonomy in this fashion, the film is then unable to reconcile her resourcefulness with the need for her to react in approved *Perils of Pauline* fashion whenever danger strikes. And because the film has, in any event, much less time than the novel at its disposal to show us how Erica uses her specialist knowledge to unravel the mystery, and thus to inevitably re-encounter the other characters involved, what we see here is more like two parallel plots—one in which she is dragged more or less impotently through a murder and smuggling plot, and another in which she vacillates drippily between two suspicious love interests: a French journalist who is clearly not all he seems[14] and Frank Langella's dishy but troubled director general of the Egyptian Department of Antiquities. As a result, it's possible that the mixed messages Erica sends out in the movie alienated audiences on both sides of the ideological divide. Robin Cook feels it "turned an exciting, action thriller into a syrupy 1930s-style romance."[15]

The casting of Lesley-Anne Down necessitated the most obvious change from page to screen: Erica is now British. (For some reason this *does* make a difference, possibly a bigger one that it should, and I suspect an even bigger one for American audiences than it does for British ones.) Therefore when we eventually encounter her (after two flashbacks in succession—the first to the Eighteenth Dynasty and then to Carter and Carnarvon in the tomb in 1922—a delaying tactic lifted direct from the novel that plays a bit too much like time-wasting on screen) she is engaged in some bluntly functional dialogue with a museum colleague:

CURATOR: 21 other people associated with the beginning of the tomb died in inexplicable ways. Scientific interest in the strange disarray of the objects in the tomb was replaced by a lot of nonsense about the curse of the Pharaohs. And that was that.

ERICA: Which of course you're going to incorporate in your notes at the exhibition...

CURATOR: It may not be science but it certainly sells tickets!

ERICA: It's the same everywhere. The minute I mention in Boston to anyone that I'm an Egyptologist, all they want to talk about is Pyramid Power!

CURATOR: I've always wanted to visit America.

ERICA: You should! I've lived there for five years and I love it![16]

Erica's specialist subject is Menephta, a fictional New Kingdom architect from the reign of Seti I. The name sounds indebted to Merneptah (a.k.a. Merenptah, the fourth ruler of the Nineteenth Dynasty, thirteenth son of Rameses II and supposedly pharaoh during the Exodus), but from the dialogue we get the feeling that he may have been modeled on (the real) Imhotep: "This Menephta, he was just an architect, nothing more?" asks the soon to be murdered shopkeeper Abu-Hamdi (John Gielgud, fourth-billed in a one-scene cameo). "Good gracious no, he was lots of things," replies Erica. "A physician, a scientist...." ("Look, do you really want to hear about this?" she asks. "It does make most people look as though they've taken a quaalude.") Oddly, he is named Nenephta in the source novel, and is not her specialist subject; it's possible screenwriter John Byrum felt that because he appears in the film's first flashback prologue it was necessary to make a little more of him than Cook does. (The sequence, depicting the apprehension of robbers

Lesley-Anne Down among the dead men: *Sphinx* **(1981).**

in Tutankhamen's tomb, ends with the chief miscreant being tied to four horses and gruesomely torn to pieces, and boasts supposedly authentic ancient dialogue, sadly rendered juicily comic by being translated into modern English via subtitles, e.g.: "I only wanted one statue to pay for the embalming of my parents!")

For audiences who know something of the background, the melding of Egyptological speculation, and details from the story of the Tutankhamen discovery, with the modern plot is genuinely adroit. The book's central conceit is that Nenephta, disturbed by the ease with which even the most ingenious tomb fortifications are overcome by determined plunderers, vows to create the ultimate security device for the tomb of Seti I, then in construction. Using the layered structure of the Pyramids as his inspiration, he opts to build it underneath the tomb of Tutankhamen, so that the one (already violated when the story begins) serves as cover for the other. As a final touch, he also installs an anonymous mummy in a second, fake Seti tomb, built deliberately so as to be found and plundered. (This phony tomb, therefore, is the one that was discovered in 1817 and which is still considered the authentic one by Egyptologists.) The real Seti tomb, so unimaginably lavish as to make Tutankhamen's look meager in comparison, remained lost until Carter and Carnarvon rediscovered the latter in 1922. As they attempted to make sense of the chaotic first chamber, with its randomly scattered contents (the results, Cook suggests, of the disturbed attempt at robbery with which book and film begin) their foreman Sarwat Raman spirits away a parchment which—Erica has spotted—is mentioned in Carnarvon's account of the opening but not Carter's. This, which she eventually locates in the cottage of Raman's widow, is a cryptic message from Menephta, somewhat carelessly left in the very place he would surely have least wanted it found, which Raman duly deciphered. This led him to discover the real Seti tomb, the contents of which he and his descendants have been quietly filtering into the black market ever since. Anyone who comes close to discovering their guilty secret—Erica being only the latest—is quietly disposed of, accounting for several of the deaths attributed to the curse of Tutankhamen! "Was Lord Carnarvon one of the people that had to be 'dealt with'?" asks Erica of the book's semi-surprise villain. "I'm not certain," he replies. "It was a long time ago, but I think so." (This hedge-betting is a neat trick of Cook's that he uses elsewhere: an ancient tomb-robber "half-expected to be set upon by demons of the underworld," the clever use of "half-expected" cunningly side-stepping the whole issue of how reverence and sacrilege could have co-existed.)

The central idea of *Sphinx*—a family supporting itself with the proceeds of robbing tombs of which only they know the location, and passing the secret on from generation to generation—recalls an exceptional Egyptian film from 1969. In fact, Shadi Abdel Salam's *The Night of Counting the Years* (1969, "based on the story of the discovery of the cache of mummies in Dayr-Al-Bahri in 1881") is by any sober measure a work of extraordinary insight, and the most important film to fall under the purview of this enquiry, so it is only appropriate to save it for last.

A detailed account of the lives and work of a family of Egyptian tomb robbers, filled with extraordinary imagery and brilliant compositions, and making exceptional use of landscape, the film is shot in long, meditative takes in a bleached white desert, dotted with human figures entirely in black amidst the toppled monuments. Scene after scene is shot in narrow passageways, or huge, empty stone rooms, with dust and sand constantly blowing, and the soundtrack intense with birdsong and howling wind. Dialogue scenes play out in small apertures defined by vast, enclosing architecture, the perfect metaphor for the characters' relationship to their land, their past, and the sheer weight of historical and mythological meaning pressing on them at all times. It is by no means a horror film (despite being widely known under the incredibly misleading alternate title *The Mummy*). Nonetheless, the scenes set in the tomb interiors, as the family furtively go about their business by flickering candlelight, have a unique and authentic potency.

The question of sacrilege, key to the story we have been telling, is the film's central theme, mediated through the crisis of conscience experience by the two sons tasked with continuing the family business after the death of their father. The younger tries to honor his duties to his family, even as he watches in horror as bodies are defiled for artefacts, slashed with knives and dismembered with axes to make their treasures come free. The elder rejects the family creed entirely, leaving the village to join the police tasked with stamping out the robbers' trade, earning the enmity of his mother and peers. A key dialogue scene articulates perfectly the issues which, I have been suggesting, all of the films in this book must ultimately address. "Those whom you call 'the dead' are only dust and wood from thousands of years ago," his uncles tell him. "They do not have parents, or children." "To you it's a piece of gold," he replies, picking up a piece of jewelry that he has pointedly refrained from handing over to the black market dealers. "But I see it as an eye that pursues me."

Poster for *The Night of Counting the Years* (1969), sometimes misleadingly known as *The Mummy*.

Epilogue:
Graves and Dead Men

> Looking down at the dried-up face, Erica felt a little sick. It was the kind of image Hollywood makeup artists strove to imitate for countless horror movies, and she noticed that the ears had fragmented and that the head was no longer attached to the torso. Instead of ensuring immortality, the remains suggested that the horror of death was permanent.
>
> Glancing around at the other royal mummies contained within the room, Erica thought that instead of making ancient Egypt come alive, the petrified bodies emphasized the enormous time that had elapsed and the remoteness of ancient Egypt.—Robin Cook, *Sphinx* (1979)

I began this study by asking what it was about Ancient Egypt that made it so fascinating to modern and Western sensibilities, to the extent that enthusiasm for its ideas radiated far outside the bounds of academia to the most disposable forms of popular culture, and endure, in our own time, as instantly understood generic currency. The mummies themselves, I have proposed, are the essence of this distinction, but for more than one reason.

The fact that specialists are able to learn and tell us so much about this extraordinary culture is in first measure a happy accident, resulting from the fact that the perceived need to pack the tombs with so much information and material has enabled the compiling of a vastly completer record of Egyptian thought and history than would otherwise be even conceivable (colored, of course, by the inevitable emphasis on funerary matters which has helped us assume, doubtless mistakenly, that there was something especially morbid and "spooky" about them).

The idea of the archaeologists themselves first searching for these buried tombs, then entering them and discovering in half-light this mass of hidden, eerie art and funerary material adds to the fascination, of course. Even the most elaborate tombs of other cultures do not possess this same quality: they are still monuments to the dead, demonstrations of the power, influence and acclaim their inhabitants commanded in life, designed to serve as reminders of their status and markers of their presence, but the Egyptian tombs are more. They are living quarters for their dead inhabitants, encompassing their bodies in a unique state between vivification and decomposition, just as their spirit exists in a unique state between corporeality and incorporeality, the here and the elsewhere.

The immediate fascination of the mummy, to Egyptological specialist and thrill-hungry layman both, is the degree to which it retains the physical appearance of the deceased. Unlike most ancient bodies they are not mere mortal remains but still recognizable human forms, in which such details as hair, facial features and expression might still be clearly discerned. Here too, then, academic importance and imaginative potential continue to march hand in hand, and continue to insulate us from a very simple fact: that it seems, or should seem, an unlikely notion now that any excavated remains of ancient cultures displayed in museums should also include the corpses of their buried dead.

Indeed the whole idea seems quite unconscionable, when put so baldly. We no longer pay to see freak shows, or to gawk at the inmates of mental asylums, so why has our appetite for gazing at mummies not likewise died away? Modern sensitivities have revised museum displays, descriptions and practice in countless ways, and yet the mummies remain, starkly on show, with the guilty allure of pornography. A corpse, per se, remains a shocking thing, and its public display remains a sensitive and divisive proposition. But an Egyptian mummy is simultaneously something more and something less than just a corpse; it is an integral part of the iconography of its subject in the way that, say, the corpse of a Viking would never be presumed to be.

The accepted route to take from here is in the direction of Edward Said and his concept of "Orientalism," a supposed Western pathology which places a distancing barrier between our treatment of our own mortal remains and those of a fundamentally "other" culture to which we have correspondingly fewer moral obligations.[1] But I wonder if there is not a more fluid and symbiotic process at work here. Isn't there a sense in which our seemingly callous disregard for the Egyptian dead, and appropriation of mummies as showpieces in exhibitions, is not so much because we perceive them as a product of a different culture to our own but rather, on the contrary, because we do not?

Could it be that the mummy movies, at first innocently informed by the insensitivities of their day, now *themselves* inform the perpetuation of what seems, on the face of it, to be something of a double standard? Only extreme familiarity (what Richard Dawkins termed, in an unrelated context, "the anaesthetic of familiarity") can account for this seeming hypocrisy. The mummy is too familiar, and too much *a part of our own culture,* to even fully register as its true self any more. It has been robbed of its humanity, first by the colonial disregard of the original excavators, and now by its spurious but indelible association with mystery and the supernatural and, in a general sense, with Western, Anglophone popular culture. The mummy is one of us, and too much a part of our own cultural repertoire to be permitted the possibility of returning to its own with dignity restored ... though how long such will remain the case is an interesting subject for conjecture.

Such calls to our better nature are heard from time to time, and indeed always were. Jasmine Day in *The Mummy's Curse* quotes a letter written to the London *Times* by Martin Conway, Director-General of the Imperial War Museum in 1923, in which he opines that nobody could observe "the dismal and dilapidated remains of the great Pharaohs ... without disgust." By all means display the artefacts, he says, "but let the bones of the Pharaohs be re-interred." Persuasive sentiments, but one can only wonder if the world's fascination would have long survived any decision to act upon them.

They were unexpectedly re-echoed in 1980, when Egypt's President Sadat gave a speech in which he urged that the 27 royal mummies on display in Egypt's museums should be reburied with full honors, explaining that "exposing the remains of Egypt's pharaohs in exhibitions for people to view ... is against our religious concept." The Mummy Room at the Cairo Museum was immediately closed to visitors, and ripples of unease pulsed through the Egyptological world.

The response shone an interesting light on the attitudes of British, French and American experts who, nearly three decades after Nasser's revolution, were still essentially proprietorial in their attitude to the relics. As a result, a purely domestic initiative stirred up a hornet's nest of old-fashioned interventionism, couched in language that carefully sought to avoid any trace of condescension ... and only intermittently pulled it off. "Egyptologists Shocked By Sadat Proposal To Rebury Royal Mummies" blazed the *Gettysburg Times*,[2] going on to quote an archaeologist "who asked not to be quoted by name": "Any decent human being would agree that the mummies should be treated with dignity. But what I'm worried about is that this sentiment might spill over and stop scientific research."

Two things should immediately strike us in the above quote. First, that less than sixty years after the greatest treasure hunt of all time, the whole purpose of archaeology is now stated without question to be "scientific research." And second, that this is then by convenient implication presumed to automatically equate with the "treating with dignity" that "any decent human being would agree" is the mummies' entitlement. But how should dignity be defined if it is to be allied with the compassionless enactment of scientific research? The question is not even contemplated, let alone pursued. Rather, it is fudged: Sadat had pulled the rug from under generations of complacency.

"It's a decision that doesn't help science," complained French archaeologist Guillemette Andreu in the same news report, "but we have to do our work without annoying or bothering our hosts." A meeting of Egyptian archaeologists ("they didn't ask for any advice from foreign experts," complained Andreu) came up with three possible measures to implement the plan: that the mummies should be returned to their individual tombs (which was deemed impractical on account of the physical condition of many of the structures and the cost of restoring them), a mass burial in one grave (which horrified the foreign experts) and the closure of the mummy room to all but scientific experts (which didn't bother them anything like as much). In the event, the whole grandiose gesture stalled—perhaps when the potential cost to the tourism industry was calculated. Today Egypt still tops the international package tour hit list, and museums know that an Egypt show is one of the surest ways of drawing crowds. And so the mummies remain, the big come-on, by public demand. Nonetheless, this is not an issue that is going to go away.

On the movie screens, however, the mummy seemed to me essentially an anachronism as I began this book, as much a living force in the cinematic lexicon as the Keystone Kops. True, there had been a popular revival at the turn of the century from director Stephen Sommers, but that was a million years ago to modern sensibilities, and I think it is fair to say that popular memory seems not to have kept its place warm, on account perhaps of the films' iconoclast spirit, and refusal to produce the objects of trade seemingly promised by their titles (no "proper" mummies).

Although I had seen the first two on general release I had no clear memory of them at all when I began writing this book, so I acquired a DVD of *The Mummy Returns*, and managed about a half-hour or so before conceding defeat. It's certainly eager to please, and has plenty of resources at its disposal to do so. Fans of fire, water, explosions, shouting, machine guns, people running about and jumping, computer-generated effects, vehicles crashing and huge sets falling over will have a ball. But there is nothing here for the kind of sensibility that tingles as Karloff's mummy comes to life, or ponders the mysteries of time and memory while observing Valerie Leon in her gilded coffin. What was yet more surprising, perhaps, was that even as late as the millennium these films were still blithely offering the same chauvinistic, unreconstructed attitudes we associate with the original mummy movies and the deeply unpleasant "Indiana Jones" films that are their primary inspiration.

So the traditional mummy film, I had assumed, was long gone, cursed by too much familiarity on the one hand and too much revisionism on the other. Their most notable recent screen appearance, in *Les Aventures Extraordinaires d'Adèle Blanc-Sec* (2010), a full circle return to Poe's *Some Words with a Mummy* with the mummies portrayed as unthreatening, urbane and well-spoken, was perhaps a necessary corrective to a century of mindless mayhem, but unlikely to start a new tradition. But it seemed that as soon as I put finger to keyboard, strange things began to occur, and by the time 2016 was half-over, it looked like Egyptomania was gearing up to make another of its periodic reappearances.

As always, there was the nudge from real life, the big excitement of 2015 being the suggestion that radar scanning may have revealed the presence of a still hidden area behind Tutankhamen's burial chamber. British archaeologist Nicholas Reeves has speculated that it may be the tomb of Nefertiti, and the painted wall covering what he believes to be another corridor was a ruse to fool tomb robbers. This was more or less exactly what Robin Cook had posited in *Sphinx*, so I asked the author if there was anything more to it than a flight of the imagination: "I wanted to write *Sphinx* since I had been intrigued by Ancient Egyptian history as a young boy. I even wanted to become an archaeologist for a number of years. After the success of *Coma*, I decided to prove to myself that I could write a book that wasn't about medicine. I got the idea of a tomb being hidden by another tomb on my research trip to Egypt, when I visited the tomb of Seti I. I used percussion, like in medicine, on the floor of one of the major rooms. I was convinced that there was a hollow space below the floor. Of course, I never followed up in presenting the idea to the Egyptian authorities, but just used it for the story."[3]

Next came the suggestion by an international team that "thermal anomalies" in adjacent stones at the base of the Giza pyramids may likewise indicate hidden chambers (shades this time of *Land of the Pharaohs*). Others have disputed both these assertions, however, and the debates continue at time of writing.

Then, incredibly, came news that Universal were making yet another big-budget "remake" of the 1932 movie—and this time with Tom Cruise! Universal claimed they had learned a hard lesson with *Van Helsing* (2004) and would be reviving what is invariably now referred to (in the ugly but no doubt appropriate terms of the trading room) as the "franchise" with respect and imagination. But skepticism gave way to despair when the film appeared in the summer of 2017. Doggedly intent upon making all the same mistakes as the previous reboot *and* adding its own, it offered another non-bandaged, shape-shifting mummy in place of the iconic version, zombie armies, and more boringly huge-scale explosive action rather than scares. Apart from a couple of CGI shots of the Gaza plateau Egypt is absent, the film being set in England and Iraq. Russell Crowe plays Dr. Jekyll and Mr. Hyde. Thankfully, audiences seem to have given all this the wide berth it merited.

As was the fact that Sunday night television then likewise waded into the renaissance: in the slot that British television habitually reserves for its take on "quality" historical drama, ITV mounted a four part adaptation of the Tutankhamen discovery, with a preposterously young and hunky Howard Carter romancing Lady Evelyn, and South Africa standing in as Egypt. Titled simply *Tutankhamen*, it aired in October and November of 2016 and received reassuringly dubious reviews, but at least it allowed the newspapers to dust off the old curse stories yet again.

Lastly, and perhaps most surprisingly of all, 2016 brought us a re-imagined remake of *Blood Feast*! Now set in Paris, it gave Fuad Ramses a wife and daughter and some overt mental health issues, and the Goddess Ishtar made an actual corporeal appearance in the form of actress Sadie Katz. Most usefully, the 87-year-old Herschell Lewis contributed a Skype cameo as the Professor who helps explain the Egyptian blood cult. It proved his last screen work: the curse of Ishtar finally claimed Lewis in September of 2016, just as I was putting the finishing touches to this manuscript.[4]

So yes, this might be a moment of resurgence … or it might not. It may be that the naysayers are right, and there are no more mummies, treasure or revelations to be discovered in the Pyramids or Tutankhamen's tomb. It may be that there are no more movies. Such things, ultimately, are of no more than temporary importance when compared to the monuments and artefacts themselves. But as it turns out, even their future is uncertain.

Right back in 1924, Arthur Weigall contributed this far-sighted observation to his *Tutankhamen and Other Essays*:

> It is to be argued that Lord Carnarvon's discovery put Egypt under a great obligation to him; and though we consider this true, thoughtful Egyptians have expressed an opposite view. The tomb, they say, was so safely buried beneath tons of rock that it was in no danger, and its treasures might well have been left to the better handling of a future generation. As it is, a mass of material has been discovered at a time when there is no proper place to house it, and when our knowledge of how to preserve it is very limited.… Have these wonderful objects survived the siege of nearly thirty-three centuries, only to be shown to us of this one generation and then to fall to pieces because conditions are not ready for their preservation?

Despite their exceptional fragility, the ancient sites of Egypt are daily subjected to rigors that even modern attractions engineered for mass tourism would struggle to withstand. The visitors who arrive in their millions inadvertently—and in some cases deliberately—add to the destruction of the very things they have paid small fortunes and travelled vast distances to experience. Like everything else in this story, this is also nothing new. As far back as 1882, the *New York Times* had published a polemic entitled "Tourists Who Infest Egypt."

> In the thirty years that Egypt has been thus visited, more harm has been done to its old buildings than in the centuries of so much abused neglect which have passed over the country. The destruction caused by the tourists is really serious; piece by piece the inscriptions and the wall paintings have been chipped away to supply "mementoes" … How is it possible to censure this wanton and petty mischief when the removal of noble obelisks to London and New York is thought worthy of public applause and national honors? What is the difference in stupidity between knocking off the nose of a statue, defacing a tomb, or ravaging an inscription and carrying away one or more of the few obelisks left?

Indeed—what is the difference? Modern archaeology is less changed since the bad old days than one might suppose, too, and the amount of insensitive excavation taking place around the ancient sites is no less intensive. We tend to imagine modern international teams working hand in hand with Egyptian conservators, and with the safety of the already excavated tombs and monuments a top priority. But as John Romer's terrifying book *The Rape of Tutankhamun* revealed, this is by no means to be presumed. Many modern expeditions are engaged solely in the documenting of visibly crumbling sites on the grounds that this in itself is an act of conservation. Some of those old jealousies still bubble under the surface, too, limiting effective collaboration with all relevant parties and (vested) interests.

Meanwhile, the burden of conservation is stretching the Egyptians' own resources to breaking point, as seen in the pitiful condition of the Tutankhamen relics in Cairo, visibly decaying in broken and buckling showcases, amidst poisonous levels of humidity and air pollution. Again, Weigall spotted the problem early:

> The staff at Cairo is too small and too hard-worked to deal with the rapidly increasing mass of antiquities, and ruinous confusion grows ever more confused. The building, though fairly new, is dilapidated, and part of the roof fell in a short time ago, destroying many fine objects. If antiquities removed from a tomb where they were perfectly safe are thrown pell-mell into an understaffed museum in a damp climate and left there to rot, excavation becomes utterly immoral...

Another news story that landed in my in-box while writing this book (in January 2016) concerned the sending to trial of six restorers and two former heads of restoration at Cairo Museum, accused of negligence and incompetence in their attempts to glue back the beard on Tutankhamen's golden mask. (Apparently the beard had snapped off as a result of it being dropped during cleaning.) But it is too easy and comfortable to blame the Egyptian authorities for the pitiful present state of the treasures, monuments and tombs (so many of which are "closed for restoration," quite possibly a euphemism for "beyond hope"). The sad fact is that Ancient Egypt is an enterprise so vast and nebulous that only the world acting in concert can save it, and the will to do so seems sadly lacking, perhaps reasonably in the light of other priorities. Add to this the death-and-dynamite iconoclasm of resurgent monotheist fascism and the ancient relics and sites could be largely consigned to memory in a matter of generations.

Then all that will be left will be Egyptomania itself—an irony indeed, but perhaps one that the Ancients saw coming. They knew that eventually their sacred sites and beliefs would become mere curiosities. As one ancient text warned:

> There will be a time when it will be manifest that it was in vain that the Egyptians cherished godhead with pious will and constant devotion, and all holy reverence for the gods will vanish and be made of no effect. Godhead will go back from earth to heaven. Egypt will be abandoned, and the land which was the home of worship will be stripped of the presence of the deities and left bare. Foreigners will fill this region and the land.... Then this most holy land, the abode of shrines and temples, will be most full of graves and of dead men.[5]

And one of those dead men will be called Kharis.... For if two and a half centuries of Egyptomania have taught us anything, it is that reality is only a springboard: what really endure are the fantasies evoked. In many forms shall we return—Oh, mighty one.

The Mummy List: A Chronological Concordance of Egyptomania at the Movies, 1849–2015

Panorama of Egypt **(1849, British).** Illuminated transparency by Egyptologist Joseph Bonomi, exhibited at London's Egyptian Hall. The moment when Egyptomania and the pop-cultural projected image first meet.

Robbing Cleopatra's Tomb **(1899, France).** Georges Melies trick quickie, in which an archaeologist chops up and resurrects a mummy in a tomb.

The Haunted Curiosity Shop **(1901, Britain).** An Egyptian appearing from a mummy case and turning into a skeleton is one of the delights in this trick film from British visionaries Walter R. Booth and R.W. Paul.

Antony and Cleopatra **(1908, U.S.).** Maurice Costello and Florence Lawrence bring Shakespeare's lovers to the screen for the first time, and just as the Bard intended: silent, and all over in ten minutes.

The Mummy **(1908, France).** Short comedy in which a man unwrapping a mummy with a knife is mistaken for a murderer mutilating a corpse. Laughs all the way.

The Egyptian Mystery **(1909, U.S.).** Split-reel Edison comedy about an amulet found in an Egyptian tomb that makes anything its wearer touches disappear.

The Mummy of the King Rameses **(1909, France).** A professor brings Rameses's mummy to life in tempting but lost French fancy.

The Mummy's Foot **(1910, France).** Listed in some sources: a not-vouched-for adaptation of Gautier's yarn that may also incorporate parts of his *Romance of the Mummy*.

The Mummy **(1911, U.S.).** One of at least two, possibly three films made with this title in 1911. In this one, a female mummy revived by electricity gets the hots for an archaeologist, mummifies him when he rejects her, then returns to

The Mummy (1911, U.S.)

save him from the dissector's knife and ends up marrying the Egyptologist who was about to cut up the first one. Laughs all the way.

***Romance of the Mummy* (1911, France).** Another short you'll never see.

***Cleopatra* (1912, U.S.).** Cleo makes her feature film debut in the form of Helen Gardner; supporting cast includes "Mr. Howard," "Mr. Brady" and "Mr. Corker."

***The Mummy* (1912, Britain).** Lost British effort about which nothing is known beyond that it was one of over 250 film credits notched up by director A. E. Coleby.

***The Mummy and the Cowpuncher* (1912, U.S.).** Another of those titles that makes you genuinely undecided as to whether you're happy or sad that the accompanying film is lost. Otto Lederer stars as "Dr. Quack the Fakir," if that helps any.

***The Vengeance of Egypt* (1912, France).** During Napoleon's campaign, a ring is stolen from a mummy's finger but curse-based complications ensue.

***Antony and Cleopatra* (1913, Italy).** Italian take on the yarn, with epic action scenes, alligators, and the forbiddingly-named Gianna Terribili-Gonzales as Cleo.

***The Egyptian Mummy* (1913, U.S.).** When an Egyptologist takes consignment of the mummy of Rameses III, his daughter's ne'er-do-well boyfriend gets in the case and impersonates it, so as to supernaturally command to the professor to view him favorably. Lost split-reel oddity.

***When Soul Meets Soul* (1913, U.S.).** Romance among the sarcophagi, as Egyptologist Francis X. Bushman discovers he is the reincarnation of the lover of an Egyptian princess.

***An Egyptian Princess* (1914, U.S.).** Fill-in-the-blanks lost comedy that appears to be about the titular tootsie being revived by a funny chemist.

***The Egyptian Mummy* (1914, U.S.).** A man hires a bum to pretend to be a mummy so he can sell the body for dissection. Laughs all the way.

***The Mummy* (1914, U.S.).** Mysterious lost short from the Melies company.

***The Necklace of Rameses* (1914, U.S.).** A jewel thief is cursed for stealing a necklace from the mummy of Rameses's daughter; Edison effort with Robert Brower as Rameses and Rex Ingram as "English Jim."

***Slim and the Mummy* (1914, U.S.).** Short comedy. Who is Slim? Beats me.

***Through the Centuries* (1914, U.S.).** Dead princess is revived in this romantic comedy short.

***The Avenging Hand* (1915, Britain).** An archaeologist steals a mummy's hand, but her ghost follows to seek revenge.

***The Dust of Egypt* (1915, U.S.).** An Ancient Egyptian princess takes a sleeping potion on the banks of the Nile and wakes up in a mummy case in contemporary New York. The fun begins as she encounters modern mysteries like telephones and cigars. Turns out it was all a dream at the end.

***The Live Mummy* (1915, Britain).** Short in which a man pretends to be a mummy to fool a scientist. Does he succeed? Get used to never finding out.

***Too Much Elixir of Life* (1915, U.S.).** Short comedy with Freddie Fralick as a scientist who accidentally revives a mummy with an elixir.

***When the Mummy Cried for Help* (1915, U.S.).** Despite the harrowing title, a comedy from Al Christie, with Lee Moran.

***Elixir of Life* (1916, U.S.).** A different short comedy about a scientist who accidentally revives a mummy with an elixir.

***The Missing Mummy* (1916, U.S.).** Short comedy from director William Beaudine.

***Cleopatra* (1917, U.S.).** The lavish and tragically lost Theda Bara version, filmed near Long Beach. The two last-known prints were destroyed in separate fires many miles apart. A curse? No, nitrate.

***The Undying Flame* (1917, U.S.).** Mme. Olga Petrova ("the world's greatest emotional actress") as an Ancient Egyptian princess who loves a humble shepherd: their love is cruelly denied but reincarnation gives them a break. Sadly lost Paramount melodrama.

The Undying Flame (1917, U.S.)

The Eyes of the Mummy **(1918, Germany).** Lubistch movie with Emil Jannings and a high kitsch factor, striking low-budget visuals.

Mercy, the Mummy Mumbled **(1918, U.S.).** All-black one-reel comedy with possibly the best title of any film ever made.

The Beetle **(1919, Britain).** One of the first serious films to use the plot of supernatural vengeance for the desecration of a tomb; from the novel by Richard Marsh.

The Lure of Egypt **(1921, U.S.).** Melodrama opportunistically (and very successfully) reissued in the wake of the Tutankhamen excavations.

Burning Sands **(1922, U.S.).** Adaptation of Arthur Weigall's novel *The Dweller in the Desert*, from the director of *The Sheikh*.

The Loves of Pharaoh **(1922, Germany).** A revturn to the tombs for Jannings and Lubitsch in the latter's last German film. A much more lavish affair, in standard epic mode.

Bella Donna **(1923, U.S.).** Pola Negri walks like an Egyptian amidst heavily Tutankhamen-inspired art direction.

Dancer of the Nile **(1923, U.S.).** The one certain and authentic Tutankhamen extravaganza of the initial Tutmania period and, according to

Burning Sands (1922, U.S.)

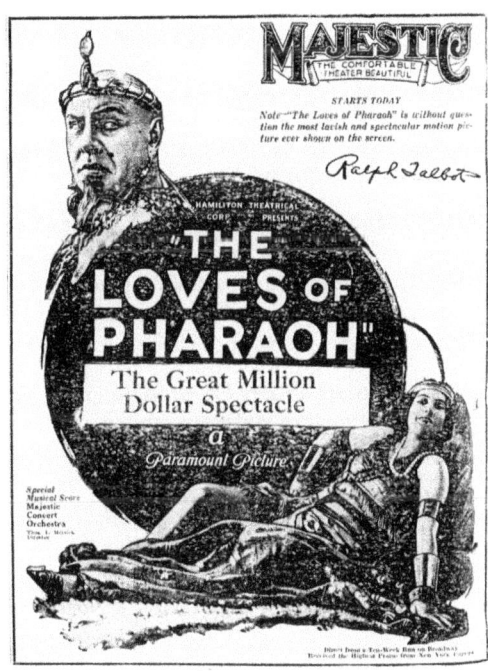

The Loves of Pharaoh (1922, Germany)

reviews, something of a damp squib. Exoticism factor doubtless high, however.

Fires of Fate **(1923, Britain).** From Conan Doyle's lesser-known third contribution to Egyptian lore; a melodrama with authentic location photography and the mischievous Tom Terriss in the director's chair. Remade in 1932.

For the Love of Tut **(1923, U.S.).** Mummy mirth in short comedy with Eddie Lyons. (Photograph appeared in *Exhibitor's Herald*.).

For the Love of Tut (1923, U.S.)

Lawful Larceny **(1923, U.S.).** Nita Naldi also walks like an Egyptian, also amidst heavily Tutankhamen-inspired art direction.

The Mummy **(1923, U.S.).** "Whenever a comedy director runs low on ideas he makes a picture with the action taking place in a wax works or a museum…. Not much sense to it, and few laughs."—Exhibitor's Herald

The Mystery of Dr. Fu Manchu **(1923, Britain).** A 15-part chapterplay and, according to Chris Elliott in his book *Egypt in England*, the first film to use the Cleopatra Needle as a location. It later appears in *Indiscreet* (1958) and *What a Crazy World* (1963), among others.

The Mystery of King Tut-Ankh-Amen's Eighth Wife **(1923, U.S.).** Audacious cash-in supposedly anticipating the death of Lord Carnarvon; apparently made and exhibited, but lost within seconds.

Land of Tut-Ankh-Amen **(1923, U.S.).** One-reel travelogue-cum-newsreel-cum-cash-in, with optional hit song accompaniment.

The Shepherd King **(1923, U.S.).** Rival Exodus adaptation to DeMille's, supposedly really filmed in Egypt. Do we believe them?

The Ten Commandments **(1923, U.S.).** Moses leads the Israelites to Hollywood; no mistaking Tutankhamen's influence on the décor.

Tut Tut King **(aka: *Oh Mummy*) (1923, U.S.).** Neely Edwards and Bert Roach play it for laughs in this two-reeler. (Photo appeared in *Exhibitor's Herald*.).

Tut Tut King (aka *Oh Mummy*) (1923, U.S.)

Tutankhamen **(1923, Austria).** Two-reel comedy with French comedian Raymond Dandy.

The Vengeance of King Tut-Ankh-Amen **(1923, U.S.).** Extravagantly advertised but probably never actually made thrill-a-second spectacular.

Shadow of Egypt **(1924, Britain).** An adventurer tries to rob a tomb and gets cursed: British silent boasts real Valley locations—just imagine Howard Carter's face when the van turned up.

Made for Love (1926, U.S.). Misleadingly titled romantic melodrama, in which husband and wife archaeologists barely escape being buried alive by a wily Egyptian prince-cum-tomb robber. *Motion Picture News* liked the Ancient Egypt flashback sequence and suggested exhibitors should "mention King Tut." Supporting cast includes Neely Edwards from *Tut Tut King* and Bertram Grassby, previously Tut himself in *Dancer of the Nile*.

Mummy Love (1926, U.S.). Short comedy from the Joe Rock company. Alyce Ardell stars; Neely Edwards joins her for his third Egypt-based movie!

That's My Mummy (1927, U.S.). Buddy Messinger and the Sunquist Bathing Beauties take to the tombs.

Through Oil Lands of Europe and Africa—Poland, Greece and Egypt (1927, U.S.). Forty-five minute educational travelogue with extensive Egyptian footage, including of Tutankhamen's tomb. "Made in cooperation with the American oil company."

Lloyd of the C.I.D. (1931, Britain). Scotland Yard's ace Detective Lloyd battles a gang of international crooks who have stolen an amulet originating in Tutankhamen's tomb. An all-action serial, cut into a feature and released in America in 1932 as *The Green Spot Mystery*.

The Mummy (1932, U.S.). The film that *really* started it all. Karloff the Uncanny as a revived, unwrapped mummy with the Egyptological hots for Zita Johann.

The Ghoul (1933, Britain). Karloff returns in British old dark house mystery with a thin layer of Egyptian bandaging.

Cleopatra (1934, U.S.). DeMille at his best: a delicious romp through the imagined world of

Cleopatra (1934, U.S.)

Egypt as conjured by a decade of Tutmania. Claudette Colbert shines amidst a barrage of amazing visuals, sets and costume design.

***The Curse of Tutankhamen* (1934, U.S.).** Much-to-be-mourned mystery project, announced but never made; from the director of *Fires of Fate* (1923).

***Kid Millions* (1934, U.S.).** Eddie Cantor, in Egypt to collect the treasure he has inherited from his archaeologist father, enters a tomb and encounters a chorus of singing mummies.

***My Mummy's Arms* (1934).** Vitaphone short with Harry Gribbon and Shemp Howard on the expedition to find the mummy of King Phooey.

***Charlie Chan in Egypt* (1935, U.S.).** Warner Oland as the venerable detective finds a fresh corpse in a sarcophagus. With Stepin Fetchit and Rita Hayworth.

***Mummy's Boys* (1936, U.S.).** Wheeler and Woolsey comedy with cursed tomb theme and villain dressed as mummy; Barbara Pepper co-stars. Weakest of all W&W films, says Ed Watz in his book on the team.

***Professor Beware* (1938, U.S.).** Harold Lloyd stars as an Egyptologist who doesn't climb tall buildings.

***We Want Our Mummy* (1939, U.S.).** The Three Stooges excavate the tomb of King Rootentooten, hit each other with shovels, etc.

***Mr. Moto Takes a Vacation* (1939, U.S.).** Possibly your only chance to see a Hungarian actor play a Japanese detective pretending to be a German archaeologist. No wonder he needed a vacation.

***The Mummy's Hand* (1940, U.S.).** First Universal sequel introducing Kharis, the quintessential movie mummy.

***Whistling in the Dark* (1941, U.S.).** Egyptology-themed comedy mystery with Red Skelton.

***The Mummy's Tomb* (1942, U.S.).** Lon Chaney takes over as Kharis, waking up in an alternate 1970 where World War II still rages.

Mummy's Boys (1936, U.S.).

The Mummy's Hand (1940, U.S.).

The Mummy's Ghost **(1944, U.S.).** Chaney again, still on the leaves. John Carradine and George Zucco are the Egyptians.

The Mummy's Curse **(1944, U.S.).** The final Chaney-as-Mummy vehicle, location switch to Cajun country for no reason offered or discernible.

Caesar and Cleopatra **(1945, Britain).** Vivien Leigh and Claude Rains and George Bernard Shaw, shot in England on imported Egyptian sand.

Mummy's Dummies **(1948, U.S.).** The Three stooges hit each other with hammers, etc., in a film actually set during the reign of Rootentooten, making it a kind of prequel to *We Want Our Mummy*. Shemp briefly dresses up as a mummy.

Serpent of the Nile **(1953, U.S.).** William Castle directs and Sam Katzman produces on leftover sets from Rita Hayworth's *Salome*: Raymond Burr as Mark Antony and Rhonda Fleming as Cleopatra. They didn't make them like this anymore even at the time.

The Egyptian **(1954, U.S.).** Hokey but solemn Hollywood epic, with Edmund Purdom and Victor Mature, plus Michael Wilding as Akhenaten. Unusually authentic backgrounds.

Valley of the Kings **(1954, U.S.).** Robert Taylor involved in tomb-related mystery shot in Egypt and California. "Suggested by historical data."

Abbott and Costello Meet the Mummy **(1955, U.S.).** Bud and Lou meet Klaris [*sic*] in the scariest of the Universal series.

Land of the Pharaohs **(1955, Italy/U.S.).** Period epic, supernatural infused climax shows up again in the 1999 *Mummy* remake.

The Ten Commandments **(1956, U.S.).** DeMille goes back to Moses for his last film, this time with the parallel contemporary plot snipped off.

***Pharaoh's Curse* (1957, U.S.).** Slow-moving, highly unconvincing but unusual and interesting American anomaly: a straight horror in the age of Abbott and Costello, with a bizarre semi-mummy creature on the prowl.

***The Mummy* (1959, Britain).** Hammer remake with Victorian setting and Christopher Lee as Kharis, in which the mummy keeps falling in a bog.

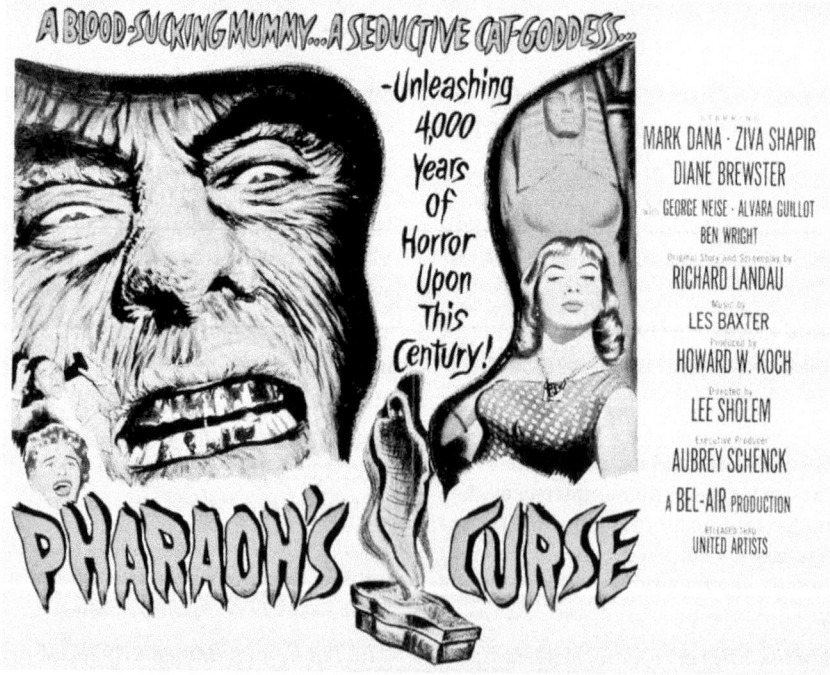

Abbott and Costello Meet the Mummy (1955, U.S.). Pharaoh's Curse (1957, U.S.).

***The Pharaohs' Woman* (1960, Italy).** Typical Italian "peplum" set shortly after the unification of Upper and Lower Egypt, with Drew Barrymore's dad John as Sabaku, Prince of Bubastis.

***Nefertiti, Queen of the Nile* (1961, Italy).** Another Italian job, opportunistically uniting Edmund Purdom from *The Egyptian* and Vincent Price from *The Ten Commandments*. Jeanne Crain takes the title role.

***Cleopatra's Daughter* (1963, Italy).** Debra Paget is the chip off the old block in a lavish peplum confusingly set after the deaths of Antony and Cleopatra but also during the reign of Khufu two and a half thousand years earlier.

***Blood Feast* (1963, U.S.).** Herschell Gordon Lewis's seminal gore film. An Egyptian caterer uses cannibalistic feasts to attempt to revive a goddess before accidentally falling into the back of a truck.

***Cairo* (1963, U.S.).** Master-criminal George Sanders attempts to steal Tutankhamen's treasures from the Cairo Museum. Advertising promised: "Egypt—the Land of Mystery, Evil and Veiled Women…. The Priceless Jewels of

Nefertiti, Queen of the Nile (1961, Italy)

Blood Feast (1963, U.S.)

Tutankhamen Disappear Under the Eyes of the Watching Police…. Thieving Hands and Veiled Faces."

Cleopatra **(1963, U.S.).** If ever an Egyptian-themed movie had a curse on it, this was it: apparently the only time in film history that the number one box-office hit of its year lost money. Dick and Liz cast sheep's eyes at each other as budgets spiral out of control, directors resign, and the same sets are built and rebuilt in different countries.

Carry On Cleo **(1964, Britain).** Spoof of the Liz Taylor version, making audacious use of some of its abandoned sets. Better in every conceivable way.

The Curse of the Mummy's Tomb **(1964, Britain).** Second Hammer vehicle with Jeanne Roland and Terence Morgan (below) encountering an all-new mummy, played by Dickie Owen, originally intended to be giant-sized. You may not see the final twist coming.

Kiss Me Quick **(1964, U.S.).** Softcore quickie involving various monsters.

Secret of the Sphinx **(1964, Italy).** Maria Perschy (below) in Italian murder mystery with authentic locations.

Secret of the Sphinx **(1964, Italy)**

The Curse of the Mummy's Tomb **(1964, Britain)**

Orgy of the Dead (1965, U.S.). Ed Wood film with random mummy appearance.

Carry On Screaming (1966, Britain). Another installment in the long-running UK comedy series, mostly a *House of Wax* parody in the Hammer style, features a mummy called Rubbatiti.

Pharaoh (1966, Poland). Unlikely but highly regarded Polish recreation of the epoch of Rameses XIII, starring, directed by and photographed by three different people all called Jerzy. Some real Egyptian location photography.

The Glass Sphinx (1967, Italy/U.S.). Robert Taylor leads an expedition to find an elixir of eternal life inside a glass sphinx buried in an Egyptian tomb, and picks up Anita Ekberg en route.

The Mummy's Shroud (1967, Britain). Hammer's third mummy on a cheap and cheerful rampage.

The Mummy and the Curse of the Jackals (1969, U.S.). John Carradine appears in Vegas-shot twaddle involving a mummy fighting a were-jackal which resembles two drunk fathers fighting at a wedding. Real and plainly befuddled bystanders serve as unpaid extras. Unfinished and unreleased until an illicit video crept out in 1985. Director Oliver Drake was an uncredited screenwriter of *The Mummy's Curse*.

The Night of Counting the Years (1969, Egypt/Italy). Haunting, beautifully made and massively recommended insight in the life of a family of tomb robbers.

Cleopatra (1970, Japan). Pornographic cartoon version which, retitled *Cleopatra, Queen of Sex* in 1972, would have been the first X-rated cartoon released in America if *Fritz the Cat* had not beaten it to the title by six days.

Dracula versus Frankenstein (1970, Spain/Italy). Monster rally with Paul Naschy and Michael Rennie.

Secrets of Sex (1970, Britain). Valentine Dyall–voiced mummy narrates British supernatural sex anthology from the director of *Horror Hospital*.

Santo and Blue Demon Against the Monsters (1970, Mexico). Mexican wrestlers team up (no tagging, sadly) to fight off a madman and his army of monsters. There's a mummy in there somewhere.

Antony and Cleopatra (1972, Britain/Spain/Switzerland). Charlton Heston directs and stars in a Shakespearean adaptation shot in Spain; off-cuts from *Ben Hur* provide the action.

Blood from the Mummy's Tomb (1972, Britain). *The Jewel of Seven Stars* adapted by Hammer in the modern day, with Valerie Leon (below) as Queen Tera, a mummy upon whom rotting bandages would be a sacrilege.

Blood from the Mummy's Tomb (1972, Britain)

Dr. Phibes Rises Again **(1972, Britain).** Mostly set in Egypt, shot in Spain, involves the search for a hidden tomb beneath a pyramid.

The Cat Creature **(1973, U.S. TV).** Fun Egyptian cat lady piece; Kent Smith gets what's been coming to him since 1942.

Chabelo y Pepito contra los monstruos **(1973, Mexico).** Riff on *Abbott and Costello Meets Frankenstein.*

Love Brides of the Blood Mummy **(1973, Spain/France).** Revived mummy gropes women and drinks their blood in British-set caper; the main character is a scientist called Dartmoor.

Vengeance of the Mummy **(1973, Spain).** Paul Naschy plays the Mummy in London-shot mock-UK Victorian potboiler.

Night Ferry **(1976, Britain).** Children's Film Foundation lark—about your usual gang of kids pitching in to stop a robbery—in this case Bernard Cribbins is trying to steal an Egyptian boy king's corpse.

The Dragon Lives Again **(1977, Hong Kong).** Bruce Lee–alike fights mummies.

The Spy Who Loved Me **(1977, U.S./Britain).** James Bond yarn with Roger Moore. Steel-toothed Jaws kills Nadim Sawalha on the Giza plateau and fights Bond and Barbara Bach in the Royal Necropolis. Plus a British Intelligence base in a pyramid.

Cruise into Terror **(1978, U.S. TV).** Mummy on a cruise ship turns out to be the Antichrist. Lively U.S. TV movie with a pre–*Dynasty* John Forsythe as a priest.

Death on the Nile **(1978, Britain).** Agatha Christie all-starrer with Peter Ustinov as Poirot and your one chance to see Jane Birkin and Bette Davis in the same film. Scrumptiously photographed locations, an attempted murder via crumbling masonry from the top of a pyramid.

The Awakening **(1980, Britain).** Charlton Heston in a big-budget adaptation of *The Jewel of Seven Stars.* With Susannah York and the inevitable Nadim Sawalha.

Love Brides of the Blood Mummy (1973, Spain/France)

The Curse of King Tutankhamen's Tomb **(aka: *The Curse of King Tut's Tomb*, 1980, U.S./Britain TV).** Spectacular international co-production with an all-star cast; much of it is played for laughs, perhaps accidentally.

Fade to Black **(1980, U.S.).** Features a serial killer disguised as various movie villains including a mummy.

Dawn of the Mummy **(1981, U.S./Egypt/Italy).** Gore, cannibalism, lots of fashion models asking for trouble, and one effective scene (showing the mummies rising from the sand) about forty-five minutes in. Shot in Egypt by the director of *Queen Kong*.

The National Mummy **(1981, Spain).** Spanish spoof from the director of 1974's *Vampyres*.

Saturday the 14th **(1981, U.S.).** Monster rally spoof comedy with Richard Benjamin and Paula Prentiss.

Sphinx **(1981, U.S./Netherlands).** Lesley-Anne Down among the tombs in a series of thoroughly drab outfits and a haircut that looks unfinished; John Gielgud fourth-billed as an Egyptian who gets killed after one scene; Nadim Sawalha for continuity. Hugely entertaining and beautifully photographed.

Manhattan Baby **(1982, Italy).** Typical, incontinently violent horror from Lucio Fulci with an evil spirit loosed from a tomb going to work in America.

O Segredo da Múmia **(1982, Brazil).** Spoof, with a female mummy.

Time Walker **(1982, U.S.).** Roger Corman–produced ancient astronaut mummy on college rampage flick.

Scarab **(1983, Spain/U.S.).** Early straight to video horror, with Rip Torn—Nazis revive Egyptian god.

Devil Story **(1985, France).** French splatter movie with a random mummy.

Pyramids of Mars **(1985 video, Britain).** Four-part *Doctor Who* serial first televised in 1975,

Dawn of the Mummy (1981, U.S./Egypt/Italy)

edited into a most agreeable 90 minute feature for home video by the BBC. An obvious low budget compensated for by plentiful imagination and patent enthusiasm in all departments: highly recommended.

***Transylvania 6-5000* (1985, U.S./Yugoslavia).** Jeff Goldblum comedy featuring a mummy.

***Young Sherlock Holmes and the Pyramid of Fear* (1985, Britain/U.S.).** Typically remote house-of-Spielberg fluff, with Egyptian cult in underground pyramid below London. As if by magic, Nadim Sawalha appears.

***Mummy a Gore Gore* (1986 Video, U.S.).** Home-made antics.

***The Tomb* (1986, U.S.).** Fred Olen Ray quickie about a murderous Egyptian goddess raging through LA.

***The Monster Squad* (1987, U.S.).** Mummy appears as one of the band of famous monsters fighting against monster fan kids in 1980s California.

***Howl of the Devil* (1988, Spain).** Paul Naschy plays all of the monsters in pseudo-biographic piece, with Caroline Munro.

***Saturday the 14th Strikes Back* (1988, U.S.).** They said it couldn't be done!

***Waxwork* (1988, U.S./Britain).** Includes a lengthy segment set in a mummy's tomb.

***Encounters of the Spooky Kind 2* (1989, Hong Kong).** Sammo Hung fights a mummy.

***Mummy Dearest* (1990).** Egyptian queen rises from the dead in porno variation on the standard mummy plot. One of the characters is called Dr. Banning. *Mummy Dearest 2* appeared the same year; *Mummy Dearest 3* followed in 1991.

***Puppetmaster II* (1990, U.S.).** Second in long-running video franchise. Features trip to Egypt, supernatural wizardry relating to Egyptian re-animation curse.

***Tales from the Darkside—The Movie* (1990, U.S.).** Anthology horror, linked by Debbie Harry eating some kids. One story adapts Arthur Conan Doyle's *Lot No. 249* with the advantage of Steve Buscemi in the cast: not great but not bad.

***Bloodsucking Pharaohs in Pittsburgh* (1991, U.S.).** Low-budget farce.

***I Was a Teenage Mummy* (1992, U.S.).** Direct to video cheapjack semi-amateur piece.

***Nightmare Asylum* (1992, U.S.).** More direct to video homemade horror hi jinx.

***The Mummy's Dungeon* (1993, U.S.).** Egyptian-themed bondage video: just what the doctor ordered for someone, presumably.

***The Mummy Lives* (1993, U.S./Britain/Israel).** Cannon/Harry Alan Towers production, with Tony Curtis in the title role. Not a comedy but possibly an all-time classic.

***Stargate* (1994, U.S.).** Big studio plodder, involves Egyptian gods, people went to see it at the time.

***Teenage Catgirls in Heat* (1994, U.S.).** Troma rip-off of *The Cat Creature* with a slightly better title.

***Monster Mash: The Movie* (1995, U.S.).** Thrill as Bobby Pickett turns his novelty song into a film thirty years too late.

***Frankenstein and Me* (1996, Canada).** Burt Reynolds and Ryan Gosling appear in monster fan fantasy.

***Tales from the Crypt: Bordello of Blood* (1996, U.S.).** Vampire horror spinoff of TV series, host segment features William Sadler as a mummy.

***Bram Stoker's Legend of the Mummy* (1997, U.S.).** *Seven Stars* adaptation with TV aesthetics and confusing Mid-Atlantic setting.

***The Creeps* (1997, U.S.).** The famous monsters are revived as dwarves. At last!

***The Fifth Element* (1997, France).** Big budget sci-fi, begins in early 20th century Egypt with John Bluthal and John Bennett contacting ancient astronauts in a pyramid. Anticlimax inevitably follows.

***Legend of the Lost Tomb* (1997, U.S. TV).** Roger Corman–produced family adventure with Stacy Keach, about the search for the treasure of Ramessess II [*sic*].

***Under Wraps* (1997, U.S. TV).** Kiddy mummy slapstick.

Talos the Mummy (1998, Britain/U.S./Luxembourg). Louise Lombard and Lysette Anthony join forces in all-star Europudding creepo-caper. Christopher Lee dies early via weird, unfinished CGI. With special effects makeup by Dave Myers of TV chef duo the Hairy Bikers.

The All New Adventures of Laurel & Hardy in "For Love or Mummy" (1999, U.S.). Reasonably good impersonators of the great screen comics face a marauding mummy in a film that makes you wonder.

Ancient Desires (1999, U.S.). Jenna Bodnar plays a mummy that can stay alive only by having sex. Luckily for all, she doesn't resemble Boris Karloff.

The Mummy (1999, U.S.). Mega-budget Indiana Jones–style revamp, a big hit with the masses but not so much with its core audience.

The Mummy Theme Park (2000 Video, Italy). Ultra-low-budget shot-on-video schlock.

Belphégor—Le Fantôme du Louvre (2001, France). Sophie Marceau follows her pet cat into the Louvre after closing time and becomes possessed by an Ancient Egyptian spirit.

Lara Croft—Tomb Raider (2001, U.S./Britain). Angelina Jolie as video game heroine; would that the rest of the film could somehow disappear and just leave her standing there. They probably made a sequel.

The Mummy Returns (2001, U.S./Britain). London-set sequel that spawned its own spin-off series in the *Scorpion King* (2002, U.S.) and its sequels. Donna Air appears for a few seconds towards the start.

The Pharaoh Project (2001, U.S.). Seemingly unreleased immortality-themed thriller featuring Ramses as a character. Stars Conan Lee, one of the later Bruce Lee imitators.

Bubba Ho-Tep (2002, U.S.). A mummy terrorizes a Texan nursing home, runs afoul of Bruce Campbell as a geriatric Elvis Presley.

Detective Lovelorn und die Rache des Pharao (2002, Germany). Rampaging mummy comedy, with Horst Buchholz in his last role.

It's a Haunted Happenin'! (2002 Video, U.S.). It's a no-budget horror musical.

Lust in the Mummy's Tomb (2002 Video, U.S.). Misty Mundae, with endearing English accent, plays an archaeologist's daughter who finds a mummy with a big erection, and revives it by sitting on it and rubbing herself up and down, while the ghost of Cleopatra watches from behind some shelves. Suspense only slightly dissipated by the creaking of the tripod whenever the camera moves. The trick is not to tighten it quite so much.

Mummy Raider (2002 Video, U.S.). Misty Mundae again, shooting at mummies and stopping to have sex in a Lara Croft–inspired softporn quickie, shot in a Massachusetts garage full of cardboard boxes.

The Mummy's Kiss (2003, U.S.). Softcore directed by Donald F. Glut, the dinosaur guy; earns points for opening with the *Swan Lake* theme from the Karloff original.

Evil Unleashed (2003 Video, U.S.). Low-budgeter in 3-D, with a dancing mummy.

Attack of the Virgin Mummies (2004 Video, U.S.). Undead Egyptian hotties revived in a future where sex is illegal. Two directors were necessary to bring it off.

Min Søsters Børn i Ægypten (2004, Denmark). One in a long running series of Danish comedies, begun in the 1960s, this features the recurring characters on holiday in Egypt and getting involved in mystery and intrigue.

Anubis: Guardian of the Underworld (2005 Video, U.S.). Low-budget semi-comedy.

The Fallen Ones (2005, U.S. TV). Features a giant mummy, as Hammer once promised.

The Kung Fu Mummy (2005 Video, U.S.). A mummy is resurrected in present day Hollywood on a budget of $500. The curse this time? Inadequate sound recording.

Legion of the Dead (2005, U.S.). Asylum Studios cash-in on the *Mummy* remake and its sequels.

Night of Anubis (2005, U.S.). The mummy of a 3000-year-old criminal goes on the rampage.

Scooby Doo in Where's My Mummy? (2005, U.S.). Virginia Madsen as the voice of Cleopatra in a lively cartoon adventure with a decidedly eccentric sense of modern Egypt.

Tales from the Grave, Volume 2: Happy Holidays (2005 Video, U.S.). Direct to video anthology. Features a mummy stalking on Halloween night.

The Worst Horror Movie Ever Made (2005 Video, U.S.). If only.

The Curse of King Tut's Tomb (2006, U.S. TV). Russell "*Talos The Mummy*" Mulcahy heads back to the tombs, this time riffing on Indiana Jones and the recent Mummy remake. Not an account of the actual discovery but an all-new fantasy.

The Mummy's Kiss: 2nd Dynasty (2006 Video, U.S.). More slow-motion softcore from Donald Glut and his crew of pneumatic charmers.

Night at the Museum (2006, U.S./Canada). Features some Egyptian wizardry and too many comedians.

Petrified (2006 Video, U.S.). Charles Band production with an alien mummy.

The University of Illinois vs. a Mummy (2006, U.S.). Exactly what you'd expect from the title.

All Wrapped Up (2007 Video, U.S.). Four mummies and a vampire or two in a low budget monster rally.

Sands of Oblivion (2007, U.S. TV). Now here's a novelty: a real Egyptian artefact is left in the sand after the sets of DeMille's *Ten Commandments* were bulldozed: now, years later, the avenging Egyptian spirit attached to it pops up for vengeance.

Blood Scarab (2008 Video, U.S.). Donald F. Glut again, this time with Countess Bathory, Dracula and Renfield getting involved with the mummy of an Egyptian sorceress with the same name as the one in *The Mummy's Kiss*.

The Boneyard Collection (2008, U.S.). Anthology featuring a mummy that has started acting and sues a movie studio for not being typecast. (I can't personally vouch for that synopsis.).

My Mummy (2008 Video, U.S.). Comedy in which a joke shop mummy is brought to life by an enchanted scarf: expect all the thrills a camcorder can capture.

The Mummy: Tomb of the Dragon Emperor (2008, U.S./China/Canada). China-set sequel to the other two that nobody knew was even made.

Riddles of the Sphinx (2008, Canada TV). Dina Meyer in a Sci-Fi Channel TV movie about a wild sphinx let loose by archaeologists.

Hank Danger and the Space Mummy's Tomb! (U.S., 2009). Semi-amateur, semi-comic serial spoof.

Night at the Museum: Battle of the Smithsonian (2009, U.S./Canada). More Egyptian wizardry in remakey sequel.

The Tomb Robbery Papyrus: Notes of a Past (2009, Spain/Germany). Children's Film Foundation-styled Europudding about the search for a royal tomb, "based on a true story."

The Extraordinary Adventures of Adèle Blanc-Sec (2010, France). Luc Besson comic book adaptation with usual excess of style and talkative unmenacing mummies. Lead Louise Bourgoin (facing page) resembles violinist Nicola Benedetti.

Monster Brawl (2011, Canada). Wrestlers versus monsters. Lance Henriksen miscast as God.

Baby Geniuses and the Lost Treasures of Egypt (2013, U.S.). One in a seemingly infinite series with CGI-assisted "babies" dancing around badly green–screened images of Giza. London setting also keenly established via the magic of green-screen: Jon Voight appears as an evil Professor pulling faces outside a blown-up photograph of Boots the Chemist.

Isis Rising: Curse of the Lady Mummy (2013, U.S.). Semi-amateur fare based with unexpected fidelity on the actual legend of Isis, Osiris and Set.

Prisoners of the Sun (2013, U.S.). Unreleased International co-production fantasy adventure with John Rhys-Davies and *EastEnders*' Shane Richie as an Egyptian.

Day of the Mummy (2014, U.S.). Danny Glover's entire performance recorded via Skype.

Dummie de Mummie (2014, Netherlands). A kid finds a mummy in his bedroom and they team up to play cute. According to the IMDB, it's "the start of an amazing friendship learning the boy more than any friend could."

The Extraordinary Adventures of Adèle Blanc-Sec (2010, France)

The Mummy Resurrected (2014, U.S.). Not the easiest thing in the world to lose a pyramid, you might think, but according to the blurb this one's about some explorers who find a lost pyramid, with obligatory mummy and curse antics to follow.

Night at the Museum: Secret of the Tomb (2014, U.S./Canada). Mostly filmed in Vancouver, set in London, conceived in desperation.

The Pyramid (2014, U.S.). Found-footage mainstream horror, set in haunted pyramid.

Frankenstein vs. the Mummy (2015, U.S.). Frankenstein reanimates a madman while his colleague revives the mummy of an evil pharaoh—when these two get together it's mayhem aplenty.

Chapter Notes

References to authors by surname relate
to the works listed in the bibliography.

Chapter 1

1. Davies
2. The Egyptians attached no special importance to the brain, and seem to have had no awareness of the nervous system or blood circulation; neither did they perform major surgery. J. R. Harris notes in *The Legacy of Egypt* that the word "mt" was "used indifferently of sinews, veins, arteries, and other vessels" and that "the process of mummification would have afforded little opportunity for the study of internal anatomy."
3. In Hammer's 1959 version of *The Mummy*, Eddie Byrne's skeptical policeman likens the idea of living mummies to "fiction straight out of Edgar Allan Poe!"—a clever point of reference to give him, given that the film's setting of 1898 precludes mention of most more relevant sources!

Chapter 2

1. Wolfe
2. Indeed, we tend to think of Egyptomania as beginning at this time, but it actually stretches back to antiquity itself. As James Steven Curl notes in his study *Egyptomania*: "It is clear that Egyptian elements were of immense importance during the Roman Empire. The many obelisks that grace the squares and open spaces of Rome itself, for example, provide evidence of the esteem in which these Egyptian objects were held in Imperial times.... The collections of Egyptian pieces and of Roman works in the Egyptian style in the Vatican and Capitoline Museums indicate how widespread were such objects during the Roman Empire, and study of the literature dealing with the sites where ancient artefacts were discovered reveals that Egyptian cults had a powerful influence on Imperial Rome.... We are often brought up to consider Ancient Rome in the light of a pure Classicism, but such a view is unbalanced because the Rome of the Emperors was embellished with many items from Egypt and elsewhere, and in the matters of art and architecture the motifs used became more and more eclectic, drawn from every corner of the Empire."
3. Even its popular name reflects casual disregard of the historical record. One of a pair, it was originally erected in front of the Temple of the Sun at Heliopolis around 1460 BC, about a millennium and a half before Cleopatra. It was transported to Alexandria around 10 BC, probably by Augustus, some twenty years after her death.
4. July 14, 1923
5. March 20, 1924
6. The "Roman temple" from the exhibition is, incidentally, still to be found within the botanical gardens of Bath's Victoria Park, not far from my friendly sphinxes.
7. *Los Angeles Herald*, December 5, 1917
8. July 17, 1917
9. January 29, 1918
10. August 27, 1918
11. December 8, 1924
12. October 10, 1924
13. March 10, 1924. Oddly, Arthur Weigall, in his *Tutankhamen and Other Essays* also says of Tutankhamen that "I believe him to be the Pharaoh of the Exodus," so it possible that DeMille had derived the idea not from his quixotic imagination but rather from contemporary sources.

Chapter 3

1. March 18, 1923
2. *Variety*, March 22, 1923
3. April 21, 1923
4. April 14, 1923
5. May 23, 1923
6. March 10, 1923
7. March 17, 1923
8. June 30, 1923

9. June 23, 1923
10. March 10, 1923
11. *Film Daily* March 17, 1923
12. *Film Daily*, April 12, 1923
13. *Motion Picture Magazine*, January 1921
14. June 23, 1923
15. *Film Daily*, May 29, 1923
16. November 17, 1923
17. *Picture Play*, January 1924
18. E.g.: *Moving Picture World*, April 14, 1923
19. April 28, 1923
20. May 5, 1923
21. April 1, 1923
22. June 30, 1923
23. *Film Daily*, May 2, 1923
24. July 31, 1926
25. May 12, 1923

Chapter 4

1. The squeaky flapper voice, Helen Kane by way of Jean Arthur, belongs to Carla Laemmle, a.k.a. Rebekah Laemmle, Uncle Carl's bob-haired and twinkle-toed niece. An enthusiastic totem of the Universal horror legacy, sprightly and vivacious almost to the very last, she passed away in 2014 at the age of 104.

2. Though it was not known that Tutankhamen would be so young, it had already been noted how small his gloves and headgear were, and how low his stool, leading Weigall to speculate in his 1924 *Tutankhamen and Other Essays* that he may perhaps have been a dwarf.

3. It is significant how often the downfall of the mummy occurs not through the invention, or even intervention, of the heroes, but by chance, or nature, or as a result of the villains' own misreading or violation of their lore. The "curses tend not to be defeated from without by moral arguments but to collapse from within" notes Jasmine Day in *The Mummy's Curse*. The most extreme example of this occurs at the end of *The Mummy's Shroud*, in which the mummy literally tears itself to pieces on hearing an incantation from an ancient scroll.

4. She only made seven movies in her three-year career between 1931 and 1934; *The Mummy* being her third (after *The Struggle* [1931] for D.W. Griffith, and macho fishing drama *Tiger Shark* [1932] for Howard Hawks.) The most interesting is *The Sin of Nora Moran* (1933), one of the most unusual and provocative independent oddities of the pre–Code years, which casts her as an innocent woman about to be executed for murder. It's an oddly structured and relentlessly gloomy meditation on fate and mortality, told partly in flashback and partly in semi-symbolic form, in dreams and fantasies, which constantly butt into each other, and lead to an overtly supernatural climax. This is pre-Code so, innocent though she is, she dies anyway, the real killer puts a gun to his head, and a character who has perverted the course of justice twice sums up for us and walks free. It should have been Johann's springboard to stardom, but maybe the studios weren't looking, or maybe her style is just that bit too unusual. To get the most from Johann's performance in *The Mummy* it's good to come to it after watching *Nora Moran* rather than the other way round. That abrupt cut to our first glimpse of her, eighteen minutes in, seems instantly loaded with portent if you've just watched her grappling with destiny for an hour, if you already know what those soulful eyes are capable of conveying.

5. January 14, 1933
6. *Chicago Tribune*, May 19, 1935
7. September 24, 1932
8. May 1933
9. February 4, 1933
10. "Rubber Shortage Bad For Business But Still A Comfort, Avers Chaney" (*Montreal Gazette*, February 8, 1943)
11. *Amarillo Globe-Times*, March 30, 1924
12. Sydney *World's News*, April 19, 1924
13. One of a number of odd coincidences that I noted while writing this book was a peculiar news story that a number of friends sent me in February of 2016, according to which a night watchman at the Smithsonian Museum was arrested after security cameras recorded him obtaining carnal knowledge of a 2,500-year-old mummy. The bizarre story made its way to a number of news outlets before being revealed as a bizarre hoax: as far as I am aware, none of the reports made any connection to *The Ring of Thoth*, but one wonders if it in any way inspired the outlandish scam.

14. December 20, 1932. Some writers (e.g., Carter Lupton: "Mummymania for the Masses" in MacDonald/Rice) have cited these differences to support the contention that Doyle was not a primary source—on the contrary, I feel it is precisely the unreconciled and contradictory nature of these interpolations that make the case for Doyle's centrality.

15. It's no wonder that recent years have seen a revisionist effort to reduce Imhotep's reputation to more earthly proportions, partly in due deference to the sketchiness and ambiguity of the historical record but also from that characteristic modern resentment of the very idea that history might occasionally be shaped by individuals of genius, rather than masses in productive concert. John Romer insists that "the provision of a single ancient name offers no convincing explanation of the creation of (Djoser's) pyramid" in a somewhat peevish section of his *History of Ancient Egypt*. The truth almost certainly lies where it usually does—somewhere between the twin perils of hagiography and iconoclasm.

16. Thoth is one of the chief beneficiaries of the tendency among later cultures of continuing to accord a vestigial respect and awe to the Egyptian traditions. A surprising dialogue in Plato's *Phaedrus* even sees Socrates articulating something of this sentiment:

> I heard, then, that at Naucratis, in Egypt, was one of the ancient gods of that country, the one whose sacred bird is called the ibis, and the name of the god himself was Theuth. He it was who invented

numbers and arithmetic and geometry and astronomy, also draughts and dice, and, most important of all, letters. Now the king of all Egypt at that time was the god Thamus, who lived in the great city of the upper region, which the Greeks call the Egyptian Thebes, and they call the god himself Ammon. To him came Theuth to show his inventions, saying that they ought to be imparted to the other Egyptians. But Thamus asked what use there was in each, and as Theuth enumerated their uses, expressed praise or blame, according as he approved or disapproved. The story goes that Thamus said many things to Theuth in praise or blame of the various arts, which it would take too long to repeat; but when they came to the letters, "This invention, O king," said Theuth, "will make the Egyptians wiser and will improve their memories; for it is an elixir of memory and wisdom that I have discovered." But Thamus replied, "Most ingenious Theuth, one man has the ability to beget arts, but the ability to judge of their usefulness or harmfulness to their users belongs to another; and now you, who are the father of letters, have been led by your affection to ascribe to them a power the opposite of that which they really possess. For this invention will produce forgetfulness in the minds of those who learn to use it, because they will not practice their memory. Their trust in writing, produced by external characters which are no part of themselves, will discourage the use of their own memory within them. You have invented an elixir not of memory, but of reminding; and you offer your pupils the appearance of wisdom, not true wisdom, for they will read many things without instruction and will therefore seem to know many things, when they are for the most part ignorant and hard to get along with, since they are not wise, but only appear wise.

17. In fact, burial alive as a theme is so potent that it transcends the mummy genre, and even the horror genre, to reappear in mainstream melodramas such as *Land of the Pharaohs* (1955).

18. There is one anomaly worth noting: *The Ghoul* (1933). This British movie marked Karloff's return to his homeland after his American triumph, but he is given so little to do he feels distinctly grafted on. The same goes for the echoes of the previous year's *The Mummy* in the scenario: his character is made an Egyptologist, with a splendid statue of Anubis looming commandingly in the corner of his room, and he is buried in a tomb decorated with hieroglyphs. Little other Egyptian influence is to be found in the set dressings, however, and the story itself is in essence an old dark house mystery, revolving around a stolen jewel and a seemingly beyond-the-grave revenge. The seemingly supernatural elements of the story are hurriedly rationalized in the finale, and the Egyptian aspects are pure window dressing, not deriving from Frank King's source novel, and quite likely added at the last minute, to make a worthier Karloff vehicle out of a project that had probably been set up before the opportunity of its Hollywood casting arose.

Chapter 5

1. Dr. Kathlyn Cooney, *Coffin Reuse in the 21st Dynasty: How and why did the Egyptians reuse the Body Containers of Their Ancestors?* (http://arce.org/news/u115)
2. Hankey
3. Interview with author, 2016
4. July 21, 1934
5. October 16, 1932
6. March 17, 1923
7. December 22, 1923
8. *Morning Telegraph*, September 23, 1923
9. February 27, 1930
10. *Film Daily*
11. Hankey
12. January 26, 1934
13. *Los Angeles Herald*, January 8, 1909
14. In 1913 his wife, according to a report in the *Chicago Tribune* of March 9, was sentenced to a fine of twenty-five pounds or fifteen days in prison for the crime of obtaining money by pretending to tell fortunes. When in her defense she pointed out that the pregnant woman whose child she predicted would die did indeed suffer such a calamity, the judge told her that it was a "monstrous" thing to have said, which "only illustrates the mischief of this practice."
15. He had kept the old stories alive in a series of radio lectures between 1938 and 1940, entitled *Letters from Abroad*. Several have Egyptian settings (*Tom Terriss tells a beautiful story about Egypt, the Sphinx in the moonlight and a mysterious woman.... Tom Terriss explores a treasure pit in the Temple of Karnak, in Luxor, Egypt.... Tom Terriss bamboozles an Egyptian General while finishing his movie in the desert with the famous Camel Corps.... While Tom Terriss is in the Arabian desert directing a Lionel Barrymore film; he hears the story about a battle in the desert with a five-thousand-year-old mummy*) though some of those which do not are, if anything, even more tempting (*Tom Terriss is taken on a tour of torture chambers in the chateau region of France.... Tom Terriss visits the land of the Satan worshipers in the desert outside Baghdad.... Tom Terriss is trapped by ferocious blind men in a prison in Canton, China.... An old man in Louisiana tells Tom Terriss the tale about an embezzler who cannot remember the name needed to retrieve his loot.... Tom Terriss and a friend spend the night in a weird castle in northern Spain and find a madwoman.... Tom Terriss makes an enemy in Saigon who then tries to kill him with Oriental subtlety....*) There's a touch of "physician, psychoanalyze thyself" about this one: "*While visiting historical sites in Paris associated with the Three Musketeers, Tom Terriss imagines himself to be D'Artagnon, the swashbuckler.*")
16. March 15, 1946
17. London *Daily Mail*, January 26, 1898

Chapter 6

1. Woolsey had visited Egypt in 1933: W&W expert Ed Watz has shown me a delightful photograph

of him astride a camel, with pith helmet and cigar, next to the Sphinx and pyramids at Giza.

2. This made the mummy the ideal monster for the times, which perhaps explains why, uniquely among the Universal first eleven, he was revived in no fewer than four solo starring adventures between 1940 and 1944, greater than Dracula, Frankenstein or the Wolf Man. Even if we factor in the monster rally films in which they shared with each other the burden of a single film, only Frankenstein outranks Kharis for ubiquity. In fact, initial plans for 1944's *House of Frankenstein* were to have the mummy take his place alongside the other three, but the concept proved unworkable even to scenarists this imaginative; instead he appeared by extension, when the film went out on a double-bill with *The Mummy's Curse*.

3. Sydney *World's News*, January 21, 1939
4. *Los Angeles Herald*, September 20, 1892
5. *Sacramento Union*, August 20, 1924
6. Brisbane *Daily Mail*, October 10, 1924
7. *Reading Eagle*, July 12, 1930
8. *Adelaide News*, August 14, 1934
9. *News Chronicle*, July 6, 1937
10. Rockhampton *Evening News*, August 5, 1937
11. Sydney *World's News*, April 5, 1924
12. Brisbane *Telegraph* from July 30, 1938, and elsewhere
13. We might even wonder if the phenomenon of the crawling severed hand in horror fiction generally, familiar to film fans from such as *The Beast With Five Fingers*, *Dr Terror's House of Horrors* and *And Now the Screaming Starts* may have emerged from the foundations laid down by these "racial hand" revenge yarns.
14. February 15, 1941
15. *Ocala Star-Banner*, April 23, 1963
16. *Chicago Tribune*, August 18, 1944
17. This claim doesn't survive much scrutiny, however. In the first place, the glass appears to be broken not by Chaney's hand but by the head of the unfortunate museum guard he is throttling at the time. The latter, in any case, is far too near the glass to make it even remotely safe had real glass broken in such menacingly large shards as we see in the film. To these eyes, the pane breaks with the unmistakable dynamics of sugar glass, and in any event, even if a sugar glass pane had not been installed in the frame in time, why would there be a real one there instead? There does appear to be a spot of blood on Chaney's chin, glimpsed very briefly on screen but more clearly in stills, but there seems no obvious way in which it could have been caused by the glass breaking, which his head is not remotely near—unlike that of the mummy's unfortunate victim, which should by rights have been shredded if that were the case. Whatever the truth of the matter, it can't be as clear cut as the accepted story would have you believe.
18. *Deseret News*, September 1, 1944
19. http://www.haaretz.com/news/israel/paying-homage-to-pioneering-archaeologist-who-lost-his-head-1.456689
20. Hankey

Chapter 7

1. http://www.smithsonianmag.com/history/ancient-egypt-shipping-mining-farming-economy--pyramids-180956619/
2. Posters depicted an enormous, Kong-sized mummy with heroine Jeanne Roland in his fist: apparently this was not merely Hammer's customary visual hyperbole but a wisely discarded original intention of the film.

Chapter 8

1. Belford
2. This is the general opinion, but, like almost every assertion regarding Hatshepsut, has been disputed.
3. See Zawi Hawass: http://www.drhawass.com/events/quest-hatshepsut-discovering-mummy-egypts-greatest-female-pharaoh
4. See Cooney, *The Woman Who Would Be King*
5. Champollion: *Lettres écrites d'Égypte et de Nubie en 1828 et 1829*
6. Sydney *World's News*, April 5, 1924
7. *Bram Stoker's Legend of the Mummy* is a generally cheap and forgettable attempt to cash in on the hype surrounding Francis Coppola's 1992 version of *Dracula*, distinguished only by the curious fact that Aubrey Morris is cast in the same role he played in the Hammer film.
8. The TV version, an episode of the anthology series *Mystery and Imagination*, is the only version to retain the correct Edwardian setting of Stoker's original, but somewhat straitened by its budget, as David L. Rattigan notes in a perceptive essay: "Where the novel had flashbacks to Trelawny's Egyptian expeditions and a finale in a Cornish cavern, this adaptation is constrained almost solely to the house, resulting in a very stagebound feel. The boom mic frequently drops into the frame, cameras and equipment are often reflected in mirrors, the supposedly dead Queen Tera can't help blinking and breathing…. When the fumes from Trelawny's relics overcome the characters … the surreal haze is suggested by what appears to be something like a translucent candy wrapper being waved in front of the lens, an effect that is both risible and confusing."
9. Details on Omm Seti: Sattin
10. All Leon quotes: interview with author, 2016.
11. Kinsey: *Elstree Studios Years*
12. Valerie's memory is entirely correct: Margaret can be clearly heard saying "Knickairs!" in one scene. While it is true that Leon is for the most part dubbed throughout the film, it is unlikely in the extreme that the dubbing actress would have likewise intoned "Knickers!" in the recording booth (especially with Holt now dead and unable to repeat the instruction, even as a joke). Therefore it seems more than possible that this one sequence preserves Leon's original voice track.

Chapter 9

1. Topless, what's more, in European prints.
2. In an excavation at Abydos in 1921, Petrie also found evidence to suggest that some of the bodies he uncovered had been buried alive.
3. Romer: *History of Ancient Egypt*
4. e.g., in Humphrey: *The Mind Made Flesh* (Oxford: Oxford University Press, 2002)

Chapter 10

1. January 5, 1979
2. December 21, 1976
3. The song itself is treat enough, with its cod-Egyptian woodwind motifs layered over wocca-wocca guitars, squealing sax and hand claps. But for full enjoyment you have to see Mr. Wolf deliver it: there is video footage and I urge you to track it down on YouTube or wherever. Dressed all in skin-hugging black, bearded, with luxurious hair and his arms folded across his chest, moving to the beat in an attitude of dazed rapture, he is unmistakably reminiscent of the actor Andreas Voutsinas in *The Producers*.
4. Wilson: *From Atlantis to the Sphinx* (London: Virgin, 1996)
5. Bovis: *Exposé de M.A. Bovis au Congrès International de Radiotellerie à Nice* (c. 1935)
6. *Evening Independent*, December 18, 1973
7. December 18, 1973
8. *Reading Eagle*, December 1, 1973
9. February 5, 1977. Toth seems to have been a disarmingly likeable and down to earth fellow. A mutual friend who encountered him not long before his death in 2011 found him to be enthusiastic still about his ideas, but also winningly self-deprecating and kind-hearted.
10. April 24, 1976
11. *Beaver County Times*, May 14, 1977
12. *Evening Independent*, December 18, 1973
13. August 1980
14. Played by Maurice Ronet, who looks like a good deal of high living has been enjoyed since essaying the sexy Gallic archetype of Malle's *Ascenseur pour L'échafaud*.
15. Interview with author, 2017.
16. Peter Benchley had to graft on some similar expository dialogue as we get here to his adaptation of *The Island* in 1980 so as to explain the sudden Britishness of his lead character Blair Maynard, once Michael Caine signed on to play it.

Epilogue

1. Said: *Orientalism* (1978). Said's work has been widely and convincingly challenged: see in particular Roger Scruton: *Fools, Frauds and Firebrands* (London: Bloomsbury, 2015).
2. October 17, 1980
3. Interview with author, 2017.
4. Sadly, the new *Blood Feast* proved a tawdry and unworthy tribute, desiring not so much to shock as to give succor to those who enjoy the sight of others in prolonged pain. Lewis once stressed that, if nothing else, the victims in his films died quickly. No more. And yet such entertainments are no longer even renegade but of the unexceptional general fabric.
5. Quoted in Romer: *Romer's Egypt*.

Bibliography

Over the thirty years this book has been brewing in my mind, literally hundreds of books and other sources have contributed to the form it eventually took. In the list below, I have confined myself to those which have been specifically mentioned, or on which I relied for a specific fact, or which prompted or aided a specific train of thought.

Belford, Barbara. *Bram Stoker: A Biography of the Author of Dracula*. London: Weidenfeld & Nicolson, 1996.

Briefel, Aviva. *The Racial Hand in the Victorian Imagination*. Cambridge: Cambridge University Press, 2015.

Brier, Bob. *Egyptomania: Our Three Thousand Year Obsession with the Land of the Pharaohs*. New York: Palgrave Macmillan, 2013.

Carter, Howard and A.C. Mace. *The Discovery of the Tomb of Tutankhamen*, Vols. 1–3. London: Cassell & Company, 1923, 1927, 1933.

Cooney, Kara. *The Woman Who Would Be King: Hatshepsut's Rise to Power in Ancient Egypt*. London: Oneworld, 2015.

Curl, James Stevens. *Egyptomania, The Egyptian Revival: A Recurring Theme in the History of Taste*. Manchester: Manchester University Press, 1994.

Curry, Christopher Wayne. *A Taste of Blood: The Films of Herschell Gordon Lewis*. London: Creation, 1999.

Davies, Vivian and Renee Friedman. *Egypt*. London: British Museum Press, 1998.

Day, Jasmine. *The Mummy's Curse: Mummymania in the English-Speaking World*. Abingdon: Routledge, 2006.

El Mahdy, Christine. *The Pyramid Builder*. London: Headline, 2003.

Elliott, Chris. *Egypt in England*. Swindon: English Heritage, 2012.

Frank, Alan. *Horror Movies*. London: Octopus, 1974.

Frayling, Christopher. *The Face of Tutankhamun*. London: Faber & Faber, 1992.

Halliwell, Leslie. *The Dead That Walk*. London: Paladin, 1988.

_____. *Halliwell's Hundred*. London: Granada, 1982.

Hankey, Julie. *A Passion for Egypt: Arthur Weigall, Tutankhamun and the Curse of the Pharaohs*. New York: Tauris Parke, 2007.

Harris, J.R., ed. *The Legacy of Egypt*. Oxford: Oxford University Press, 1971.

James, T.G.H. *Ramesses II*. Vercelli: White Star, 2002.

Kinsey, Wayne. *Hammer Films: The Bray Studios Years*. Surrey, UK: Reynolds & Hearn, 2002.

_____. *Hammer Films: The Elstree Studios Years*. Sheffield, UK: Tomahawk Press, 2007.

Macdonald, Sally and Michael Rice, eds. *Consuming Ancient Egypt*. Walnut Creek, CA: Left Coast Press, 2009.

Meikle, Denis. *A History of Horrors: The Rise and Fall of the House of Hammer*, Revised Edition. Lanham, MD: Scarecrow Press, 2007.

Pirie, David. *A Heritage of Horror: The English Gothic Cinema, 1946–1972*. London: Gordon Fraser, 1973.

Reeves, Nicholas. *The Complete Tutankhamun*. London: Thames & Hudson, 1990.

_____, and Richard H. Wilkinson. *The Complete Valley of the Kings*. London: Thames & Hudson, 1996.

Romer, John. *Ancient Lives: The Story of the Pharaohs' Tombmakers*. London: Guild, 1984.

_____. *A History of Ancient Egypt from the First Farmers to the Great Pyramid*. London: Allen Lane, 2012.

_____. *The Rape of Tutankhamun*. London: Michel O'Mara, 1993.

_____. *Romer's Egypt*. London: Michael Joseph, 1982.

_____. *Valley of the Kings*. London: Michael O'Mara, 1981.

Sattin, Anthony. *The Pharaoh's Shadow: Travels in Ancient and Modern Egypt*. London: Victor Gollancz, 2000.

Schablitsky, Julie M. *Box Office Archaeology: Refining Hollywood's Portrayals of the Past*. Walnut Creek, CA: Left Coast Press, 2007.

Shaw, Ian, ed. *The Oxford History of Ancient Egypt*. Oxford: Oxford University Press, 2000.

Spencer, A.J. *Death in Ancient Egypt*. Middlesex, UK: Penguin, 1982.

Tyldesley, Joyce. *Ramesses: Egypt's Greatest Pharaoh.* London: Penguin, 2000.

Weigaall, Arthur. *Tutankhamen and Other Essays.* New York: Doran, 1924.

Wilson, John A. *The Culture of Ancient Egypt.* Chicago: University of Chicago Press, 1951.

Winstone, H.V.F. *Howard Carter and the Discovery of the Tomb of Tutankhamun.* London: Constable, 1991.

Wolfe, S. J. and Robert Singerman. *Mummies in Nineteenth Century America: Ancient Egyptians as Artefacts.* Jefferson, NC: McFarland, 2009.

Index

Numbers in ***bold italics*** indicate pages with photographs.

Abbott and Costello Meet the Mummy (film) 108, ***166***
Aggasi, Louis 21
America Is Ready (film) 49
Ames, Ramsay ***104***
Andrews, Harry 145
Arnold, Mal 92
"Art Deco" 29, 55; *see also* "Nile Style"
Ascher, Sydney 52–53
The Avenging Hand (film) 95
The Awakening (film) 124, 128, 145–***146***

Balderston, John L. 67, 69, 71, 105, 125
Bara, Theda 32, ***33***, 46
Bella Donna (film) 45–46
Belzoni, Giovanni 15
Benchley, Peter 181
Binney, Neil 128
Bird in a Gilded Cage (song) 50
Bitzer, John 50
The Black Cat (film) 91
The Black Room (film) 61
Bloch, Robert 125
Blood Feast (1963 and 2016 films) 92, 131–134, ***132***, ***135***, ***167***, 181
Blood from the Mummy's Tomb (film) 78, ***79***, 96, 112, 124, 127–130, ***129***, 131, ***169***
Bluebeard's Eighth Wife (film) 50
Bolling, Claude 145
Bonomi, Joseph 30
Bourgoin, Louise 175
Bovis, Antoine 143
Bow, Clara 29
Bower, Frederick B. 50
Bram Stoker's Legend of the Mummy see Legend of the Mummy
Brewster, Diane ***81***
Brooks, Louise 59
Brugsch, Emile 16

Budge, E.A. Wallis 85, 123, 127; *Egyptian Tales and Romances* 11
Burning Sands (film) ***73***, ***161***
Burns, Frederick M. 50–51
Burr, Raymond 144
Bushman, Francis X. 124
Byrne, Eddie 177
Byrum, John 149

Cantor, Eddie 89
Cardiff, Jack 145
Carnarvon, Lord 3, 26, 30, 43, 72, 84, 95, 148, 150; death of and curse theory 51–52, 77–78, 83, 85–88; sells media rights to excavation 39
Carradine, John 92
Carter, Howard 1, 2, 3, ***27***, ***28***, 34, 39, 55, ***58***, 67, 69, 72, 73, 74, 77, 83, 86, 91, 105, 106, 116, 119, 122, 148, 150; discovers tomb 25–27; lecture tour 54; publishes account 37, 72, 85; on Tutmania 27–28, 29–30
The Cat Creature (TV film) 125
Chaney, Lon 101
Chaney, Lon, Jr. 10, ***11***, 14, 25, 63, 89, 101–103, ***102***, ***104***, 112, 180
Chaplin, Charles 54, 82
Cheiro *see* Warner, John
Clark, Fred 21, 119
Cleopatra (1917 film) 32–33, 46
Cleopatra (1934 film) 34, 59, ***163***
Cleopatra (1963 film) 132
Cleopatra Had a Jazz Band (song) 33, ***38***
Cleopatra's Needle Waltz (song) 24
Coburn, James 144
Cohen, Max 49–52, 53
Colbert, Claudette 34, 59, ***163***
Collins, Joan 108, ***109***, 110
Conan Doyle, Arthur 65, ***68***, 83, 120, 178; *Lot No. 249* 96–98, 99, 100, 111–112; promotes curse myth 78; *Ring of Thoth* 67–69, 70, 71, 96, 97, 111, 125, 178; *Tragedy of the Korosko (Fires of Fate)* 82
Cook, Robin 146, 148, 149, 150, 152, 155; *Coma* 146, 155; *see also Sphinx*
Coolidge, Calvin 54
Cooney, Kathlyn (Kara) 76–77, 124
Corlette, Dudley S. 46
Crain, Jeanne ***167***
Crowe, Russell 155
Cruise, Tom 155
Curse of Frankenstein (film) 131
Curse of King Tut's Tomb (TV film) 81, 144
Curse of the Mummy (TV film) 124, 180
Curse of the Mummy's Tomb (film) 21, 79, 96, 113–115, ***114***, 119, 131, ***168***
Cushing, Peter 78, 99, 111, ***112***, 116, 117, 119, 128

Dancer of the Nile (film) 46–49, ***48***, ***49***
Dandy, Ramond 53
Daniken, Erich Von 143, 144
Dawkins, Richard 153
Dawn of the Mummy (film) 131, 135, ***171***
Death on the Nile (film) 145
DeMille, Cecil B. 1, 34–36, 46, 59, 108, 110
Dixon, Waynham 24
Doctor Who (TV series) 142
Dodge, Paul 46
Down, Lesley-Anne 146, ***147***, 148, ***149***
Dracula (film) 49, 55, ***56***–57, 58, 61, 66, 67, 110
Drbal, Karl, 143
Dream Girl (film) 34

185

"EA6704" (unidentified mummy) 64-*65*
Eady, Dorothy ("Omm Seti") 127, 129
Earle, W. P. S. 46, 47, 43
Eden, Anthony 117
Edwards, Neely 53, *162*
Egypt: Quest for Eternity (TV film) 127
The Egyptian (film) 108
Egyptian life and custom 9–14, 109–110, 134–140
Egyptian mythology 10, 11–12, 69, 70–71, 100, 124; corruption of by Western popular culture 2, 69, 70–71, 74, 124–126
Ellis, Robin 145
El Mahdy, Christine 70
Elvidge, June 49
Englin, Maureen 37–38
The Extraordinary Adventures of Adele Blanc-Sec (film) 155, *175*
Eyes of the Mummy (film) 31–32

Fairbanks, Douglas 54
Faulkner, William 108
Fires of Fate (film) 82–83; see also Conan Doyle, Arthur
Fisher, Terence 113
Flanagan, G. Patrick 144
Fletcher, Bramwell *59*, 61
The Flying Deuces (film) 53
For the Love of Tut (film) 53, *162*
Foran, Dick *93*, 103, *165*
Ford, Henry 54
Ford, Wallace 103
Frank, Alan 102
Frankenstein (film) 55, 58, 61, 63, 66, 67, 91, 110
Freud, Sigmund 2
Freund, Karl 69
Friedman, David F. 132
Fulci, Lucio 131
Furneaux, Yvonne 125, *126*

Gallagher and Shean 37
Gautier, Theophile 20, 31, 93; *The Mummy's Foot* 16–17, 96; *Romance of the Mummy* 17, 20
George, Jack 37
The Ghoul (film) 179
Gielgud, John 149
Gilling, John 116
The Glacier's Secret (film) 84
Gliddon, George 21–22, 30–31
Golden, Ray 134
The Gorilla (play and films) 53
Grassby, Bertram *46*–47, 49
Green Hell (film) 100
Gribbon, Harry 89

Halliwell, Leslie 91, 98, 100
Hammer, Arthur (and Hammer Film Productions) 84
Hatshepsut 122–123, 130, 145
The Haunted Palace (film) 102
Hawkins, Jack 108

Herbert, George (Earl of Carnarvon) *see* Carnarvon, Lord
Heston, Charlton 34, 124, 128, 145, *146*
Holt, Seth 78, 127, 128
Hoover, Herbert 29
Howard, Shemp 89
Humphrey, Nicholas 139

I'll Do Without Meat, I'll Do Without Wheat, But I Can't Do Without Love (song) 50
Imhotep 70, 178
Inner Sanctum (film series) 101
It May Be Your Daughter (film) 49

Jack the Ripper (TV mini-series) 144
Jannings, Emil 31
Jenzen, Doug 1
Johann, Zita 34, 59–*60*, 67, 178
Jones, Buck 52
Justice, James Robertson 108

Karloff, Boris 3, 12, 13, 34, 58, *59*, 61–64, *62*, *66*, 67, 68, 69, 70, 78, 91, 92, 98, 102, 103, 110, 112, 117, 125, 128, 145, 155
Keir, Andrew 78, 128
Kimberly, Maggie *65*, *115*, 116
King Tut (alligator) 55
King Tut (dog) *29*
King Tut (lightweight boxer) 29
Knox, Elyse *102*, 103

Laemmle, Carl, Jr. 67
Lamb, Arthur J. 50
Land of the Pharaohs (film) 87, 108–110, *109*, *111*, 135, 142, 155, 179
Land of Tut-Ankh-Amen (film) 42–45, *43*
Lane, Tamar 46
Langdon, Harry 29
Langella, Frank 148
Laurel and Hardy 53
Lawful Larceny (film) 45
Lee, Christopher 13, 14, 80, 111, *112*, *118*, 133, *137*
Legend of the Mummy (film) 124, 180
Leon, Valerie 78, *79*, 128–*129*, 130, 155, *169*, 180
Lewis, Herschell Gordon 132, 133, 134, 156
Lewton, Val 61
Lloyd, Harold 29
Logan, Jacqueline 73
Longfellow, Henry Wadsworth 21
Loudon, Jane C. (and *The Mummy! A Tale of the 22nd Century*) 9, 17–18
Love Brides of the Blood Mummy (film) 25, *170*
The Loves of Pharaoh (film) 45, 53, *161*
Low, Andrew 113

Lubitsch, Ernst 31, 34, 45, 53
The Lure of Egypt (film) 45
Lyons, Eddie 53, *162*
Lythgoe, Albert 85, 86

Madison, James 37
Male and Female (film) 34
The Man from Glengarry (film) 42
Manetho 5, 123
Manners, David 67
Martin, Steve 142
Mason, Connie 133
McGregor, Malcolm 49
McNally, Robert Aquinas 143
McShane, Ian 145
Merrick, George M. 50, 52
Mix, Tom 52
Mixx, Ernest 53
Mochado, Xavier 46
Morgan, Terence *168*
mummies: alternate uses 15; appearance of (in museums) 13; changing designs 14, 65; and coffin re-use 65, 76–77; destruction and disregard for 14–15; history and meaning 10–14; moral responsibility towards 153–154; "mummy's hand" in folklore and fiction 92–96; 124; and tomb robbery 74–76; unwrapping 18
The Mummy (1911 film) *159*
The Mummy (1923 film) 53
The Mummy (1932 film) 3, *4*, 121, 34, 57, 58–64, *59*, *60*, *62*, *66*–67, 69–71, 78, 89, 91, 92, 96, 98, 100, 103, 105, 113, 125
The Mummy (1959 film) 79–81, *80*, 92, 98, 99, 107, 110–113, *112*, 116–117, *118*, 119, 125, *126*, 131, 133, 135, *136*, 177
The Mummy (2017 film) 155
The Mummy Returns (film) 154–155
Mummy's Boys (film) 89, *164*
The Mummy's Curse (film) 89, 102, 103, 107
The Mummy's Ghost (film) 102, 103, *104*, 125
The Mummy's Hand (film) 14, 91, 92, *93*, 98, 100–101, 103, 105, 133, *165*
The Mummy's Shroud (film) 64, *65*, 96, *115*–116, 119, 131
The Mummy's Tomb (film) *11*, *101*, 103
Mundstuk, Dave 52
Murders in the Rue Morgue (film) 56, 91
My Mummy's Arms (film) 89
Myers, Carmel 47, *48*, 49
Mystery of King Tut-Ankh-Amen's Eighth Wife (film) 50–52, *51*

Naldi, Nita 45
Naschy, Paul 131
Nasser, Gamal Abdel 116–117

Index

Negri, Pola 31, 45
Nielsen, Greg 144
Night of Counting the Years (film) 150-*151*
"Nile Style" 29; *see also* "Art Deco"
North of Sahara (film) 84

The Old Dark House (film) 61, 63
Old King Tut (song) 42-43, *44*, 51
Old King Tut Was a Wise Old Nut (song) 29, 142
The Omen (film) 145
Onan, Jim 144
"Orientalism" 2, 153, 181
The Orion Mystery (book) 142
Ostrander, Sheila 143

Panorama of Ancient Egypt (theatrical presentation) 30-31
Papyrus (horse) 39
Parker, Eddie 102
Parsons, Louella 83
Partlean, George 64, 66
Pasolini, Pier Paolo 131
Pastell, George 92, 112, 116, 17, *118*, 119, 131
Patton (film) 148
Perschy, Maria 168
Petrie, Wiliam Flinders 17, 105-*106*, 123, 136, 137
Petrova, Olga 125, 161
Pharaoh's Curse (film) *81*, 108, 118-119, 125, *166*
Pierce, Jack 61-64, 66, 98, 101
Pirie, David 112
Planet of the Apes (film) 148
Poe, Edgar Allan *18*, 21, 177; *Some Words with a Mummy* 18-19, 21, 155
Pogany, William 66
Powell, Eddie *65*, *115*
Psychic Discoveries Behind the Iron Curtain (book) 143
Punch (magazine) 30, 94
Putnam, Nina Wilcox 67
Pyramid Power 142-144
Pyramid Power (books) 144
Pyramid Quest (book) 143

Queen of the Nile (film) *167*
Quest of the Perfect Woman (film series) 84, 86

Rattigan, David L. 180
The Raven (film) 91
Rees, Angharad *145*
Remo, Andrew 50
Roach, Bert 53, *162*

Robinson, Bernard 113
Robinson, Margaret 113
Roland, Jeanne *114*, *168*
Romer, John 75, 123, 139, 157, 178
Said, Edward *see* "Orientalism"
Saint, Eva Marie 145
Salam, Shadi Abdel 150
Salo (film) 131
Salt, Henry 65, 66
Sangster, Jimmy 112, 113
Schaffner, Franklin J. 148
Schoch, Robert M. 143
Schroeder, Lynn 143
Scofield, Paul 145
Secret of the Sphinx (film) 168
Selznick, Lewis J. 53
The Shepherd King (film) 46
Shipman, Ernest 39-42, *40*, 45, 82
The Shriek of Araby (film) 49
Siegel, Shelly 144
Slater, Christian *97*
Slaughter, Tod 110
Sloan, Edward Van 67
Soane, John 65
Sommers, Stephen 12, 155
Song of the Voodoo (film) 84
Spence, Ralph 53
Sphinx (book and film) 156-150, *147*, *149*, 152, 155
Stargate (film) 142
Steele, Barbara 59
Stittler, Daryl 144
Stoker, Bram 121, *122*, 123, 124, 125, 127; *The Jewel of Seven Stars* 95, 121, 122-124, 128, 130, 145
Stumar, Charles 62
Swanson, Gloria 34, 50, 144

Tales from the Darkside (film) 96, *97*
Talos the Mummy (film) 12
Taurog, Norman 53
Taylor, Elizabeth 6, 132, 141
The Ten Commandments (1923 and 1956 films) 1, 34-*36*, 46, 108
Terriss, Tom 81-85, *83*, 86-88, 113, 179
The Three Stooges 2, 89, *90*
Tilzer, Harry Von 42-43, 50, 51
Titzel, Elizabeth 108
Toth, Max 144, 181
Trowbridge, Charles *93*
Tucker, Sophie 43, 44
Turpin, Ben 49
Tut Tut King (film) 53, *162*
Tutankhamen 2, 3, 67; and curse theories 2, 67, 73, 74, 77-78, 85-88; discovery 26-27; as Lost Generation and Jazz Age icon 27; modern theories regarding 150, 155; as New Age icon 142; reality versus fantasy regarding 26, 35-36, 42-43, 57; on tour 117, 141-2
Tutankhamen (film) 53
Tutankhamen (TV series) 156
The Tutankhamen Deception (book) 2
Tutankhamen, King of the Nile (song) 142, 181
Tyler, Tom 13, 14, 98, *99*, 102, 103, 133, *165*

The Undying Flame (film) 125, *160*

Valley of the Kings (film) 108
The Vampire of Marrakesh (film) 85
Van Helsing (film) 155
The Veiled Dancer of Eloued (film) 85
Vengeance of the Mummy (film) 131
Vengeance of Tut-Ankh-Amen (unmade film) 52-*53*
Vulliamy, George John 23
Warner, John 85-86, 95, 124, 179
We Want Our Mummy (film) 2, 89, *90*
Weigall, Arthur 30, 66, 67, 72-73, 77-78, 85, 105, 130, 157, 177, 178; *Dweller in the Desert* 73; *Tutankhamen and Other Essays* 72, 75, 107, 156
When Soul Meets Soul (film) 125
White Zombie (film) 84
Who Did the Strut for Old King Tut (When He Said Tut Tut to the Queen)? (song) 51, 55
Wicking, Christopher 127, 128, 130
Wilde, William 121-122, 123
Williams, Charles W. 143-144
Wilson, Betty 29
Wilson, Colin 143
Wilson, Keppel 29
Winlock, Herbert 86
Wolf, Riccardo 142
The Wolf Man (film) 61

Yorke and King ("the only living relatives of Old King Tut") 37

Zimbalist, Stephanie *146*
Zombie Flesh Eaters (film) 131
Zucco, George 98, 103

www.ingramcontent.com/pod-product-compliance
Ingram Content Group UK Ltd.
Pitfield, Milton Keynes, MK11 3LW, UK
UKHW050524150426
5217IPUK00026B/1783